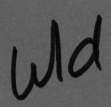

W9-APX-636

wd

BEST OF
Country Cooking

Tangy Cranberry Chicken (p. 82)

© 2019 RDA Enthusiast Brands, LLC.
1610 N. 2nd St., Suite 102, Milwaukee WI 53212-3906
All rights reserved. Taste of Home is a registered trademark of RDA Enthusiast Brands, LLC.
Visit us at tasteofhome.com for other Taste of Home books and products.

ISBN:
D 978-1-61765-875-4
U 978-1-61765-876-1
ISSN: 2166-0522
Component Number:
D 116700089H
U 117000060H

Deputy Editor: Mark Hagen
Senior Art Director: Raeann Thompson
Editor: Hazel Wheaton
Designer: Arielle Jardine
Copy Chief: Deb Warlaumont Mulvey

Front Cover
Photographer: Dan Roberts
Senior Set Stylist: Melissa Franco
Food Stylist: Lauren Knoelke

Pictured on front cover:
Peach and Berry Cobbler, p. 180

Pictured on title page:
Split Pea Soup with Ham, p. 54

Pictured on back cover:
Italian Pasta Bake, p. 81; Garlic-Herb Pattypan Squash, p. 24; Citrus-Mustard Roasted Chicken, p. 88;

Printed in China
1 3 5 7 9 10 8 6 4 2

The Best Meals the Country Has to Offer

SERVE UP THE BEST OF DOWN-HOME COUNTRY COOKING TO YOUR FAMILY TONIGHT!

When we talk country cooking, we're talking hearty, satisfying and comforting food. It means no frills, no nonsense—and no complaints! Your family will love every bite of these mouthwatering main courses, savory casseroles, warming soups and stews, scrumptious sides and irresistible desserts. From traditional favorites to fresh takes, these are the recipes that will be happily passed around and passed down.

This edition of **Best of Country Cooking** is filled with recipes home cooks across the country have shared with their families for generations—and now have shared with you. Homemade salsas and jams, from-scratch breads and pies, farm-fresh vegetable dishes, tasty soups you'll have simmering on the stove all day...every recipe in this collection is a keeper. You'll find delicious traditional dishes and new spins on old favorites, with every recipe approved by the experts in the *Taste of Home* Test Kitchen.

LOOK INSIDE FOR:

Blue-Ribbon Recipes

Keep an eye out for the blue-ribbon icon—it identifies a recipe chosen by a special tasting panel as a *Taste of Home* contest winner. These dishes are guaranteed to please!

Freeze It!

Recipes with the FREEZE IT icon can be made in advance and kept in the freezer—so you'll always have a satisfying, delicious dinner on hand, even on jam-packed days.

With the great recipes in **Best of Country Cooking,** serving up great-tasting food is as easy as can be. You'll always have the perfect dish for family dinners, cozy nights in, potlucks, parties and more—so come and get it!

CONTENTS

Snacks & Beverages

For a backyard family get-together, a holiday celebration or a game-day gathering with friends, great food helps make the occasion special. Check out the 30 recipes in this chapter for the appetizers and drinks—either cold or hot—that will make your party perfect.

HOT HOLIDAY CIDER

This slightly tart apple cider is perfect for a holiday open house or winter party. It fills the house with a wonderful aroma.
—*Cindy Tobin, West Bend, WI*

Prep: 10 min. • **Cook:** 3 hours
Makes: 16 servings

    8   cups apple cider or juice
    4   cups cranberry juice
    2   cups orange juice
    ½   cup sugar
    3   cinnamon sticks (3 in.)
    1   tsp. whole allspice
    1   tsp. whole cloves

1. Place first four ingredients in a 5- or 6-qt. slow cooker. Place spices on a double thickness of cheesecloth. Gather corners of cloth to enclose spices; tie securely with string. Add to slow cooker.
2. Cook, covered, on low until heated through, 3-4 hours. Discard spice bag. Serve warm.

¾ cup: 127 cal., 0 fat (0 sat. fat), 0 chol., 14mg sod., 32g carb. (30g sugars, 0 fiber), 1g pro.

PIZZA EGG ROLLS

We gave traditional pizza a twist by rolling up the usual toppings in egg roll wrappers, then deep-frying them. Yum!
—Taste of Home *Test Kitchen*

Prep: 20 min. • **Cook:** 5 min./batch
Makes: 14 egg rolls

    1   pkg. (3½ oz.) sliced
        pepperoni, chopped
    1   cup chopped fresh mushrooms
    1   medium green pepper, chopped
    ½   cup grated Parmesan cheese
    ½   tsp. pizza seasoning or
        Italian seasoning
   14   egg roll wrappers
   14   pieces string cheese
        Oil for deep-fat frying
    1   can (15 oz.) pizza sauce, warmed

1. In a small bowl, combine pepperoni, mushrooms, green pepper, Parmesan cheese and pizza seasoning. Place an egg roll wrapper on a work surface with a point facing you; place a piece of string cheese near the bottom corner. Top with about 2 Tbsp. of the pepperoni mixture.
2. Fold bottom corner over filling. Fold sides toward center over filling. Using a pastry brush, wet the top corner with water; roll up tightly to seal. Repeat with remaining wrappers, cheese and filling.
3. In an electric skillet or deep-fat fryer, heat oil to 375°. Fry egg rolls, a few at a time, for 1-2 minutes on each side or until golden brown. Drain on paper towels. Serve with pizza sauce.

1 egg roll: 326 cal., 21g fat (7g sat. fat), 31mg chol., 682mg sod., 21g carb. (1g sugars, 1g fiber), 13g pro.

SALMON PARTY SPREAD

We're proud to serve our delicious Alaskan salmon to guests. Set out some crackers, and this slightly smoky spread will be gone in no time!
—*Kathy Crow, Cordova, AK*

Prep: 10 min. + chilling • **Makes:** 2 cups

- 1 pkg. (8 oz.) cream cheese, softened
- 1 can (7½ oz.) pink salmon, drained, flaked and cartilage removed
- 3 Tbsp. chopped fresh parsley
- 2 Tbsp. finely chopped green pepper
- 2 Tbsp. finely chopped sweet red pepper
- 2 tsp. lemon juice
- 1 tsp. prepared horseradish
- ½ tsp. liquid smoke, optional
- Finely chopped pecans or additional parsley, optional
- Crackers

In a bowl, combine first eight ingredients; stir until well blended. Cover and chill for up to 24 hours. Transfer to a serving bowl; if desired, sprinkle with pecans or parsley. Serve with crackers.

2 Tbsp.: 71 cal., 6g fat (3g sat. fat), 21mg chol., 115mg sod., 1g carb. (0 sugars, 0 fiber), 4g pro.

ASPARAGUS BRUSCHETTA

I really like asparagus, so I'm always trying it in different things. It makes a delicious and crunchy spin on traditional bruschetta.
—*Elaine Sweet, Dallas, TX*

Takes: 30 min. • **Makes:** 12 servings

- 3 cups water
- ½ lb. fresh asparagus, trimmed and cut into ½-in. pieces
- 2 cups grape tomatoes, halved
- ¼ cup minced fresh basil
- 3 green onions, chopped
- 3 Tbsp. lime juice
- 1 Tbsp. olive oil
- 3 garlic cloves, minced
- 1½ tsp. grated lime zest
- ¼ tsp. salt
- ¼ tsp. pepper
- 1 French bread baguette (8 oz.), cut into 12 slices and toasted
- ½ cup crumbled blue cheese

1. In a large saucepan, bring water to a boil. Add the asparagus; cover and boil for 2-4 minutes. Drain and immediately place asparagus in ice water. Drain and pat dry.
2. Combine the asparagus, tomatoes, basil, onions, lime juice, oil, garlic, lime zest, salt and pepper. Using a slotted spoon, spoon the asparagus mixture onto bread slices. Sprinkle with blue cheese.

1 piece: 88 cal., 3g fat (1g sat. fat), 4mg chol., 237mg sod., 13g carb. (1g sugars, 1g fiber), 3g pro.

ZESTY MARINATED SHRIMP

These easy shrimp look impressive on a buffet table and taste even better! The zesty marinade has a wonderful spicy citrus flavor. I especially like this recipe because I can prepare it ahead of time.

—*Mary Jane Guest, Alamosa, CO*

Prep: 10 min. + chilling
Makes: about 4½ dozen

- 12 lemon or lime slices
- ½ cup thinly sliced red onion
- 1 Tbsp. minced fresh parsley
- ½ cup canola oil
- ½ cup lime juice
- ½ tsp. salt
- ½ tsp. dill weed
- ⅛ tsp. hot pepper sauce
- 2 lbs. peeled and deveined cooked shrimp (26-30 per lb.)

Place the first eight ingredients in a large bowl; toss with the shrimp. Refrigerate, covered, for 4 hours, stirring occasionally. Drain before serving.

1 shrimp: 28 cal., 1g fat (0 sat. fat), 26mg chol., 36mg sod., 0 carb. (0 sugars, 0 fiber), 3g pro.

GERMAN BEER CHEESE SPREAD

We love the bold flavors of our German heritage. Cheddar and beer make a tangy spread to serve with pretzels, pumpernickel, crackers and sausage. Choose your favorite beer; the flavor really comes through in the finished recipe.

—*Angela Spengler, Tampa, FL*

Takes: 15 min. • **Makes:** 2½ cups

- 1 lb. sharp cheddar cheese, cut into ½-in. cubes
- 1 Tbsp. Worcestershire sauce
- 1½ tsp. prepared mustard
- 1 small garlic clove, minced
- ¼ tsp. salt
- ⅛ tsp. pepper
- ⅔ cup German beer or nonalcoholic beer
  Assorted crackers or vegetables

1. Place cheese in a food processor; pulse until finely chopped, about 1 minute. Add Worcestershire sauce, mustard, garlic, salt and pepper. Gradually add the beer while continuing to process until the mixture is smooth and spreadable, about 1½ minutes.
2. Transfer to a serving bowl or gift jars. Refrigerate, covered, up to 1 week. Serve with crackers or vegetables.

2 Tbsp.: 95 cal., 8g fat (5g sat. fat), 24mg chol., 187mg sod., 1g carb. (0 sugars, 0 fiber), 6g pro.

BOURBON HAM BALLS

Growing up, I loved my Grandma Nette's homemade ham balls. I make them salty-sweet with a bourbon and vinegar kick. Serve them alone, in a sandwich or over pasta or rice as a change from regular meatballs.

—*Kimla Carsten, Grand Junction, CO*

- -

Prep: 70 min. + freezing • **Bake:** 15 min.
Makes: about 3½ dozen

- 2 **lbs. fully cooked boneless ham**
- 1 **thick boneless pork loin chop (8 oz.)**
- ½ **lb. bacon strips**
- 1 **cup panko (Japanese) bread crumbs**
- 1 **cup 2% milk**
- 2 **large eggs, lightly beaten**
    Oil for frying

SAUCE

- 1½ **cups packed brown sugar**
- ½ **cup white vinegar**
- ½ **cup bourbon**
- 2 **tsp. spicy brown mustard**

1. Cut ham, pork chop and bacon into 1-in. pieces; arrange in a single layer in a foil-lined 15x10x1-in. pan. Freeze for 30 minutes or until partially frozen.
2. Preheat oven to 350°. Working in batches, transfer the meat to a food processor; pulse until coarsely ground, about 20-24 pulses. In a large bowl, combine the bread crumbs, milk and eggs. Add the pork mixture; mix lightly but thoroughly. Shape mixture into 1½-in. balls.

3. In a large skillet, heat ¼ in. of oil over medium heat. Add the ham balls in batches; cook for 3-4 minutes or until cooked through, turning occasionally. Remove from pan; drain on paper towels.
4. In a large bowl, whisk the sauce ingredients; reserve 1 cup for serving. Add the ham balls to the remaining sauce a few at a time, allowing them to soak for 1-2 minutes before transferring them to a foil-lined 15x10x1-in. baking pan.
5. Bake 15-20 minutes or until heated through, brushing occasionally with the sauce used for soaking. Serve with the reserved sauce.

1 ham ball with 1 tsp. sauce: 138 cal., 8g fat (2g sat. fat), 27mg chol., 276mg sod., 9g carb. (8g sugars, 0 fiber), 6g pro.

SAUSAGE-STUFFED JALAPENOS

If you like foods that pack a bit of a punch, you'll love these jalapeno poppers filled with sausage and cheese. This is one of my favorite recipes for parties.

—Rachel Oswald, Greenville, MI

- -

Prep: 20 min. • **Bake:** 15 min.
Makes: 44 appetizers

- 1 lb. bulk pork sausage
- 1 pkg. (8 oz.) cream cheese, softened
- 1 cup shredded Parmesan cheese
- 22 large jalapeno peppers, halved lengthwise and seeded
   Ranch salad dressing, optional

1. Preheat oven to 425°. In a large skillet, cook the sausage over medium heat until no longer pink; drain. In a small bowl, combine cream cheese and Parmesan cheese; fold in sausage.

2. Spoon about 1 tablespoonful filling into each jalapeno half. Place in two ungreased 13x9-in. baking dishes. Bake, uncovered, for 15-20 minutes or until filling is lightly browned and bubbly. Serve with ranch dressing if desired.

Note: Wear disposable gloves when cutting hot peppers; the oils can burn exposed skin. Avoid touching your face.

1 appetizer: 56 cal., 5g fat (2g sat. fat), 13mg chol., 123mg sod., 1g carb. (0 sugars, 0 fiber), 2g pro.

HOT CRAB DIP

I have a large family, work full time and coach both soccer and football, so I really value recipes that are easy to assemble. This rich, creamy dip is a fun appetizer to whip up for any gathering.

—Teri Rasey, Cadillac, MI

- -

Prep: 5 min. • **Cook:** 3 hours
Makes: about 5 cups

- ½ cup whole milk
- ⅓ cup salsa
- 3 pkg. (8 oz. each) cream cheese, cubed
- 2 pkg. (8 oz. each) imitation crabmeat, flaked
- 1 cup thinly sliced green onions
- 1 can (4 oz.) chopped green chiles
   Assorted crackers or fresh vegetables

In a small bowl, combine milk and salsa. Transfer to a greased 3-qt. slow cooker. Stir in the cream cheese, crab, onions and chiles. Cover and cook on low for 3-4 hours, stirring every 30 minutes. Serve with crackers.

¼ cup: 148 cal., 12g fat (7g sat. fat), 38mg chol., 274mg sod., 6g carb. (2g sugars, 0 fiber), 5g pro.

HOT SPICED LEMON DRINK

I received this recipe from a lady in our church who is an excellent cook and who has shared several of her slow-cooker recipes with us. We really enjoy the sweet-tangy flavor of this warm citrus punch.
—*Mandy Wright, Springville, UT*

Prep: 10 min. • **Cook:** 2 hours
Makes: about 3 qt.

   2½ qt. water
   2   cups sugar
   1½ cups orange juice
   ½   cup plus 2 Tbsp. lemon juice
   ¼   cup pineapple juice
   1   cinnamon stick (3 in.)
   ½   tsp. whole cloves

In a 5-qt. slow cooker, combine the water, sugar and juices. Place the cinnamon stick and the cloves on a double thickness of cheesecloth; bring up the corners of the cloth and tie with kitchen string to form a bag. Place bag in slow cooker. Cover and cook on low for 2-3 hours or until heated through. Discard spice bag.
1 cup: 149 cal., 0 fat (0 sat. fat), 0 chol., 1mg sod., 38g carb. (36g sugars, 0 fiber), 0 pro.

SPICED NUT MIX

One Christmas, a good friend gave me this recipe and a bag of the ingredients needed to make them as a gift. I think of her every time I stir up these delicious pumpkin-spiced nuts.
—*Patti Holland, Parker, CO*

Takes: 30 min. • **Makes:** about 10 cups

   3   large egg whites
   2   tsp. water
   2   cans (12 oz. each) salted peanuts
   1   cup whole blanched almonds
   1   cup walnut halves
   1¾ cups sugar
   3   Tbsp. pumpkin pie spice
   ¾   tsp. salt
   1   cup raisins

1. Preheat oven to 300°. In a bowl, beat egg whites and water until frothy. Add nuts; stir gently to coat. Combine sugar, pie spice and salt; add to nut mixture and stir gently to coat. Fold in raisins. Spread into two greased 15x10x1-in. baking pans.
2. Bake, uncovered, for 20-25 minutes or nuts are until lightly browned, stirring every 10 minutes. Let cool; store in an airtight container.
¼ cup: 134 cal., 8g fat (1g sat. fat), 0 chol., 87mg sod., 15g carb. (11g sugars, 2g fiber), 4g pro.

Wingin' It

Chicken wings are the ultimate party food—savory and perfect for serving up on a platter or in a basket for guests to eat their fill. Spicy, flavorful sauces are key to creating irresistible wings, and the mess is half the fun!

GRILLED JERK CHICKEN WINGS

I've been making these wings for as long as I can remember. They're simple to fix, don't require a lot of ingredients and always score big with my guests.

—*Caren Adams, Fontana, CA*

Takes: 30 min. • **Makes:** about 2 dozen

- ½ cup Caribbean jerk seasoning
- 2½ lbs. chicken wingettes and drumettes
- 2 cups honey barbecue sauce
- ⅓ cup packed brown sugar
- 2 tsp. prepared mustard
- 1 tsp. ground ginger

1. Place jerk seasoning in a large bowl; add chicken, a few pieces at a time, and toss to coat. In a small bowl, combine the barbecue sauce, brown sugar, mustard and ginger; set aside.

2. Grill chicken wings, covered, on an oiled grill rack over medium heat or broil 4 in. from the heat for 12-16 minutes, turning occasionally.

3. Brush with the sauce mixture. Grill or broil 8-10 minutes longer or until the juices run clear, basting and turning several times.

1 wing: 119 cal., 4g fat (1g sat. fat), 33mg chol., 670mg sod., 12g carb. (12g sugars, 0g fiber), 8g pro.

GRILLED CHERRY-GLAZED CHICKEN WINGS

Whenever I take these grilled wings to parties and events, there are never any leftovers! Friends and family love them.

—*Ashley Gable, Atlanta, GA*

Prep: 20 min. • **Grill:** 15 min. • **Makes:** 1 dozen

- 12 chicken wings (about 3 lbs.)
- 3 Tbsp. canola oil, divided
- 1 garlic clove, minced
- 1 cup ketchup
- ½ cup cider vinegar
- ½ cup cherry preserves
- 2 Tbsp. Louisiana-style hot sauce
- 1 Tbsp. Worcestershire sauce
- 3 tsp. coarse salt, divided
- 1 tsp. coarsely ground pepper, divided

1. Using a sharp knife, cut through the two wing joints; discard wing tips. In a small saucepan, heat 1 Tbsp. oil over medium heat. Add garlic; cook and stir for 1 minute. Stir in ketchup, vinegar, preserves, hot sauce, Worcestershire sauce, 1 tsp. salt and ½ tsp. pepper. Cook and stir until heated through. Brush wings with the remaining oil; sprinkle with the remaining salt and pepper.

2. Grill, covered, over medium heat for 15-18 minutes or until juices run clear, turning occasionally and brushing with glaze during the last 5 minutes of grilling. Serve with the remaining glaze.

1 wing (2 sections): 214 cal., 12g fat (3g sat. fat), 36mg chol., 867mg sod., 15g carb. (14g sugars, 0g fiber), 12g pro.

Contest Winner

SWEET SRIRACHA WINGS

Serve my fiery hot wings on game day or any time friends and family gather. If you don't like a ton of sweetness, add the honey slowly and taste as you go.
—*Logan Holser, Clarkston, MI*

- -

Prep: 20 min. + marinating • **Grill:** 15 min.
Makes: 1 dozen

- 12 chicken wings (about 3 lbs.)
- 1 Tbsp. canola oil
- 2 tsp. ground coriander
- ½ tsp. garlic salt
- ¼ tsp. pepper

SAUCE
- ¼ cup butter, cubed
- ½ cup orange juice
- ⅓ cup Sriracha Asian hot chili sauce
- 3 Tbsp. honey
- 2 Tbsp. lime juice
- ¼ cup chopped fresh cilantro

1. Place chicken wings in a large bowl. Mix oil, coriander, garlic salt and pepper; add to the wings and toss to coat. Refrigerate, covered, 2 hours or overnight.
2. For the sauce, in a small saucepan, melt butter. Stir in orange juice, chili sauce, honey and lime juice until blended.
3. Grill wings, covered, over medium heat 15-18 minutes or until juices run clear, turning occasionally; brush with some of the sauce during the last 5 minutes of grilling.
4. Transfer chicken to a large bowl; add the remaining sauce and toss to coat. Sprinkle with cilantro.
1 wing: 201 cal., 13g fat (5g sat. fat), 46mg chol., 321mg sod., 8g carb. (7g sugars, 0 fiber), 12g pro.

SRIRACHA SWAP
Sriracha is a spicy Thai sauce made from peppers, vinegar, garlic, sugar and salt. You can also use chili sauce or Tabasco instead.

TANGY BARBECUE WINGS

I took these slow-cooked wings to work, and they vanished before I even got a bite! The tangy sauce is lip-smacking good.
—*Sherry Pitzer, Troy, MO*

- -

Prep: 1 hour • **Cook:** 3 hours
Makes: 2 dozen wings

- 5 lbs. chicken wings
- 2½ cups ketchup
- ⅔ cup white vinegar
- ⅔ cup honey
- ½ cup molasses
- 2 to 3 Tbsp. hot pepper sauce
- 1 tsp. salt
- 1 tsp. Worcestershire sauce
- ½ tsp. onion powder
- ½ tsp. chili powder
- ½ to 1 tsp. liquid smoke, optional

1. Preheat oven to 375°. Using a sharp knife, cut through the two wing joints; discard wing tips. Arrange remaining wing pieces in two greased 15x10x1-in. baking pans. Bake 30 minutes; drain. Turn wings; bake 20-25 minutes longer or until juices run clear.
2. Meanwhile, in a large saucepan, combine remaining ingredients; bring to a boil. Reduce heat; simmer, uncovered, 30 minutes, stirring occasionally.
3. Drain wings. Place one-third of the chicken in a 5-qt. slow cooker; top with one-third of the sauce. Repeat layers twice. Cook, covered, on low 3-4 hours. Stir before serving.
Note: Uncooked chicken wing sections (wingettes) may be substituted for whole chicken wings.
1 wing (2 sections): 178 cal., 7g fat (2g sat. fat), 30mg chol., 458mg sod., 19g carb. (19g sugars, 0 fiber), 10g pro.

SMOKED PIMIENTO CHEESE CROSTINI

We always have appetizers on Christmas Eve, and each year I try new recipes. Pimiento cheese is a family favorite, so baked cheese made bite-sized was a great idea! To save time, you can use store-bought jalapeno pimiento cheese and prep the cheese and onions up to five days in advance.
—Caitlyn Bunch, Trenton, GA

- -

Prep: 50 min. • **Bake:** 10 min. • **Makes:** 4 dozen

48	slices French bread baguette (¼ in. thick)

CARAMELIZED ONIONS

2	Tbsp. canola oil
2	large onions, chopped
½	cup beef broth
2	Tbsp. balsamic vinegar
1½	tsp. sugar
¼	tsp. salt
¼	tsp. pepper
	Dash dried rosemary, crushed
	Dash dried thyme

PIMIENTO CHEESE

2½	cups shredded smoked Gouda cheese
2½	cups shredded sharp cheddar cheese
½	cup mayonnaise
2	jars (4 oz. each) diced pimientos, drained
1	tsp. Worcestershire sauce
1	tsp. hot pepper sauce
½	tsp. garlic powder
½	tsp. pepper
9	bacon strips, cooked and crumbled

1. Preheat oven to 400°. Place bread on baking sheets. Bake 4-6 minutes or until light brown.

2. In a large skillet, heat oil over medium heat. Add the onions; cook and stir for 4-6 minutes or until softened. Stir in broth, vinegar, sugar and seasonings. Reduce heat to medium-low; cook for 12-15 minutes or until the liquid is evaporated, stirring occasionally.

3. In a large bowl, toss the cheeses; beat in mayonnaise, pimientos, Worcestershire sauce, pepper sauce and seasonings. Spread 1 Tbsp. of the mixture over each baguette slice; top with 2 tsp. of the onion mixture. Sprinkle with bacon. Bake for 3-4 minutes or until the cheese is melted.

1 appetizer: 87 cal., 6g fat (3g sat. fat), 14mg chol., 174mg sod., 4g carb. (1g sugars, 0 fiber), 4g pro.

ROSEMARY & THYME LEMON COCKTAIL

A bubbly drink means it's time to celebrate! Try dressing up the usual hard lemonade with sprigs of rosemary and thyme for a refreshingly different cocktail any time of year.

—Moffat Frazier, New York, NY

Prep: 5 min. + chilling • **Makes:** 15 servings

- 5 fresh rosemary sprigs
- 5 fresh thyme sprigs
- 1 bottle (1¾ liters) lemonade

ADDITIONAL INGREDIENTS (FOR EACH SERVING)

- 1½ oz. vodka
- Ice cubes
- 2 oz. carbonated water, chilled

GARNISH

- Lemon zest strips and fresh rosemary sprigs

1. In a 2-qt. pitcher, muddle rosemary and thyme; add lemonade. Cover and refrigerate overnight. Strain lemonade; discard the herbs.

2. To prepare cocktail: In a mixing glass or tumbler, combine ½ cup lemonade and the vodka. Place ice in a highball glass; add the lemonade mixture. Top with carbonated water. Garnish with a lemon zest strip and rosemary sprig if desired.

1 cup: 152 cal., 0 fat (0 sat. fat), 0 chol., 8mg sod., 14g carb. (13g sugars, 0 fiber), 0 pro.

CANDIED PECANS

I like to pack these crispy pecans in jars, tied with pretty ribbon, for family and friends. My granddaughter gave some to a doctor at the hospital where she works—he said they were too good to be true!

—Opal Turner, Hughes Springs, TX

Prep: 25 min. • **Bake:** 30 min.
Makes: about 1 lb. (8 servings)

- 2¾ cups pecan halves
- 2 Tbsp. butter, softened, divided
- 1 cup sugar
- ½ cup water
- ½ tsp. salt
- ½ tsp. ground cinnamon
- 1 tsp. vanilla extract

1. Place pecans in a shallow baking pan in a 250° oven for 10 minutes or until warmed. Grease a 15x10x1-in. baking pan with 1 Tbsp. butter; set aside.

2. Grease the sides of a large heavy saucepan with the remaining butter; add sugar, water, salt and cinnamon. Bring to a boil, stirring constantly to dissolve the sugar. Cover; cook 2 minutes to dissolve any sugar crystals that may form on the sides of the pan.

3. Cook, without stirring, until a candy thermometer reads 236° (soft-ball stage). Remove from the heat; add vanilla. Stir in warm pecans until evenly coated.

4. Spread pecans onto the prepared baking pan. Bake at 250° for 30 minutes, stirring every 10 minutes. Spread on a waxed paper-lined baking sheet to cool.

Note: We recommend you test your candy thermometer before each use by bringing water to a boil; the thermometer should read 212°. Adjust your recipe temperature up or down based on your test.

2 oz. pecans: 380 cal., 30g fat (4g sat. fat), 8mg chol., 177mg sod., 30g carb. (26g sugars, 4g fiber), 3g pro.

HONEY HORSERADISH DIP

We love having a light dinner of appetizers on Friday night instead of a full meal, and during the summer we enjoy cooler foods. This has just the right amount of zing.
—*Ann Marie Eberhart, Gig Harbor, WA*

Prep: 10 min. + chilling • **Makes:** 1 cup

- ½ cup fat-free plain Greek yogurt
- ¼ cup stone-ground mustard
- ¼ cup honey
- 2 Tbsp. prepared horseradish
- 1 lb. cold peeled and deveined cooked shrimp (16-20 per lb.), optional
- ½ lb. cold fresh sugar snap peas, optional

Combine yogurt, mustard, honey and horseradish; refrigerate 1 hour. If desired, serve with cold cooked shrimp or sugar snap peas.

2 Tbsp.: 54 cal., 1g fat (0 sat. fat), 0 chol., 177mg sod., 11g carb. (10g sugars, 0 fiber), 2g pro. **Diabetic exchanges:** 1 starch.

CHILI-LIME ROASTED CHICKPEAS

Looking for a lighter crowd-pleasing snack? You've found it! These crunchy chickpeas will have everyone happily munching away.
—*Julie Ruble, Charlotte, NC*

Prep: 10 min. • **Bake:** 40 min. + cooling
Makes: 2 cups

- 2 cans (15 oz. each) chickpeas or garbanzo beans, rinsed, drained and patted dry
- 2 Tbsp. extra virgin olive oil
- 1 Tbsp. chili powder
- 2 tsp. ground cumin
- 1 tsp. grated lime zest
- 1 Tbsp. lime juice
- ¾ tsp. sea salt

1. Line a 15x10x1-in. baking sheet with foil. Spread the chickpeas in a single layer over the foil, removing any loose skins. Bake at 400° until very crunchy, 40-45 minutes, stirring every 15 minutes.

2. Meanwhile, whisk the remaining ingredients. Remove chickpeas from oven; let cool 5 minutes. Drizzle with the oil mixture; shake pan to coat. Cool completely. Store in an airtight container.

⅓ cup: 178 cal., 8g fat (1g sat. fat), 0mg chol., 463mg sod., 23g carb. (3g sugars, 6g fiber), 6g pro.

Rosemary-Sea Salt variation: Prepare chickpeas according to step 1 in the recipe above. Toss with 2 Tbsp. extra virgin olive oil, 1 Tbsp. minced fresh rosemary and ½ tsp. sea salt.

Orange-Curry variation: Prepare chickpeas according to step 1 in the recipe above. Whisk 2 Tbsp. extra virgin olive oil, 1 tsp. grated orange zest and 1 Tbsp. curry powder. Toss chickpeas with oil mixture. Cool completely.

Lemon-Pepper variation: Prepare chickpeas according to step 1 in the recipe above. Whisk 2 Tbsp. extra virgin olive oil, 1 tsp. grated lemon zest and 2 tsp. freshly cracked pepper. Toss chickpeas with oil mixture. Cool completely.

ORANGE JUICE SPRITZER

This is a nice twist on regular orange juice; it's great that it's not overly sweet.

—Michelle Krzmarzick, Torrance, CA

Takes: 5 min. • **Makes:** 8 servings

- 4 **cups orange juice**
- 1 **liter ginger ale, chilled**
- ¼ **cup maraschino cherry juice**
  Orange wedges and maraschino cherries, optional

In a 2-qt. pitcher, mix orange juice, ginger ale and cherry juice. Serve over ice. If desired, top individual servings with orange wedges and cherries.

1 cup: 103 cal., 0 fat (0 sat. fat), 0 chol., 9mg sod., 25g carb. (23g sugars, 0 fiber), 1g pro.

HONEY COFFEE

This pleasantly sweet coffee, inspired by the taste of a traditional Spanish latte, makes a soothing pick-me-up.

—Taste of Home Test Kitchen

Takes: 10 min. • **Makes:** 4 servings

- 2 **cups hot strong brewed coffee (French or other dark roast)**
- ½ **cup whole milk**
- ¼ **cup honey**
- ⅛ **tsp. ground cinnamon**
  Dash ground nutmeg
- ¼ **tsp. vanilla extract**

In a small saucepan, combine coffee, milk, honey, cinnamon and nutmeg. Cook and stir until heated through. (Do not boil.) Remove from the heat; stir in vanilla. Pour into cups or mugs; serve immediately.

½ cup: 86 cal., 1g fat (1g sat. fat), 4mg chol., 18mg sod., 19g carb. (18g sugars, 0 fiber), 1g pro.

SWISS MUSHROOM LOAF

Whenever I serve this outstanding loaf stuffed with Swiss cheese and mushrooms, I know people will ask for the recipe. It's excellent as an appetizer or served alongside pasta or chili.

—Heidi Mellon, Waukesha, WI

Prep: 15 min. • **Bake:** 40 min.
Makes: 12 servings

- 1 **loaf (1 lb.) Italian bread, unsliced**
- 1 **block (8 oz.) Swiss cheese, cut into cubes**
- 1 **cup sliced fresh mushrooms**
- ¼ **cup softened butter, cubed**
- 1 **small onion, finely chopped**
- 1½ **tsp. poppy seeds**
- 2 **garlic cloves, minced**
- ½ **tsp. seasoned salt**
- ½ **tsp. ground mustard**
- ½ **tsp. lemon juice**

1. Preheat oven to 350°. Cut bread diagonally into 1-in. slices to within 1 in. of the bottom of the loaf. Repeat cuts in opposite direction. Place cheese cubes and mushrooms in the cuts.

2. In a microwave-safe bowl, combine the remaining ingredients; microwave, covered, on high until butter is melted, 30-60 seconds. Stir until blended. Spoon over the bread.

3. Wrap loaf in foil; place on a baking sheet. Bake until the cheese is melted, about 40 minutes.

1 piece: 214 cal., 11g fat (6g sat. fat), 28mg chol., 372mg sod., 21g carb. (2g sugars, 1g fiber), 9g pro.

CHIPOTLE SLIDERS

This recipe has to be the ultimate in a fast-fix mini burger with simply fabulous flavor! Creamy mayo, cheese and sweet Hawaiian rolls help tame the heat of the chipotle peppers.

—Shawn Singleton, Vidor, TX

- -

Takes: 30 min. • **Makes:** 10 sliders

  1 pkg. (12 oz.) Hawaiian sweet rolls, divided
  1 tsp. salt
  ½ tsp. pepper
  8 tsp. minced chipotle peppers in adobo sauce, divided
  1½ lbs. ground beef
 10 slices pepper Jack cheese
  ½ cup mayonnaise

1. Place 2 rolls in a food processor; process until crumbly. Transfer to a large bowl; add salt, pepper and 6 tsp. chipotle peppers. Crumble beef over the bread mixture; mix well. Shape into 10 patties.
2. Grill burgers, covered, over medium heat for 3-4 minutes on each side or until a thermometer reads 160° and juices run clear. Top with cheese. Grill 1 minute longer or until the cheese is melted.
3. Split the remaining rolls and grill, cut side down, over medium heat for 30-60 seconds or until toasted. Combine mayonnaise and the remaining chipotle peppers; spread over roll bottoms. Top each with a burger. Replace roll tops.
1 slider: 377 cal., 25g fat (8g sat. fat), 67mg chol., 710mg sod., 16g carb. (3g sugars, 1g fiber), 20g pro.

HOT CHEESE DIP

When a colleague brought this cheesy dip to school for a teachers' potluck, I immediately gave it an A-plus. I had to have this irresistibly creamy recipe!

—Ardyce Piehl, Poynette, WI

- -

Takes: 30 min. • **Makes:** 3 cups

  2 cups shredded part-skim mozzarella cheese
  2 cups shredded cheddar cheese
  2 cups mayonnaise
  1 medium onion, minced
  1 can (4-4½ oz.) chopped green chiles, drained
  ½ cup sliced ripe olives
 1½ oz. sliced pepperoni
    Assorted crackers and fresh vegetables

Preheat oven to 325°. Combine the first five ingredients; spread into a greased shallow baking dish or pie plate. Top with olives and pepperoni. Bake until bubbly, about 25 minutes. Serve with crackers and fresh vegetables.
2 Tbsp.: 201 cal., 19g fat (5g sat. fat), 18mg chol., 285mg sod., 2g carb. (0 sugars, 0 fiber), 5g pro.

- -

SHARE THE PEPPERONI!
When we make this dip, we cut the pepperoni up into bits and stir it in before we cook it—that way, everyone gets bits of pepperoni!

—GingerRae TasteOfHome.com

Contest Winner

SMOKY BACON WRAPS

These cute little sausage and bacon bites have a sweet and salty taste that's fun as an appetizer—or for breakfast!
—*Cara Flora, Kokomo, IN*

Prep: 20 min. • **Bake:** 30 min.
Makes: about 3½ dozen

- 1 lb. sliced bacon
- 1 pkg. (16 oz.) miniature smoked sausage links
- ⅓ cup packed brown sugar

Preheat oven to 400°. Cut each bacon strip in half widthwise. Wrap one piece of bacon around each sausage. Place in a foil-lined 15x10x1-in. baking pan. Sprinkle with brown sugar. Bake, uncovered, 30-40 minutes or until bacon is crisp and sausage is heated through.
1 wrap: 90 cal., 7g fat (2g sat. fat), 18mg chol., 293mg sod., 2g carb. (2g sugars, 0 fiber), 5g pro.

HAM & CHEESE BISCUIT STACKS

These finger sandwiches are a pretty addition to any spread, yet filling enough to satisfy hearty appetites. I've served them at holidays, showers and tailgate parties.
—*Kelly Williams, Forked River, NJ*

Prep: 1 hour • **Bake:** 10 min. + cooling
Makes: 40 appetizers

- 4 tubes (6 oz. each) small refrigerated flaky biscuits (5 count)
- ¼ cup stone-ground mustard

ASSEMBLY

- ½ cup butter, softened
- ¼ cup chopped green onions
- ½ cup stone-ground mustard
- ¼ cup mayonnaise
- ¼ cup honey
- 10 thick slices deli ham, quartered
- 10 slices Swiss cheese, quartered
- 2½ cups shredded romaine
- 20 pitted ripe olives, drained and patted dry
- 20 pimiento-stuffed olives, drained and patted dry
- 40 frilled toothpicks

1. Preheat oven to 400°. Cut biscuits in half to make half-circles; place 2 in. apart on ungreased baking sheets. Spread the mustard over tops of biscuits. Bake until golden brown, 8-10 minutes. Cool biscuits completely on wire racks.
2. Mix the butter and green onions. In another bowl, mix mustard, mayonnaise and honey. Split each of the biscuits into two layers.
3. Spread biscuit bottoms with the butter mixture; top with ham, cheese, romaine and biscuit tops. Spoon mustard mixture over tops. Thread one olive onto each toothpick; insert a toothpick into each stack. Serve immediately.
1 appetizer: 117 cal., 7g fat (3g sat. fat), 12mg chol., 404mg sod., 11g carb. (3g sugars, 0 fiber), 3g pro.

MUSHROOM BUNDLES

I love creating my own party starters. When I made these crispy bundles for New Year's Eve, they were gone in a flash.
—*Tina Coopman, Toronto, ON*

- -

Prep: 30 min. • **Bake:** 15 min. • **Makes:** 1 dozen

1	Tbsp. olive oil
1	cup chopped fresh mushrooms
1	cup chopped baby portobello mushrooms
¼	cup finely chopped red onion
2	garlic cloves, minced
¼	tsp. dried rosemary, crushed
⅛	tsp. pepper
4	sheets phyllo dough (14x9-in.)
3	Tbsp. butter, melted
2	Tbsp. crumbled feta cheese

1. Preheat oven to 375°. In a large skillet, heat oil over medium-high heat. Add both types of mushroom and the onion; cook and stir for 4-5 minutes or until tender. Add garlic, rosemary and pepper; cook 2 minutes longer. Remove from heat.

2. Place one sheet of phyllo dough on a work surface; brush with butter. (Keep the remaining phyllo covered with plastic wrap and a damp towel to prevent it from drying out.) Layer with three additional phyllo sheets, brushing each layer. Using a sharp knife, cut the layered sheets into twelve 3-in. squares. Carefully press each stack into an ungreased mini-muffin cup.

3. Stir feta into the mushroom mixture; spoon 1 Tbsp. of filling into each phyllo cup. Form into bundles by gathering edges of phyllo squares and twisting the centers to close. Brush tops with the remaining butter. Bake 12-15 minutes or until golden brown. Serve warm.

Freeze option: Freeze the cooled bundles in freezer containers. To use, reheat on a greased baking sheet in a preheated 375° oven until crisp and heated through.

1 pastry: 53 cal., 4g fat (2g sat. fat), 8mg chol., 50mg sod., 3g carb. (1g sugars, 0 fiber), 1g pro.

RASPBERRY ICED TEA

One sip and you'll likely agree this is the best flavored tea you've ever tasted!
—*Chris Wilson, Sellersville, PA*

- -

Prep: 10 min. + chilling • **Makes:** about 2 qt.

8¼ cups water, divided
⅔ cup sugar
5 tea bags
3 to 4 cups unsweetened raspberries

1. In a large saucepan, bring 4 cups water to a boil. Stir in sugar until dissolved. Remove from the heat; add tea bags. Steep for 5-8 minutes. Discard tea bags. Add 4 cups water.
2. In another saucepan, bring raspberries and the remaining water to a boil. Reduce heat; simmer, uncovered, for 3 minutes. Strain and discard pulp. Add raspberry juice to the tea mixture. Serve in chilled glasses over ice.
1 cup: 87 cal., 0 fat (0 sat. fat), 0 chol., 0 sod., 22g carb. (18g sugars, 3g fiber), 0 pro.

BACON, CHEDDAR & SWISS CHEESE BALL

When it's time for a party, everyone always requests this ultimate cheese ball—it's such an impressive appetizer. And if you're a party guest, it makes a fabulous gift for your hosts.
—*Sue Franklin, Lake St. Louis, MO*

- -

Prep Time: 20 min. + chilling • **Makes:** 4 cups

1 pkg. (8 oz.) cream cheese, softened
½ cup sour cream
2 cups shredded Swiss cheese
2 cups shredded sharp cheddar cheese
1 cup crumbled cooked bacon
   (about 12 strips), divided
½ cup chopped pecans, toasted, divided
½ cup finely chopped onion
1 jar (2 oz.) diced pimientos, drained
2 Tbsp. sweet pickle relish
¼ tsp. salt
¼ tsp. pepper
¼ cup minced fresh parsley
1 Tbsp. poppy seeds
   Assorted crackers

1. In a large bowl, beat cream cheese and sour cream until smooth. Stir in shredded cheeses, ½ cup bacon, ¼ cup pecans, onion, pimientos, pickle relish, salt and pepper. Refrigerate, covered, at least 1 hour.
2. In a small bowl, mix parsley, poppy seeds and the remaining bacon and pecans. Spread half of the parsley mixture on a large piece of plastic. Shape half of the cheese mixture into a ball; roll ball in parsley mixture to coat evenly. Wrap in plastic. Repeat. Refrigerate for at least 1 hour. Serve with crackers.
Note: To toast nuts, bake in a shallow pan in a 350° oven for 5-10 minutes or cook in a skillet over low heat until lightly browned, stirring occasionally.
2 Tbsp.: 116 cal., 10g fat (5g sat. fat), 22mg chol., 194mg sod., 2g carb. (1g sugars, 0 fiber), 6g pro.

Side Dishes & Condiments

A great side dish does so much more than fill the space on the plate next to the entree! Here are 33 great attention-getting sides to pair beautifully with any main course— including fabulous spreads, sauces, butters and salsas to round out your meal!

OVEN-ROASTED TOMATOES

I love tomatoes because they're both healthy and versatile. You can use these roasted tomatoes in sandwiches or omelets, or to top broiled chicken.
—*Julie Tilney, Downey, CA*

- -

Prep: 20 min. • **Bake:** 3 hours + cooling
Makes: 4 cups

- 20 plum tomatoes (about 5 lbs.)
- ¼ cup olive oil
- 5 tsp. Italian seasoning
- 2½ tsp. salt

1. Preheat oven to 325°. Cut tomatoes into ½-in. slices. Brush with oil; sprinkle with Italian seasoning and salt.
2. Place on racks coated with cooking spray in foil-lined 15x10x1-in. baking pans. Bake, uncovered, for 3-3½ hours or until tomatoes are deep brown around the edges and shriveled. Cool 10-15 minutes. Serve warm or at room temperature.
3. Store in an airtight container in the refrigerator for up to 1 week.
Freeze option: Freeze in freezer container for up to 3 months. Bring tomatoes to room temperature before using.
¼ cup: 45 cal., 4g fat (0 sat. fat), 0 chol., 373mg sod., 3g carb. (2g sugars, 1g fiber), 1g pro.

GARLIC-HERB PATTYPAN SQUASH

The first time I grew a garden, I harvested yellow summer squash and cooked it with garlic and herbs. That method works beautifully with pattypan squash.
—*Kaycee Mason, Siloam Springs, AR*

- -

Takes: 25 min. • **Makes:** 4 servings

- 5 cups halved small pattypan squash (about 1¼ lbs.)
- 1 Tbsp. olive oil
- 2 garlic cloves, minced
- ½ tsp. salt
- ¼ tsp. dried oregano
- ¼ tsp. dried thyme
- ¼ tsp. pepper
- 1 Tbsp. minced fresh parsley

Preheat oven to 425°. Place squash in a greased 15x10x1-in. baking pan. Mix oil, garlic, salt, oregano, thyme and pepper; drizzle over squash. Toss to coat. Roast 15-20 minutes or until tender, stirring occasionally. Sprinkle with parsley.
⅔ cup: 58 cal., 3g fat (0 sat. fat), 0 chol., 296mg sod., 6g carb. (3g sugars, 2g fiber), 2g pro. **Diabetic exchanges:** 1 vegetable, ½ fat.

WHAT'S A PATTYPAN?

Pattypan squash is one of the three most common varieties of summer squash, along with zucchini and yellow squash. If your store doesn't carry pattypans, you can use either of the others for this recipe instead.

CREAMY PARMESAN SPINACH BAKE

This creamy, comforting side dish rounds out Thanksgiving dinner beautifully. The rich casserole is great for large guest lists—just a little goes a long way.
—*Jennifer Bley, Austin, TX*

- -

Prep: 35 min. • **Bake:** 20 min.
Makes: 12 servings

- 3 pkg. (9 oz. each) fresh baby spinach
- 1 small red onion, chopped
- 1 Tbsp. butter
- 1 pkg. (8 oz.) cream cheese, cubed
- 1 cup sour cream
- ½ cup half-and-half cream
- ⅓ cup plus 3 Tbsp. grated Parmesan cheese, divided
- 3 garlic cloves, minced
- ⅛ tsp. pepper
- 2 cans (14 oz. each) water-packed artichoke hearts, rinsed, drained and chopped
- 1 Tbsp. snipped fresh dill
- ¼ tsp. seasoned salt
- 8 butter-flavored crackers, coarsely crushed

1. Preheat oven to 350°. Place half the spinach in a steamer basket in a large saucepan over 1 in. of water. Bring to a boil; cover and steam for 3-4 minutes or just until wilted. Transfer to a large bowl. Repeat with remaining spinach; set aside.
2. In a large saucepan, saute onion in butter until tender. Reduce heat to low; stir in the cream cheese, sour cream, half-and-half, ⅓ cup of the Parmesan cheese, the garlic and pepper. Cook and stir until cream cheese is melted. Stir in artichokes, dill, seasoned salt and spinach.
3. Transfer to an ungreased 2-qt. baking dish. Sprinkle with cracker crumbs and the remaining Parmesan cheese. Bake, uncovered, for 20-25 minutes or until edges are bubbly.
½ cup: 196 cal., 14g fat (8g sat. fat), 45mg chol., 394mg sod., 10g carb. (2g sugars, 2g fiber), 7g pro.

PICKLED SWEET ONIONS

These slightly crunchy onions are not only a great hostess or Christmas gift, but also make a terrific contribution to a backyard barbecue as a relish for burgers and hot dogs.
—*Laura Winemiller, Delta, PA*

- -

Prep: 30 min. + standing • **Process:** 10 min.
Makes: 4 half-pints

- 8 cups thinly sliced sweet onions
- 2 Tbsp. canning salt
- 1¾ cups white vinegar
- 1 cup sugar
- 1 tsp. dried thyme

1. Place onions in a colander over a plate; sprinkle with canning salt and toss. Let stand for 1 hour. Rinse and drain onions, squeezing to remove excess liquid.
2. In a Dutch oven, combine vinegar, sugar and thyme; bring to a boil. Add the onions and return to a boil. Reduce heat; simmer, uncovered, 10 minutes. Remove from heat.
3. Carefully ladle the hot mixture into four hot half-pint jars, leaving ½ in. of headspace. Remove air bubbles and adjust headspace, if necessary, by adding more hot mixture. Wipe rims. Center lids on jars; screw on bands until fingertip tight.
4. Place jars into canner with simmering water, ensuring that they are completely covered. Bring to a boil; process onions 10 minutes. Remove jars and cool.
Note: The processing time listed is for altitudes of 1,000 feet or less. For altitudes up to 3,000 feet, add 5 minutes; 6,000 feet, add 10 minutes; 8,000 feet, add 15 minutes; 10,000 feet, add 20 minutes.
2 Tbsp.: 36 cal., 0 fat (0 sat.fat), 0 chol., 395mg sod., 9g carb. (7g sugars, 1g fiber), 0 pro.

CHRISTMAS JAM

I have a passion for cooking, and it's my grandmother I can thank for it—she was a marvelous cook. You can use fresh or frozen berries to make this holiday spread. No matter how you prepare it, it's sure to be hit on Christmas morning. It also makes a tasty hostess gift any time of year!

—*Jo Talvacchia, Lanoka Harbor, NJ*

- -

Prep: 25 min. • **Process:** 10 min.
Makes: about 14 half-pints

1   pkg. (40 oz.) frozen unsweetened strawberries, thawed or 2½ qt. fresh strawberries, hulled
1   lb. fresh or frozen cranberries, thawed
5   lbs. sugar
2   pouches (3 oz. each) liquid fruit pectin

1. Grind strawberries and cranberries in a food processor or grinder; place in a Dutch oven. Add sugar. Bring to a full rolling boil; boil for 1 minute. Remove from the heat; stir in pectin and return to a full rolling boil. Boil for 1 minute, stirring constantly. Remove from heat.
2. Cool for 5 minutes; skim off foam. Carefully ladle the hot mixture into hot half-pint jars, leaving ¼-in. headspace. Remove air bubbles; wipe the rims and adjust lids. Process for 10 minutes in a boiling-water canner.
Note: This processing time is for altitudes of 1,000 feet or less. Add 1 minute to the processing time for each 1,000 feet of additional altitude.
2 Tbsp.: 84 cal., 0 fat (0 sat. fat), 0 chol., 0 sod., 22g carb. (21g sugars, 0 fiber), 0 pro.

BUTTERY ALMOND GREEN BEANS

(*PICTURED ON P. 22*)
Toasted almonds add crunch to this timeless treatment for fresh green beans.
—*Edna Hoffman, Hebron, IN*

- -

Takes: 30 min. • **Makes:** 8 servings

2   lbs. fresh green beans, trimmed
2   cups water
1   envelope onion soup mix
⅔   cup slivered almonds, toasted
2   Tbsp. grated Parmesan cheese
1   tsp. paprika
6   Tbsp. butter, melted

1. In a large saucepan, combine the green beans, water and soup mix. Bring to a boil. Reduce heat; cover and simmer until the beans are crisp-tender, 15-20 minutes.
2. In a small bowl, combine the almonds, cheese and paprika. Drain the beans; drizzle with butter and sprinkle with the almond mixture. Toss to coat.
¾ cup: 179 cal., 14g fat (6g sat. fat), 24mg chol., 407mg sod., 13g carb. (4g sugars, 5g fiber), 5g pro.

CHEESE SMASHED POTATOES

Everyone loves mashed potatoes, and cheese makes them even better. Try this slimmed-down version with any entree.
—*Janet Homes, Surprise, AZ*

- -

Prep: 10 min. • **Cook:** 25 min.
Makes: 4 servings

1   lb. small red potatoes, quartered
1   cup fresh cauliflowerets
⅔   cup shredded reduced-fat cheddar cheese
¼   cup reduced-fat sour cream
¼   tsp. salt

1. Place potatoes in a large saucepan and cover with water. Bring to a boil. Reduce heat; cover and cook 10 minutes. Add cauliflower; cook 10 minutes longer or until vegetables are tender.
2. Drain potatoes; mash with cheese, sour cream and salt.
¾ cup: 161 cal., 5g fat (3g sat. fat), 18mg chol., 292mg sod., 21g carb. (3g sugars, 3g fiber), 8g pro. **Diabetic exchanges:** 1 starch, 1 medium-fat meat.

CORN SPOON BREAD

My spoon bread is moister than corn pudding made in the oven. The cream cheese is a nice addition. We love this with Thanksgiving turkey or Christmas ham.
—*Tamara Ellefson, Frederic, WI*

Prep: 15 min. • **Cook:** 3 hours
Makes: 8 servings

- 1 pkg. (8 oz.) cream cheese, softened
- ⅓ cup sugar
- 1 cup 2% milk
- 2 large eggs
- 2 Tbsp. butter, melted
- 1 tsp. salt
- ¼ tsp. ground nutmeg
   Dash pepper
- 2⅓ cups frozen corn, thawed
- 1 can (14¾ oz.) cream-style corn
- 1 pkg. (8½ oz.) cornbread/muffin mix

1. In a large bowl, beat cream cheese and sugar until smooth. Gradually beat in milk. Beat in the eggs, butter, salt, nutmeg and pepper until blended. Stir in corn and cream-style corn. Stir in cornbread mix just until moistened.
2. Pour batter into a greased 3-qt. slow cooker. Cover and cook on high for 3-4 hours or until center is almost set.
½ cup: 391 cal., 18g fat (10g sat. fat), 100mg chol., 832mg sod., 52g carb. (19g sugars, 2g fiber), 9g pro.

SHREDDED GINGERED BRUSSELS SPROUTS

Even people who normally don't care for Brussels sprouts will ask for a second helping of these!
—*James Schend, Pleasant Prairie, WI*

Takes: 25 min. • **Makes:** 6 servings

- 1 lb. fresh Brussels sprouts (about 5½ cups)
- 1 Tbsp. olive oil
- 1 small onion, finely chopped
- 1 Tbsp. minced fresh gingerroot
- 1 garlic clove, minced
- ½ tsp. salt
- 2 Tbsp. water
- ¼ tsp. pepper

1. Trim Brussels sprouts. Cut sprouts lengthwise in half, then crosswise into thin slices.
2. In a large skillet over medium-high heat, cook and stir the sprouts until they begin to brown lightly, 2-3 minutes. Add oil and toss to coat. Stir in onion, ginger, garlic and salt. Add water; reduce heat to medium and cook, covered, until the vegetables are tender, 1-2 minutes. Stir in the pepper.
¾ cup: 56 cal., 2g fat (0 sat. fat), 0 chol., 214mg sod., 8g carb. (2g sugars, 3g fiber), 2g pro.
Diabetic exchanges: 1 vegetable, ½ fat.
Molasses-Sriracha variation: Add 1 Tbsp. molasses and 2 tsp. sriracha to the water and cook as directed.
Sesame-Ginger variation: Substitute toasted sesame oil for the olive oil and proceed as directed. Sprinkle 1 Tbsp. toasted sesame seeds over cooked sprouts before serving.
Cranberry-Pecan variation: Add ¼ cup dried cranberries with the onion and ginger. Cook as directed; sprinkle with 2 Tbsp. of chopped toasted pecans before serving.
Curry variation: Add 1 tsp. curry powder with the onion and ginger; cook as directed.

ROSE PETAL HONEY

My delicious recipe is a perfect topping for toast or English muffins. It is so simple to make and will impress guests. Always verify that the flowers have not been treated with chemicals.

—*Mary Kay Dixson, Decatur, AL*

- -

Prep: 5 min. • **Cook:** 35 min. + cooling
Makes: about 1 cup

- 1   cup packed rose petals
      (about 6 medium roses)
- 1   cup water
- 2   Tbsp. lemon juice
- 6   Tbsp. sugar
- 1   pouch (3 oz.) liquid fruit pectin

1. In a large saucepan, combine rose petals, water and lemon juice; bring to a boil. Reduce heat; simmer, uncovered, until the petals lose their color. Strain, reserving liquid and discarding petals. Return liquid to the saucepan.

2. Stir in sugar. Bring to a full rolling boil over high heat, stirring constantly. Stir in pectin. Continue to boil 1 minute, stirring constantly. Pour into a jar and cool to room temperature. Cover and refrigerate up to 3 weeks.

2 Tbsp.: 39 cal., 0 fat (0 sat. fat), 0 chol., 2mg sod., 10g carb. (9g sugars, 0 fiber), 0 pro.

ORANGE-GLAZED BEETS

Beets were popular in our house when I was growing up and this recipe was a real favorite. It's so easy, and the citrus flavor is a delight.

—*Susan Punzal, Orchard Park, NY*

- -

Takes: 25 min. • **Makes:** 8 servings

- ¾   cup orange marmalade
- 6   Tbsp. orange juice
- ⅓   cup butter, cubed
- ¼   tsp. salt
- ¼   tsp. pepper
- 3   cans (14½ oz. each) sliced
      beets, drained

In a large skillet, combine the first five ingredients. Bring to a boil; cook and stir until thickened, 3-4 minutes. Add the beets; cook and stir until most of the liquid is absorbed, 6-8 minutes longer.

½ cup: 194 cal., 8g fat (5g sat. fat), 20mg chol., 443mg sod., 32g carb. (27g sugars, 3g fiber), 2g pro.

CRANBERRY WILD RICE PILAF

This tender side dish is perfect any time you want to add a special touch to a meal. Dried cranberries, currants and almonds serve up color and texture. The ladies I work with all make this rice pilaf for their families.

—Pat Gardetta, Osage Beach, MO

- -

Prep: 25 min. • **Bake:** 50 min.
Makes: 8 servings

- ¾ cup uncooked wild rice
- 3 cups chicken broth
- ½ cup medium pearl barley
- ¼ cup dried currants
- 1 Tbsp. butter
- ⅓ cup sliced almonds, toasted
- ¼ cup dried cranberries, chopped

1. Preheat oven to 325°. In a saucepan, combine wild rice and broth; bring to a boil. Reduce heat; simmer, covered, for 10 minutes. Remove from heat; stir in barley, currants and butter. Transfer to a greased 1½-qt. baking dish.
2. Bake, covered, until wild rice and barley are tender, 50-60 minutes. Stir in almonds and cranberries.

¾ cup: 166 cal., 4g fat (1g sat. fat), 6mg chol., 382mg sod., 30g carb. (8g sugars, 4g fiber), 5g pro. **Diabetic exchanges:** 2 starch, 1 fat.

Contest Winner

JALAPENO & COTIJA CHEESE POTATO STACK PIE

Stacking thinly sliced potatoes with layers of minced jalapenos and crumbled cotija cheese helps turn ordinary spuds into something truly spectacular...especially when served with salsa and sour cream.

—Colleen Delawder, Herndon, VA

- -

Prep: 20 min. • **Bake:** 50 min.
Makes: 8 servings

- 2½ lbs. red potatoes, peeled and thinly sliced
- ¼ cup butter, melted
- ½ tsp. salt
- ¼ tsp. pepper
- 2 jalapeno peppers, seeded and minced
- 1¼ cups crumbled cotija or feta cheese
   Salsa and sour cream, optional

1. Preheat oven to 375°. Line a 15x10x1-in. pan with parchment. Remove the bottom of a 9-in. springform pan and place the round outer edge in the center of the parchment.
2. Place the potatoes, butter, salt and pepper in a large bowl; toss to coat. Layer a third of the potatoes evenly within the springform ring. Sprinkle with a third of the jalapenos and a third of the cheese. Repeat layers. Top with the remaining potatoes and jalapenos.
3. Bake for 35 minutes. Top with the remaining cheese. Bake 15-20 minutes longer or until potatoes are tender. Let stand 5 minutes before removing ring. If desired, serve with salsa and sour cream.

1 slice: 223 cal., 12g fat (7g sat. fat), 34mg chol., 477mg sod., 23g carb. (2g sugars, 3g fiber), 7g pro.

Sassy Salsas

"Salsa" just means sauce—and there's no limit to the varieties you can make. Whether served with chips or as a topping for your main course, salsas add a bit of a kick wherever they go. The secret ingredient is creativity!

STRAWBERRY TOMATO SALSA

This sweet and tangy salsa is miles away from the spicy version people expect. Serve it as an appetizer with tortilla chips for scooping, or make it part of the main event and spoon it over chicken or pork.

—Amy Hinkle, Topeka, KS

- -

Takes: 25 min. • **Makes:** 6 cups

2	pints cherry tomatoes, quartered
1	pint fresh strawberries, chopped
8	green onions, chopped
½	cup minced fresh cilantro
6	Tbsp. olive oil
2	Tbsp. balsamic vinegar
½	tsp. salt

In a large bowl, combine the tomatoes, strawberries, green onions and cilantro. In a small bowl, whisk oil, balsamic vinegar and salt; gently stir into tomato mixture. Refrigerate until serving.

¼ cup: 41 cal., 4g fat (0 sat. fat), 0 chol., 53mg sod., 3g carb. (2g sugars, 1g fiber), 0 pro.

COLORFUL CORN SALSA

It's worth the extra time it takes to grill the ears of corn when the result is this colorful salsa! The flavor goes well with barbecued meats, but it's also tasty served with chips.

—Nancy Horsburgh, Everett, ON

- -

Prep: 30 min. • **Grill:** 20 min. + cooling
Makes: about 2½ cups

2	medium ears sweet corn in husks
2	medium tomatoes, chopped
1	small onion, chopped
2	Tbsp. minced fresh cilantro
1	Tbsp. lime juice
1	Tbsp. finely chopped green pepper
1	Tbsp. finely chopped sweet red pepper
1	tsp. minced seeded jalapeno pepper
¼	tsp. salt
	Dash pepper
	Tortilla chips

1. Peel back husks of corn but don't remove; remove silk. Replace the husks and tie with kitchen string. Place corn in a bowl and cover with water; soak for 20 minutes. Drain.

2. Grill corn, covered, over medium-high heat for 20-35 minutes or until husks are blackened and corn is tender, turning several times. Cool.

3. Remove corn from cobs and place in a bowl. Add tomatoes, onion, cilantro, lime juice, peppers, salt and pepper. Serve with tortilla chips.

Note: Wear disposable gloves when cutting hot peppers; the oils can burn skin. Avoid touching your face.

¼ cup: 24 cal., 0 fat (0 sat. fat), 0 chol., 64mg sod., 5g carb. (0 sugars, 1g fiber), 1g pro.

Diabetic exchanges: 1 vegetable.

CRISP CUCUMBER SALSA

Here's a fantastic way to use cucumbers. You'll love the creamy and crunchy texture and super fresh flavors.
—*Charlene Skjerven, Hoople, ND*

- -

Takes: 20 min. • **Makes:** 2½ cups

- 2 cups finely chopped cucumber, peeled and seeded
- ½ cup finely chopped seeded tomato
- ¼ cup chopped red onion
- 2 Tbsp. minced fresh parsley
- 1 jalapeno pepper, seeded and chopped
- 4½ tsp. minced fresh cilantro
- 1 garlic clove, minced
- ¼ cup reduced-fat sour cream
- 1½ tsp. lemon juice
- 1½ tsp. lime juice
- ¼ tsp. ground cumin
- ¼ tsp. seasoned salt
   Baked tortilla chip scoops

In a small bowl, combine the first seven ingredients. In another bowl, combine the sour cream, lemon juice, lime juice, cumin and seasoned salt. Pour over the cucumber mixture and toss gently to coat. Serve immediately with chips.
¼ cup: 16 cal., 1g fat (0 sat. fat), 2mg chol., 44mg sod., 2g carb. (1g sugars, 0 fiber), 1g pro.
Diabetic exchanges: 1 free food.

SEEDING CUCUMBERS

Don't skip seeding the cucumber. Otherwise you may end up with watery salad. To make seeding a breeze, halve cucumbers lengthwise and use a spoon to scoop out the pulpy centers.

MEXICAN SALSA

I love to make this colorful salsa with fresh tomatoes and peppers from my garden. I even have a special pan that I use just for roasting the peppers!
—*Roger Stenman, Batavia, IL*

- -

Prep: 40 min. • **Makes:** 3½ cups

- 3 jalapeno peppers
- 1 medium onion, quartered
- 1 garlic clove, halved
- 2 cans (one 28 oz., one 14½ oz.) whole tomatoes, drained
- 4 fresh cilantro sprigs
- ½ tsp. salt
   Tortilla chips

1. Heat a small ungreased cast-iron skillet over high heat. With a small sharp knife, pierce jalapenos; add to hot skillet. Cook for 15-20 minutes or until the peppers are blistered and blackened, turning occasionally.
2. Immediately place jalapenos in a small bowl; cover and let stand for 20 minutes. Peel off and discard the charred skins. Remove stems and seeds.
3. Place the onion and garlic in a food processor; cover and pulse four times. Add the tomatoes, cilantro, salt and jalapenos. Cover and process until salsa reaches desired consistency. Chill until serving. Serve with tortilla chips.
¼ cup: 23 cal., 0 fat (0 sat. fat), 0 chol., 241mg sod., 5g carb. (3g sugars, 1g fiber), 1g pro.

STEAKHOUSE MUSHROOMS

I got this recipe from a friend back when we were in nursing school. Whenever my husband is cooking meat on the grill, you can bet I'll be in the kitchen preparing these delectable mushrooms!
—*Kenda Burgett, Rattan, OK*

- -

Takes: 20 min. • **Makes:** 4 servings

- ¼ cup butter, cubed
- 1 lb. medium fresh mushrooms
- 2 tsp. dried basil
- ½ tsp. dried oregano
- ½ tsp. seasoned salt
- ¼ tsp. garlic powder
- 1 tsp. browning sauce, optional

In a large skillet, heat butter over medium-high heat. Add mushrooms; cook and stir until tender. Stir in seasonings and, if desired, browning sauce. Reduce heat to medium; cook, covered, for 3-5 minutes to allow flavors to blend.

¾ cup: 131 cal., 12g fat (7g sat. fat), 30mg chol., 276mg sod., 5g carb. (2g sugars, 2g fiber), 4g pro.

MICROWAVE PICKLES

You can enjoy a small batch of these sweet, crunchy pickles anytime without the work of traditional canning methods. They're loaded with flavor and so easy to make.
—*Marie Wladyka, Land O'Lakes, FL*

- -

Prep: 10 min. + chilling • **Makes:** 6 servings

- 1 medium cucumber, thinly sliced
- 2 small onions, thinly sliced
- ¾ cup sugar
- ½ cup vinegar
- 1 tsp. salt
- ½ tsp. celery seed
- ½ tsp. mustard seed

Combine all the ingredients In a large microwave-safe bowl. Microwave, uncovered, on high for 3 minutes; stir. Cook 2-3 minutes longer or until the mixture is bubbly and the cucumbers and onions are crisp-tender. Cover and refrigerate for at least 4 hours. Serve with a slotted spoon.

1 serving: 115 cal., 0 fat (0 sat. fat), 0 chol., 395mg sod., 29g carb. (27g sugars, 1g fiber), 1g pro.

SOUTHWESTERN RICE

I created this colorful side dish after trying something similar at a restaurant. It pairs with any Tex-Mex meal wonderfully. Add cubes of grilled chicken breast to the rice to make it a meal in itself.
—*Michelle Dennis, Clarks Hill, IN*

- -

Takes: 30 min. • **Makes:** 8 servings

- 1 Tbsp. olive oil
- 1 medium green pepper, diced
- 1 medium onion, chopped
- 2 garlic cloves, minced
- 1 cup uncooked long grain rice
- ½ tsp. ground cumin
- ⅛ tsp. ground turmeric
- 1 can (14½ oz.) reduced-sodium chicken broth
- 2 cups frozen corn (about 10 oz.), thawed
- 1 can (15 oz.) black beans, rinsed and drained
- 1 can (10 oz.) diced tomatoes and green chilies, undrained

1. In a large nonstick skillet, heat oil over medium-high heat; saute pepper and onion for 3 minutes. Add garlic; cook and stir 1 minute.
2. Stir in rice, spices and broth; bring to a boil. Reduce heat; simmer, covered, until rice is tender, about 15 minutes. Stir in the remaining ingredients; cook, covered, until heated through.

¾ cup: 198 cal., 3g fat (1g sat. fat), 1mg chol., 339mg sod., 37g carb. (0 sugars, 5g fiber), 7g pro.

PEACH CHILI SAUCE

I've been eating and serving this tasty chili sauce since I was a child—it's always been a favorite.

—Barb Batten, Blenheim, ON

- -

Prep: 2¾ hours • **Process:** 20 min.
Makes: 5 pints

- 5 lbs. tomatoes (about 15 medium)
- 3 medium peaches (about 1½ lbs.)
- 3 large sweet onions, chopped (about 6 cups)
- 3 medium pears, peeled and chopped (about 3 cups)
- 2 medium green peppers, chopped (about 1½ cups)
- 2 celery ribs, chopped
- 2 jalapeno peppers, seeded and cut into matchsticks
- 3 cups sugar
- 2 cups white vinegar
- 3 tsp. salt
- 1 tsp. mixed pickling spices

1. Fill a Dutch oven two-thirds of the way with water; bring to a boil. Cut a shallow X on the bottom of each tomato and peach. Using tongs, place tomatoes and peaches, a few at a time, in the boiling water for 30-60 seconds or just until skin at the X begins to loosen. Remove; immediately drop into ice water. Pull off skins with tip of a knife; discard skins.

2. Coarsely chop tomatoes and peaches; place in a stockpot. Add onions, pears, green peppers, celery, jalapenos, sugar, vinegar and salt. Place pickling spices on a double thickness of cheesecloth. Gather the corners of the cloth to enclose spices; tie securely with string. Add to stockpot. Bring to a boil. Reduce heat; simmer, uncovered, for 2-2½ hours or until sauce is thickened, stirring occasionally. Discard the spice bag.

3. Carefully ladle hot mixture into five hot 1-pint jars, leaving ½-in. headspace. Remove air bubbles and adjust headspace, if necessary, by adding hot mixture. Wipe rims. Center lids on jars; screw on bands until fingertip tight.

4. Place jars into canner with simmering water, ensuring that they are completely covered with water. Bring to a boil; process for 20 minutes. Remove jars from canner and cool.

Note: Wear disposable gloves when cutting hot peppers; the oils can burn skin. Avoid touching your face. • The processing time listed is for altitudes of 1,000 feet or less. For altitudes up to 3,000 feet, add 5 minutes; 6,000 feet, add 10 minutes; 8,000 feet, add 15 minutes; 10,000 feet, add 20 minutes.

2 Tbsp.: 40 cal., 0 fat (0 sat. fat), 0 chol., 82mg sod., 10g carb. (9g sugars, 1g fiber), 0 pro.
Diabetic exchanges: ½ starch.

CHUNKY APPLESAUCE

There's something extra special about homemade applesauce. This simple recipe is tart and not too sweet. It makes the perfect side dish, especially with pork chops or a pork roast.

—*Deborah Amrine, Fort Myers, FL*

Prep: 15 min. • **Cook:** 30 min.
Makes: about 3½ cups

- 8   cups chopped peeled tart apples (about 3½ lbs.)
- ½   cup packed brown sugar
- 1   tsp. ground cinnamon
- 2   tsp. vanilla extract

In a Dutch oven, combine apples, brown sugar and cinnamon. Cover and cook over medium-low heat 30-40 minutes or until apples are tender, stirring occasionally. Remove from heat; stir in vanilla. Mash the apples slightly if desired. Serve warm or cold.

½ cup: 157 cal., 0 fat (0 sat. fat), 0 chol., 7mg sod., 40g carb. (36g sugars, 3g fiber), 0 pro.

Spiced Applesauce: Reduce vanilla to ½ tsp.; Add 1 Tbsp. lemon juice, ½ tsp. ground ginger, ¼ tsp. ground nutmeg, ¼ tsp. ground mace and ⅛ tsp. ground cardamom to the apples before cooking.

New England Applesauce: Use Rome Beauty or McIntosh apples. Omit brown sugar and vanilla. Reduce cinnamon to ¼ tsp.; add 1 cup honey, 1 cup water and ½ cup lemon juice to apples before cooking. If desired, stir 2 Tbsp. grenadine syrup into mashed apples.

Contest Winner

MUSHROOM MARSALA WITH BARLEY

My satisfying vegetarian recipe is a tasty mashup of chicken Marsala and mushroom barley soup. It's great as a side dish, with or without the barley, but it's also hearty enough to stand alone as a main dish.

—*Arlene Erlbach, Morton Grove, IL*

Prep: 20 min. • **Cook:** 4 hours
Makes: 6 servings

- 1½ lbs. baby portobello mushrooms, cut into ¾-in. chunks
- 1   cup thinly sliced shallots
- 3   Tbsp. olive oil
- ½   tsp. minced fresh thyme
- ¾   cup Marsala wine, divided
- 3   Tbsp. reduced-fat sour cream
- 2   Tbsp. all-purpose flour
- 1½ tsp. grated lemon zest
- ¼   tsp. salt
- ¼   cup crumbled goat cheese
- ¼   cup minced fresh parsley
- 2½ cups cooked barley

1. In a 4- or 5-qt. slow cooker, combine mushrooms, shallots, olive oil and thyme. Add ¼ cup Marsala wine. Cook, covered, on low until the vegetables are tender, 4 hours.

2. Stir in sour cream, flour, lemon zest, salt and the remaining Marsala. Cook, covered, on low 15 minutes longer. Sprinkle with goat cheese and parsley. Serve with hot cooked barley.

¾ cup: 235 cal., 9g fat (2g sat. fat), 7mg chol., 139mg sod., 31g carb. (6g sugars, 5g fiber), 7g pro. **Diabetic exchanges:** 2 starch, 2 fat, 1 vegetable.

SCALLOPED POTATOES WITH HAM

This dish is a crowd-pleaser with its smooth sauce, chunks of ham and potato slices. I always enjoyed it when my mother made it. I added the parsley and the thyme, and now my husband and five children request it.
—*Wendy Rhoades, Yacolt, WA*

- -

Prep: 15 min. • **Bake:** 1 hour 20 min.
Makes: 4 servings

- 6 Tbsp. butter, divided
- ¼ cup all-purpose flour
- 1 tsp. dried parsley flakes
- 1 tsp. salt
- ½ tsp. dried thyme
- ¼ tsp. pepper
- 3 cups 2% milk
- 6 cups thinly sliced peeled potatoes
- 1½ cups chopped fully cooked ham
- 1 small onion, grated

1. Preheat oven to 385°. In a large saucepan, melt 4 Tbsp. butter. Stir in flour, parsley, salt, thyme and pepper until smooth. Gradually add milk; bring to a boil. Cook and stir for 2 minutes.
2. Combine the potatoes, ham and onion; place half in a greased 2½-qt. baking dish. Top with half of the sauce; repeat layers.
3. Cover and bake for 65-75 minutes or until the potatoes are almost tender. Dot with the remaining butter. Bake, uncovered, 15-20 minutes longer or until the potatoes are tender.
1 cup: 521 cal., 28g fat (16g sat. fat), 99mg chol., 2343mg sod., 47g carb. (10g sugars, 5g fiber), 19g pro.

CORN ON THE COB WITH LEMON-PEPPER BUTTER

Roasting fresh-picked corn is as old as the Ozark hills where I was raised. My Grandpa Mitchell always salted and peppered his butter on the edge of his plate before spreading it on his corn. Today, I continue the tradition by serving lemon-pepper butter with roasted corn—it's a favorite!
—*Allene Bary-Cooper, Wichita Falls, TX*

- -

Prep: 10 min. + soaking • **Grill:** 25 min.
Makes: 8 servings

- 8 medium ears sweet corn
- 1 cup butter, softened
- 2 Tbsp. lemon-pepper seasoning

1. Carefully peel back corn husks to within 1 in. of bottoms; remove silk. Rewrap corn in husks; secure with kitchen string. Place in a stockpot; cover with cold water. Soak 20 minutes; drain.
2. Meanwhile, in a small bowl, mix butter and lemon pepper. Grill corn, covered, over medium heat 20-25 minutes or until tender, turning often.
3. Cut string and peel back husks. Serve corn with butter mixture.
1 ear of corn with 2 Tbsp. butter: 280 cal., 24g fat (15g sat. fat), 60mg chol., 520mg sod., 17g carb. (3g sugars, 3g fiber), 3g pro.

TWICE-BAKED SWEET POTATOES WITH BACON

This side always takes my guests by surprise because of the smoky flavor, creamy texture and pretty presentation. No doubt you'll get major kudos when you place these on your table.

—Cynthia Boberskyj, Rochester, NY

Prep: 20 min. • **Bake:** 1¼ hours
Makes: 6 servings

- 6   medium sweet potatoes (about 12 oz. each)
- ¼   cup butter, softened
- ½   tsp. salt
- ⅛   tsp. pepper
- 2   cups shredded cheddar cheese
- 6   bacon strips, cooked and crumbled

1. Preheat oven to 375°. Scrub sweet potatoes; pierce each potato several times with a fork. Place in a foil-lined 15x10x1-in. baking pan; bake until tender, 1-1¼ hours. Cool slightly.
2. Cut a thin slice off the top of each potato; discard slice. Scoop out pulp, leaving thin shells. In a large bowl, mash pulp with butter, salt and pepper; stir in cheese and bacon. Spoon into shells.
3. Return to pan. Bake until heated through, 15-20 minutes.
1 stuffed potato: 611 cal., 24g fat (13g sat. fat), 66mg chol., 683mg sod., 84g carb. (34g sugars, 10g fiber), 17g pro.

FREEZE IT
SLOW-COOKER PEAR BUTTER

This is a tasty spread for toast, muffins, biscuits or any of your favorite breads. It is easy to make and has a rich pear flavor with hints of cinnamon, star anise and lemon. For a more intense licorice flavor, use whole star anise.

—Geraldine Saucier, Albuquerque, NM

Prep: 25 min. • **Cook:** 6 hours • **Makes:** 6 cups

- 1   cinnamon stick (3 in.)
- 4-5   star anise points (about ½ whole)
- 5   lbs. pears, peeled and chopped (about 12 cups)
- 1   cup packed light brown sugar
- 1   tsp. grated lemon zest

1. Place spices on a double thickness of cheesecloth. Gather corners of the cloth to enclose the spices; tie securely with string. In a 5- or 6-qt. slow cooker, toss the remaining ingredients. Add the spice bag, covering with pears.
2. Cook, covered, on low until pears are tender, 5-6 hours. Remove spice bag.
3. Puree pear mixture using an immersion blender. Or, cool slightly and puree mixture in a blender in batches; return to slow cooker.
4. Cook, uncovered, on high until mixture is thickened to desired consistency, 1-2 hours, stirring occasionally. Store cooled pear butter in an airtight container in the refrigerator up to 1 week.
Freeze option: Freeze cooled pear butter in freezer containers up to 3 months. Liquids expand as they freeze, so leave extra room at the top of the freezer container. To use, thaw in refrigerator.
2 Tbsp.: 41 cal., 0 fat (0 sat. fat), 0 chol., 2mg sod., 11g carb. (9g sugars, 1g fiber), 0 pro.

SPICED ACORN SQUASH

Working full time, I found I didn't always have time to cook the meals my family loved. So I re-created many of our favorites in the slow cooker. This treatment for squash is one of them.
—*Carol Greco, Centereach, NY*

- -

Prep: 15 min. • **Cook:** 3½ hours
Makes: 4 squash halves

- ¾ cup packed brown sugar
- 1 tsp. ground cinnamon
- 1 tsp. ground nutmeg
- 2 small acorn squash, halved and seeded
- ¾ cup raisins
- 4 Tbsp. butter
- ½ cup water

1. In a small bowl, mix brown sugar, cinnamon and nutmeg; spoon into the squash halves. Sprinkle with raisins. Top each with 1 Tbsp. butter. Wrap each half individually in heavy-duty foil; seal tightly.
2. Pour water into a 5-qt. slow cooker. Place squash in slow cooker, cut side up (packets may be stacked). Cook, covered, on high for 3½-4 hours or until the squash is tender. Open foil carefully to allow steam to escape.
1 squash half: 433 cal., 12g fat (7g sat. fat), 31mg chol., 142mg sod., 86g carb. (63g sugars, 5g fiber), 3g pro.

CAULIFLOWER CASSEROLE

To dress up cauliflower, my mother used a delightful mixture of a cheesy sauce, bright red and green pepper pieces and crushed cornflakes. Leftovers were rare!
—*Linda McGinty, Parma, OH*

- -

Prep: 15 min. • **Bake:** 30 min.
Makes: 8 servings

- 1 medium head cauliflower, broken into florets
- 1 cup sour cream
- 1 cup shredded cheddar cheese
- ½ cup crushed cornflakes
- ¼ cup chopped green pepper
- ¼ cup chopped sweet red pepper
- 1 tsp. salt
- ¼ cup grated Parmesan cheese
  Paprika

1. Preheat oven to 325°. Place 1 in. of water in a saucepan; add cauliflower. Bring to a boil. Reduce heat; cover and simmer for 5-10 minutes or until crisp-tender. Drain.
2. In a large bowl, combine cauliflower, sour cream, cheddar cheese, cornflakes, peppers and salt; transfer to a greased 2-qt. baking dish. Sprinkle with Parmesan cheese and paprika.
3. Bake, uncovered, for 30-35 minutes or until heated through.
1 serving: 162 cal., 10g fat (7g sat. fat), 37mg chol., 503mg sod., 10g carb. (4g sugars, 2g fiber), 7g pro.

PORTOBELLO RISOTTO WITH MASCARPONE

Portobello mushrooms add an earthy flavor to this creamy classic. Each serving is topped with soft, buttery mascarpone cheese, which makes it extra special.

—*Carmella Ryan, Rockville Centre, NY*

- -

Prep: 20 min. • **Cook:** 25 min.
Makes: 6 servings

- 1½ cups water
- 1 can (14 oz.) reduced-sodium beef broth
- ½ cup chopped shallots
- 2 garlic cloves, minced
- 1 Tbsp. canola oil
- 1 cup uncooked arborio rice
- 1 Tbsp. minced fresh thyme or 1 tsp. dried thyme
- ½ tsp. salt
- ½ tsp. pepper
- ½ cup white wine or additional reduced-sodium beef broth
- 1 cup sliced baby portobello mushrooms, chopped
- ¼ cup grated Parmesan cheese
- ½ cup mascarpone cheese

1. In a large saucepan, heat water and broth and keep warm. In a large saucepan, saute the shallots and garlic in oil for 2-3 minutes or until the shallots are tender. Add the rice, thyme, salt and pepper; cook and stir for 2-3 minutes. Reduce heat; stir in wine. Cook and stir until all the liquid is absorbed.

2. Add heated broth, ½ cup at a time, stirring constantly. Allow the liquid to absorb between additions. Cook just until risotto is creamy and rice is almost tender. (Cooking time is about 20 minutes.)

3. Add mushrooms and Parmesan cheese; stir gently until cheese is melted. Garnish each serving with a tablespoonful of mascarpone. Serve immediately.

Freeze option: Before adding mascarpone, freeze cooled risotto in freezer containers. To use, partially thaw in refrigerator overnight. Heat through in a saucepan; stir occasionally and add a little broth or water if necessary. Garnish as directed.

¾ cup risotto with 1 Tbsp. marscarpone: 350 cal., 21g fat (10g sat. fat), 51mg chol., 393mg sod., 31g carb. (1g sugars, 1g fiber), 7g pro.

CHEESY GRITS

As a comforting side dish, grits have great potential but sometimes need a flavor boost. Try adding red pepper flakes, fresh rosemary or crushed garlic.

—Paula Hughes, Birmingham, AL

- -

Takes: 25 min. • **Makes:** 8 servings

- 2   cups 2% milk
- 1   cup chicken or vegetable broth
- 1   cup water
- 1   tsp. salt
- 1   cup uncooked old-fashioned grits
- 2   to 3 cups shredded sharp cheddar or Monterey Jack cheese
      Salt and pepper to taste

Combine milk, broth and water in a large saucepan; bring to a boil. Add salt. Whisk in grits; reduce heat to low. Cook, stirring frequently, until creamy, 15-20 minutes. Stir in cheese until melted. Season with pepper and additional salt to taste.

½ cup: 225 cal., 11g fat (6g sat. fat), 34mg chol., 629mg sod., 20g carb. (3g sugars, 1g fiber), 10g pro.

HONEY-THYME BUTTERNUT SQUASH

Instead of potatoes, try whipping up mashed butternut squash with honey, butter and thyme. More than a festive Thanksgiving side, this 30-minute dish will be a new favorite for weeknight meals, too.

—Bianca Noiseux, Bristol, CT

- -

Takes: 30 min. • **Makes:** 10 servings

- 1   large butternut squash (about 5 lbs.), peeled and cubed
- ¼   cup butter, cubed
- 3   Tbsp. half-and-half cream
- 2   Tbsp. honey
- 2   tsp. dried parsley flakes
- ½   tsp. salt
- ⅛   tsp. dried thyme
- ⅛   tsp. coarsely ground pepper

In a large saucepan, bring 1 in. of water to a boil. Add squash; cover and cook for 10-15 minutes or until tender. Drain. Mash squash with the remaining ingredients.

¾ cup: 145 cal., 5g fat (3g sat. fat), 14mg chol., 161mg sod., 26g carb. (9g sugars, 7g fiber), 2g pro. **Diabetic exchanges:** 1½ starch, 1 fat.

Contest Winner

SPINACH-TOPPED TOMATOES

This colorful side dish is classic for a reason! It provides a perfect taste of summer when garden-fresh tomatoes are in season, but we enjoy it year-round. My daughter especially loves this dish.

—Ila Mae Alderman, Galax, VA

- -

Prep: 20 min. • **Bake:** 15 min.
Makes: 6 servings

- 1   pkg. (10 oz.) frozen chopped spinach
- 2   chicken bouillon cubes
      Salt
- 3   large tomatoes, halved
- 1   cup soft bread crumbs
- ½   cup grated Parmesan cheese
- ½   cup chopped onion
- ½   cup butter, melted
- 1   large egg, lightly beaten
- 1   garlic clove, minced
- ¼   tsp. pepper
- ⅛   tsp. cayenne pepper
      Shredded Parmesan cheese, optional

1. In a large saucepan, cook spinach according to package directions with bouillon; drain well. Cool slightly; press out excess liquid.

2. Lightly salt tomato halves; place cut side down on a paper towel 15 minutes to absorb excess moisture.

3. In a small bowl, combine spinach, bread crumbs, cheese, onion, butter, egg, garlic, pepper and cayenne pepper.

4. Place tomato halves, cut side up, in a shallow baking dish. Divide spinach mixture over tomatoes. Sprinkle with shredded cheese if desired. Bake at 350° for about 15 minutes or until heated through.

½ tomato: 236 cal., 19g fat (11g sat. fat), 78mg chol., 649mg sod., 12g carb. (4g sugars, 3g fiber), 7g pro.

Soups, Salads & Sandwiches

Soups, salads and sandwiches combine in the most wonderful ways, whether you want something light that's suitable for a backyard picnic or a savory, comforting meal to ward off the winter chill. Check out the recipes in this chapter, and mix and match to suit the season!

SPICED SWEET POTATO SOUP

Sweet potatoes simmered in a pot with ginger, cinnamon and curry make a cheerful soup that warms our spirits.

—Lisa Speer, Palm Beach, FL

- -

Prep: 20 min. • **Cook:** 6 hours
Makes: 12 servings (2¼ qt.)

- 2 lbs. sweet potatoes (about 4 medium), peeled and chopped
- 1 large sweet onion, finely chopped
- 1 medium sweet red pepper, finely chopped
- 1½ tsp. curry powder
- 1 tsp. sea salt
- ½ tsp. ground cinnamon
- ¼ tsp. ground ginger
- ¼ tsp. ground allspice
- ¼ tsp. grated lemon zest
- ⅛ tsp. coarsely ground pepper
- 6 cups reduced-sodium chicken broth
  Salted pumpkin seeds or pepitas, optional

1. In a 5-qt. slow cooker, combine first 11 ingredients. Cook, covered, on low until the vegetables are tender, 6-8 hours.
2. Puree the soup using an immersion blender. Or, cool slightly and puree in batches in a blender; return to slow cooker and heat through. If desired, top individual servings with pumpkin seeds.
¾ cup: 86 cal., 0 fat (0 sat. fat), 0 chol., 489mg sod., 19g carb. (5g sugars, 3g fiber), 3g pro.

DILLY TURKEY MELT

This hearty grilled sandwich has a distinctive combination of ingredients. The pickle slices add a bit of fun, and the barbecue sauce provides an irresistible hint of sweetness.

—Henry Mujica, North Riverside, IL

- -

Takes: 25 min. • **Makes:** 4 servings

- 2 medium onions, sliced
- 4 Tbsp. butter, divided
- 4 Tbsp. barbecue sauce
- 8 slices sourdough bread
- 8 slices Monterey Jack cheese
- 8 slices Canadian bacon
- 8 thin slices cooked turkey
  Dill pickle slices

1. In a large skillet, saute onions in 1 Tbsp. butter until tender; remove and set aside. Spread the barbecue sauce on four slices of bread. Layer each with one slice of cheese, two slices each of bacon and turkey, pickle slices, onions and another slice of cheese. Cover with the remaining slices of bread.
2. In the same skillet over medium-low heat, melt the remaining butter. Cook sandwiches on both sides until golden brown and cheese is melted (cover the skillet during the last few minutes to help melt cheese, if necessary).
1 sandwich: 628 cal., 34g fat (19g sat. fat), 137mg chol., 1359mg sod., 42g carb. (11g sugars, 2g fiber), 39g pro.

BROCCOLI SALAD SUPREME

People can't get enough of the sweet grapes and crunchy broccoli in this colorful salad. I appreciate its make-ahead convenience.
—*Terri Twyman, Bonanza, OR*

Takes: 10 min. • **Makes:** about 20 servings

- 10 cups broccoli florets (about 3½ lbs.)
- 6 cups seedless red grapes (about 3 lbs.)
- 1 cup sliced celery
- 6 green onions, sliced
- 2 cups mayonnaise
- ⅔ cup sugar
- 2 Tbsp. cider vinegar
- 1 lb. sliced bacon, cooked and crumbled
- 1⅓ cups slivered almonds, toasted

1. In a large salad bowl, combine the broccoli, grapes, celery and onions. In a small bowl, combine the mayonnaise, sugar and vinegar. Pour over broccoli mixture and toss to coat.

2. Cover; refrigerate for at least 4 hours or overnight. Just before serving, gently stir in bacon and almonds.

1 cup: 344 cal., 26g fat (4g sat. fat), 14mg chol., 268mg sod., 25g carb. (20g sugars, 4g fiber), 7g pro.

GREEN ONIONS IN A SNIP!
I use my kitchen shears to cut green onions for salads. It's safer than using a knife, and I finish in a flash.
—**Mary P.,** Hillsboro, IN

COMFORTING CHICKEN NOODLE SOUP

A good friend made us this rich, comforting soup after the birth of our son. It was such a help to have dinner taken care of until I was back on my feet. Now I give a pot of it (along with the recipe) to other new mothers.
—*Joanna Sargent, Sandy, UT*

Takes: 25 min.
Makes: 12 servings (about 3 qt.)

- 2 qt. water
- 8 tsp. chicken bouillon granules
- 6½ cups uncooked wide egg noodles
- 2 cans (10¾ oz. each) condensed cream of chicken soup, undiluted
- 3 cups cubed cooked chicken
- 1 cup sour cream
  Minced fresh parsley

1. In a large saucepan, bring water and bouillon to a boil. Add noodles; cook, uncovered, until tender, about 10 minutes. Do not drain. Add soup and chicken; heat through.

2. Remove from the heat; stir in the sour cream. Sprinkle with minced parsley.

1 cup: 218 cal., 9g fat (4g sat. fat), 67mg chol., 980mg sod., 18g carb. (2g sugars, 1g fiber), 15g pro.

CREAMY WHITE CHILI

When I was a child, white beans were a staple at our table. My husband, Bill, also loves them. Our four children, six grandchildren and one great-grandchild are not as fond of beans, but they still enjoy this tempting chili.
—*Gloria Hutchings, Troy, MI*

- -

Prep: 20 min. + standing • **Cook:** 1 hour
Makes: 10 servings

- 1 lb. dried navy beans
- 1 medium onion, chopped
- 2 garlic cloves, minced
- 1 Tbsp. canola oil
- 1 can (10¾ oz.) condensed cream of chicken soup, undiluted
- 1 can (10¾ oz.) condensed cream of celery soup, undiluted
- 1 cup water
- 1 medium potato, peeled and cubed
- 2 Tbsp. chili powder
- 1 tsp. chicken bouillon granules
- ½ tsp. salt
- 1½ cups half-and-half cream
- 1 can (15 oz.) garbanzo beans or chickpeas, rinsed and drained

1. Place navy beans in a Dutch oven or soup kettle; add water to cover by 2 in. Bring to a boil; boil for 2 minutes. Remove from the heat; cover and let stand for 1 hour. Drain and discard liquid; return beans to pan. Add water to cover by 2 in. Bring to a boil; cover and simmer until beans are tender, about 45 minutes. Drain and discard liquid; set the beans aside.
2. In the same Dutch oven, saute onion and garlic in oil until tender. Add soups, 1 cup water, potato, chili powder, bouillon and salt; cover and cook over medium-low heat for 10 minutes. Add cream, garbanzo beans and navy beans. Cook over medium heat until heated through, about 10 minutes (do not boil).
1 cup: 331 cal., 10g fat (4g sat. fat), 22mg chol., 779mg sod., 46g carb. (6g sugars, 14g fiber), 15g pro.

CITRUS AVOCADO SALAD

This recipe nicely showcases grapefruit and oranges, making it a good year-round option and especially lovely at the holidays. The citrus pairs well with the sweet dressing.
—*Sonia Candler, Edmonton, AB*

- -

Takes: 10 min. • **Makes:** 12 servings

- 12 cups torn salad greens
- 2 medium grapefruit, peeled and sectioned
- 2 medium navel oranges, peeled and sectioned
- 2 medium ripe avocados, peeled, pitted and cut into chunks
- 1 small red onion, thinly sliced and separated into rings

DRESSING
- ½ cup canola oil
- ¼ cup sugar
- 3 Tbsp. lemon juice
- 1½ tsp. poppy seeds
- ½ tsp. salt
- ¼ tsp. ground mustard
- ¼ tsp. grated onion

Gently toss the first five ingredients. In a jar with a tight-fitting lid, combine the dressing ingredients; shake well. Drizzle over salad; toss to coat.
¾ cup: 175 cal., 13g fat (1g sat. fat), 0 chol., 136mg sod., 15g carb. (10g sugars, 4g fiber), 2g pro. **Diabetic exchanges:** 2½ fat, 1 vegetable, ½ starch.

LEMONY TURKEY RICE SOUP

While growing up in Texas, I spent a lot of time helping my grandma cook. I took her classic turkey soup recipe and gave it a delicious different twist by adding lemon and cilantro.

—*Margarita Cuellar, East Chicago, IN*

Takes: 30 min. • **Makes:** 8 servings (2 qt.)

- 2 cups diced cooked turkey
- 2 cups cooked long grain rice
- 1 can (10¾ oz.) condensed cream of chicken soup, undiluted
- ¼ tsp. pepper
- 6 cups chicken broth, divided
- 2 Tbsp. cornstarch
- ¼ to ⅓ cup lemon juice
- ¼ to ½ cup minced fresh cilantro

1. In a large saucepan, combine the first four ingredients and 5½ cups of broth. Bring to a boil; cook for 3 minutes.
2. In a small bowl, mix cornstarch and the remaining broth until smooth; gradually stir into soup. Bring to a boil; cook and stir until thickened, 1-2 minutes. Remove from heat; stir in lemon juice and cilantro.
1 cup: 166 cal., 4g fat (1g sat. fat), 42mg chol., 1047mg sod., 17g carb. (1g sugars, 1g fiber), 13g pro.

LAYERED PICNIC LOAVES

This big sandwich is inspired by one I fell in love with at a New York deli. It's easy to make ahead of time and cart to any party. Kids and adults alike say it's super.

—*Marion Lowery, Medford, OR*

Prep: 20 min. + chilling
Makes: 2 loaves (12 servings each)

- 2 unsliced loaves (1 lb. each) Italian bread
- ¼ cup olive oil
- 3 garlic cloves, minced
- 2 tsp. Italian seasoning, divided
- ½ lb. deli roast beef
- 12 slices part-skim mozzarella cheese (1 oz. each)
- 16 fresh basil leaves
- 3 medium tomatoes, thinly sliced
- ¼ lb. thinly sliced salami
- 1 jar (6½ oz.) marinated artichoke hearts, drained and sliced
- 1 pkg. (10 oz.) ready-to-serve salad greens
- 8 oz. thinly sliced deli chicken
- 1 medium onion, thinly sliced
- ¼ tsp. salt
- ⅛ tsp. pepper

1. Cut loaves in half horizontally; hollow out tops and bottoms, leaving ½-in. shells (save removed bread for another use).
2. Combine oil and garlic; brush inside bread shells. Sprinkle with 1 tsp. Italian seasoning. Layer bottom of each loaf with a fourth of the roast beef, mozzarella, basil, tomatoes, salami, artichokes, salad greens, chicken and onion. Repeat layers. Season with salt, pepper and remaining Italian seasoning.
3. Drizzle with the remaining oil mixture if desired. Replace bread tops; wrap tightly in plastic wrap. Refrigerate at least 1 hour before slicing.
1 slice: 341 cal., 18g fat (7g sat. fat), 47mg chol., 991mg sod., 26g carb. (3g sugars, 2g fiber), 19g pro.

FREEZE IT

PEPPERONI STROMBOLI

Because this stromboli starts with frozen bread dough, it comes together in no time. The golden loaf is stuffed with pepperoni, cheese, mushrooms, peppers and olives. I often add a few thin slices of ham, too. It's so tasty with warm pizza sauce for dipping.

—*Jenny Brown, West Lafayette, IN*

- -

Prep: 20 min. • **Bake:** 35 min.
Makes: 12 slices

- 1 loaf (1 lb.) frozen bread dough, thawed
- 2 large eggs, separated
- 1 Tbsp. grated Parmesan cheese
- 1 Tbsp. olive oil
- 1 tsp. minced fresh parsley
- 1 tsp. dried oregano
- ½ tsp. garlic powder
- ¼ tsp. pepper
- 8 oz. sliced pepperoni
- 2 cups shredded part-skim mozzarella cheese
- 1 can (4 oz.) mushroom stems and pieces, drained
- ¼ to ½ cup pickled pepper rings
- 1 medium green pepper, diced
- 1 can (2¼ oz.) sliced ripe olives
- 1 can (15 oz.) pizza sauce

1. Preheat oven to 350°. On a greased baking sheet, roll out dough into a 15x10-in. rectangle. In a small bowl, combine egg yolks, Parmesan cheese, oil, parsley, oregano, garlic powder and pepper. Brush over the dough.

2. Sprinkle with pepperoni, mozzarella cheese, mushrooms, pepper rings, green pepper and olives. Roll up, jelly-roll style, starting with a long side; pinch the seam to seal and tuck the ends under.

3. Position loaf with seam side down; brush with egg whites. Do not let rise. Bake until golden brown and dough is cooked through, 35-40 minutes. Warm the pizza sauce; serve with sliced loaf.

Freeze option: Freeze cooled unsliced pizza loaf in heavy-duty foil. To use, remove from freezer 30 minutes before reheating. Remove loaf from foil and reheat on a greased baking sheet in a preheated 325° oven until heated through. Serve as directed.

1 slice: 296 cal., 17g fat (6g sat. fat), 66mg chol., 827mg sod., 24g carb. (4g sugars, 2g fiber), 13g pro.

CURRIED CHICKEN & PEACH SALAD

This is a healthy and simple salad to make; even my non-cooking husband can whip it together in minutes! We've served this to friends over the years, and they always ask for the recipe.
—*Radelle Knappenberger, Oviedo, FL*

- -

Takes: 10 min. • **Makes:** 4 servings

- ½ cup fat-free mayonnaise
- 1 tsp. curry powder
- 2 cups cubed cooked chicken breasts
- ½ cup chopped walnuts
- ¼ cup raisins
- 2 medium peaches, sliced
- 1 pkg. (5 oz.) spring mix salad greens

Mix mayonnaise and curry powder; toss gently with chicken, walnuts and raisins. Serve chicken mixture and peaches over greens.

1 serving: 286 cal., 12g fat (2g sat. fat), 54mg chol., 315mg sod., 23g carb. (14g sugars, 4g fiber), 24g pro. **Diabetic exchanges:** 3 lean meat, 1½ fat, 1 vegetable, 1 fruit.

FREEZE IT
ITALIAN-STYLE LENTIL SOUP

My hearty, garlicky veggie soup is packed with tomatoes, green peppers and potatoes. If you like meat, add that, too.
—*Rachel L. Keller, Roanoke, VA*

- -

Prep: 20 min. • **Cook:** 40 min.
Makes: 6 servings

- 2 tsp. olive oil
- 2 medium onions, chopped
- 2 celery ribs, thinly sliced
- 1 medium carrot, chopped
- 1 cup dried lentils, rinsed
- ¼ cup minced fresh parsley
- 1 Tbsp. reduced-sodium beef bouillon granules
- ½ tsp. pepper
- 5¼ cups water
- 1 can (6 oz.) tomato paste
- 2 Tbsp. white vinegar
- 2 tsp. brown sugar
- ½ tsp. salt
- 2 Tbsp. shredded Parmesan cheese

1. In a large saucepan coated with cooking spray, heat oil over medium heat. Add onions, celery and carrot; cook and stir until vegetables are crisp-tender.
2. Stir in lentils, parsley, bouillon, pepper and water; bring to a boil. Reduce heat; simmer, covered, 20-25 minutes or until the lentils are tender, stirring occasionally.
3. Stir in the tomato paste, vinegar, brown sugar and salt; heat through. Serve with cheese.

Freeze option: Freeze cooled soup in freezer containers. To use, partially thaw in refrigerator overnight. Heat through in a saucepan, stirring occasionally and adding a little water if necessary.

1 cup: 122 cal., 2g fat (1g sat. fat), 1mg chol., 420mg sod., 21g carb. (11g sugars, 6g fiber), 6g pro. **Diabetic exchanges:** 2 vegetable, 1 starch.

The Best Burger Joint

Where can you get the best burger? Why not at your place? With toppings, stuffings and sauces, jazz up an ordinary burger into something that'll have friends and family coming back for seconds.

CHEDDAR CHILI BURGERS

Savory chili and french-fried onions are a fun alternative to the traditional burger fixings of ketchup and mustard. The patties are easy to assemble, making them a great weeknight meal.
—Sue Ross, Casa Grande, AZ

- -

Takes: 20 min. • **Makes:** 4 servings

- 1 lb. ground beef
- 1½ tsp. chili powder
- 1 can (15 oz.) chili with beans
- 4 hamburger buns, split and toasted
- ½ cup shredded cheddar cheese
- 1 can (2.8 oz.) french-fried onions

1. In a large bowl, combine beef and chili powder. Shape into four patties. Pan-fry, grill or broil until meat is no longer pink.
2. Meanwhile, in a small saucepan, bring chili to a boil. Reduce heat; simmer for 5 minutes or until heated through. Place burgers on bun bottoms; top with chili, cheese and onions. Replace bun tops.
1 burger: 584 cal., 28g fat (12g sat. fat), 81mg chol., 1081mg sod., 46g carb. (5g sugars, 5g fiber), 34g pro.

MUSHROOM-STUFFED CHEESEBURGERS

I never need to call my family twice when these burgers are on the menu. Get ahead of the game and stuff them ahead of time, then grill later.
—Joyce Guth, Mohnton, PA

- -

Prep: 30 min. • **Grill:** 10 min.
Makes: 8 servings

- 2 bacon strips, finely chopped
- 2 cups chopped fresh mushrooms
- ¼ cup chopped onion
- ¼ cup chopped sweet red pepper
- ¼ cup chopped green pepper
- 2 lbs. lean ground beef (90% lean)
- 2 Tbsp. steak sauce
- ½ tsp. seasoned salt
- 4 slices provolone cheese, halved
- 8 kaiser rolls, split

1. In a large skillet over medium heat, cook bacon until crisp. Remove with a slotted spoon; drain on paper towels. Cook and stir mushrooms, onion and peppers in bacon drippings until tender. Using slotted spoon, remove to a small bowl; cool completely. Stir in bacon.
2. In a large bowl, combine beef, steak sauce and seasoned salt, mixing lightly but thoroughly. Shape into 16 thin patties. Top eight patties with cheese, folding cheese to fit within ¾ in. of edge. Spread with mushroom mixture. Top with the remaining patties, pressing the edges to enclose filling.
3. Grill the burgers, uncovered, over medium-high heat or broil 4 in. from heat 5-6 minutes on each side or until a thermometer inserted in meat portion reads 160°. Serve on rolls.
1 burger: 418 cal., 17g fat (7g sat. fat), 82mg chol., 653mg sod., 33g carb. (2g sugars, 2g fiber), 31g pro.

BARBECUED BURGERS

I can't take all the credit for these winning burgers. My husband's uncle passed down his special barbecue sauce recipe. We love it on everything, and it was only natural to try it with burgers.
—*Rhoda Troyer, Glenford, OH*

Prep: 25 min. • **Grill:** 15 min.
Makes: 6 servings

SAUCE
- 1 cup ketchup
- ½ cup packed brown sugar
- ⅓ cup sugar
- ¼ cup honey
- ¼ cup molasses
- 2 tsp. prepared mustard
- 1½ tsp. Worcestershire sauce
- ¼ tsp. salt
- ¼ tsp. liquid smoke
- ⅛ tsp. pepper

BURGERS
- 1 large egg, lightly beaten
- ⅓ cup quick-cooking oats
- ¼ tsp. onion salt
- ¼ tsp. garlic salt
- ¼ tsp. pepper
- ⅛ tsp. salt
- 1½ lbs. ground beef
- 6 hamburger buns, split
- Toppings of your choice

1. In a small saucepan, combine the sauce ingredients. Bring to a boil. Remove from heat. Set aside 1 cup of the sauce to serve with burgers.

2. In a large bowl, combine the egg, oats, ¼ cup of the barbecue sauce, onion salt, garlic salt, pepper and salt. Crumble beef over the mixture and mix well. Shape into six patties.

3. Grill, covered, over medium heat for 6-8 minutes on each side or until a thermometer reads 160°, basting with ½ cup barbecue sauce during the last 5 minutes. Serve on hamburger buns with toppings of your choice and the reserved barbecue sauce.

1 burger: 626 cal., 19g fat (7g sat. fat), 121mg chol., 1146mg sod., 86g carb. (56g sugars, 2g fiber), 30g pro.

GRILLED TURKEY BURGERS

Bite into these juicy, tender patties on whole wheat buns. We especially like to grill them, but you could also pan-fry them.
—*Sherry Hulsman, Louisville, KY*

Takes: 30 min. • **Makes:** 6 servings

- 1 large egg, lightly beaten
- ⅔ cup soft whole wheat bread crumbs
- ½ cup finely chopped celery
- ¼ cup finely chopped onion
- 1 Tbsp. minced fresh parsley
- 1 tsp. Worcestershire sauce
- 1 tsp. dried oregano
- ½ tsp. salt
- ¼ tsp. pepper
- 1¼ lbs. lean ground turkey
- 6 whole wheat hamburger buns, split

In a small bowl, combine the egg, bread crumbs, celery, onion, fresh parsley, Worcestershire sauce and seasonings. Crumble turkey over mixture and mix well. Shape into six patties. On a greased grill, cook, covered, over medium heat or broil 4 in. from the heat for 5-6 minutes on each side or until a thermometer reads 165° and juices run clear. Serve on buns.

1 burger: 293 cal., 11g fat (3g sat. fat), 110mg chol., 561mg sod., 27g carb. (3g sugars, 4g fiber), 22g pro. **Diabetic exchanges:** 3 lean meat, 2 starch.

Contest Winner

TOMATO STEAK SANDWICHES

One day when we were light on groceries, I came up with steak and tomatoes over bagels. They've been a favorite ever since, particularly when we need a quick dinner.
—*Tessa Edwards, Provo, UT*

- -

Takes: 20 min. • **Makes:** 6 servings

- 2 tsp. canola oil
- 1 lb. beef top sirloin steak, cut into thin strips
- ⅛ tsp. salt
  Dash pepper
- 3 plain bagels, split
- ⅓ cup cream cheese, softened
- 6 thick slices tomato
- 6 slices part-skim mozzarella cheese

1. Preheat broiler. In a large skillet, heat oil over medium heat. Add beef; cook and stir 3-5 minutes or until browned; drain. Stir in salt and pepper.
2. Spread cut sides of bagels with cream cheese. Transfer to an ungreased baking sheet; spoon beef over the bagels. Top with tomato and mozzarella cheese. Broil 4-6 in. from heat 3-5 minutes or until cheese is melted and lightly browned.
1 open-faced sandwich: 381 cal., 15g fat (7g sat. fat), 63mg chol., 544mg sod., 31g carb. (6g sugars, 1g fiber), 30g pro.

SPINACH SALAD WITH RHUBARB DRESSING

Rhubarb adds mouthwatering flavor and rosy color to a dressing that really perks up a spinach salad. I modified a recipe that I'd received from a friend to come up with this tangy dressing.
—*Twila Mitchell, Lindsborg, KS*

- -

Prep: 20 min. + chilling • **Makes:** 6 servings

- 2 cups chopped fresh or frozen rhubarb
- ½ cup sugar
- ¼ cup white vinegar
- ¾ cup vegetable oil
- 3 Tbsp. grated onion
- 1½ tsp. Worcestershire sauce
- ½ tsp. salt

SALAD
- 6 cups torn fresh spinach
- 6 bacon strips, cooked and crumbled
- ½ cup bean sprouts
- ½ cup shredded cheddar cheese
- 1 to 2 hard-boiled large eggs, chopped

1. In a saucepan, combine the rhubarb, sugar and vinegar; cook over medium heat until the rhubarb is tender, about 6 minutes. Drain, reserving about 6 Tbsp. of the juice; discard the pulp.
2. Pour juice into a jar with tight-fitting lid; add the oil, onion, Worcestershire sauce and salt. Shake well. Refrigerate for at least 1 hour.
3. Just before serving, combine the salad ingredients in a large bowl. Add dressing and toss to coat.
Note: If using frozen rhubarb, measure it while still frozen, then thaw completely. Drain in a colander, but do not press liquid out.
1 cup: 423 cal., 35g fat (7g sat. fat), 49mg chol., 454mg sod., 21g carb. (18g sugars, 2g fiber), 8g pro.

BACKYARD RED POTATO SALAD

Here's a potato salad that has no mayonnaise. It's perfect for picnics, and looks just as good as it tastes.

—Holly Bauer, West Bend, WI

- -

Prep: 25 min. • **Grill:** 10 min.
Makes: 9 servings

2½	lbs. small red potatoes
1	medium onion, cut into ½-in. slices
½	cup olive oil, divided
1	tsp. salt, divided
½	tsp. pepper, divided
3	Tbsp. balsamic vinegar
2	Tbsp. lemon juice
1	Tbsp. Dijon mustard
2	tsp. sugar
2	garlic cloves, minced
¼	cup minced fresh tarragon

1. Place potatoes in a saucepan and cover with water. Bring to a boil. Reduce heat; cover and cook for 10 minutes. Drain; cool slightly. Cut each potato in half.

2. In a large bowl, combine the potatoes, onion, ¼ cup oil, ½ tsp. salt and ¼ tsp. pepper; toss to coat. Arrange vegetables, cut side down, on a grilling grid; place on a grill rack. Grill, covered, over medium heat for 8-10 minutes or until vegetables are tender and lightly browned, turning occasionally. Chop onion. Place the onion and potatoes in bowl.

3. In a small bowl, whisk the vinegar, lemon juice, mustard, sugar, garlic and the remaining oil, salt and pepper. Add to the potato mixture; toss to coat. Sprinkle with tarragon. Serve warm or at room temperature. Refrigerate leftovers.

Note: If you don't have a grilling grid, use a disposable foil pan. Poke holes in the bottom of the pan with a meat fork to allow any liquid to drain.

¾ **cup:** 215 cal., 12g fat (2g sat. fat), 0 chol., 312mg sod., 24g carb. (4g sugars, 3g fiber), 3g pro. **Diabetic exchanges:** 2 fat, 1½ starch.

TANGY PULLED PORK SANDWICHES

The slow cooker not only makes this an easy meal, but also keeps the pork tender, moist and loaded with flavor. The sandwiches are so comforting, they seem anything but light.
—Beki Kosydar-Krantz, Mayfield, PA

Prep: 10 min. • **Cook:** 4 hours
Makes: 4 servings

- 1 pork tenderloin (1 lb.)
- 1 cup ketchup
- 2 Tbsp. plus 1½ tsp. brown sugar
- 2 Tbsp. plus 1½ tsp. cider vinegar
- 1 Tbsp. plus 1½ tsp. Worcestershire sauce
- 1 Tbsp. spicy brown mustard
- ¼ tsp. pepper
- 4 rolls or buns, split and toasted
  Coleslaw, optional

1. Cut the tenderloin in half; place in a 3-qt. slow cooker. Combine the ketchup, brown sugar, vinegar, Worcestershire sauce, mustard and pepper; pour over the pork.
2. Cover and cook on low for 4-5 hours or until meat is tender. Remove meat; shred with two forks. Return to slow cooker; heat through. Serve on toasted rolls or buns, with coleslaw, if desired.
1 sandwich: 402 cal., 7g fat (2g sat. fat), 63mg chol., 1181mg sod., 56g carb. (18g sugars, 2g fiber), 29g pro.

Contest Winner

MEXICAN CHICKEN CORN CHOWDER

I like to make this chunky, creamy soup when company comes to visit. Its zippy flavor is full of southwestern flair. Sometimes I top it with toasted strips of leftover tortillas.
—Susan Garoutte, Georgetown, TX

Takes: 30 min. • **Makes:** 8 servings (2 qt.)

- 1½ lbs. boneless skinless chicken breasts, cut into 1-in. pieces
- ½ cup chopped onion
- 3 Tbsp. butter
- 1 to 2 garlic cloves, minced
- 1 cup hot water
- 2 tsp. chicken bouillon granules
- ½ to 1 tsp. ground cumin
- 2 cups half-and-half cream
- 2 cups shredded Monterey Jack cheese
- 1 can (14¾ oz.) cream-style corn
- 1 can (4 oz.) chopped green chiles, undrained
- ¼ to 1 tsp. hot pepper sauce
- 1 medium tomato, chopped
  Minced fresh cilantro, fried tortilla strips, optional

1. In a Dutch oven, brown chicken and onion in butter until the chicken is no longer pink. Add garlic; cook 1 minute longer. Add water, bouillon and cumin; bring to a boil. Reduce heat; cover and simmer for 5 minutes.
2. Stir in cream, cheese, corn, chiles and hot pepper sauce. Cook and stir over low heat until cheese is melted; add chopped tomato. If desired, top with cilantro and tortilla strips.
1 cup: 368 cal., 21g fat (13g sat. fat), 114mg chol., 753mg sod., 14g carb. (5g sugars, 1g fiber), 28g pro.

CAJUN SHRIMP & CUCUMBER WRAPS

Balance the heat of spicy shrimp with cool lettuce, cucumbers and parsley. This hand-held dinner is perfect for dining al fresco!
—*Chantel Beauregard, Lake Arrowhead, CA*

Takes: 20 min. • **Makes:** 4 servings

- ¼ cup lemon juice
- 4 Tbsp. olive oil, divided
- 1½ tsp. Cajun seasoning, divided
- ⅛ tsp. pepper
- 1 lb. uncooked large shrimp, peeled and deveined (tails removed)
- 8 Bibb or Boston lettuce leaves
- 4 flatbread wraps
- 2 small cucumbers, cut lengthwise into quarters
- 4 thin slices red onion
- ¼ cup fresh parsley leaves

1. In a small bowl, whisk lemon juice, 3 Tbsp. oil, 1 tsp. Cajun seasoning and pepper. Set aside. Toss shrimp with the remaining Cajun seasoning. In a large skillet, heat the remaining oil over medium-high heat. Add shrimp mixture; cook and stir until the shrimp turn pink.
2. Place lettuce on flatbread wraps; top with cucumbers, onion, fresh parsley and shrimp. Drizzle with dressing; roll up. If desired, secure with toothpicks.

1 wrap: 365 cal., 17g fat (2g sat. fat), 138mg chol., 670mg sod., 29g carb. (3g sugars, 4g fiber), 26g pro.

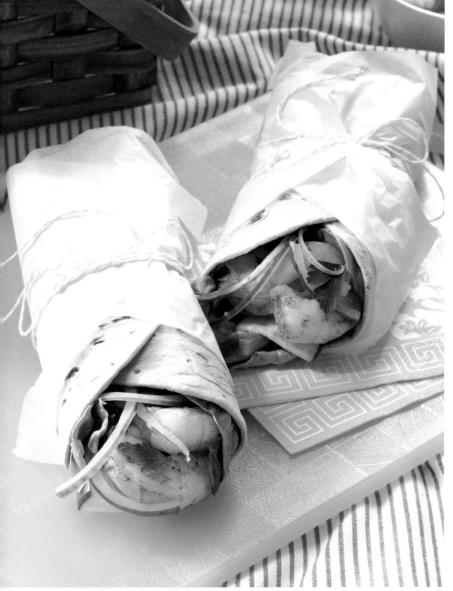

FIREHOUSE CHILI

As one of the cooks at the firehouse, I used to regularly prepare meals for 10 men. This chili was among their favorites.
—*Richard Clements, San Dimas, CA*

Prep: 20 min. • **Cook:** 1½ hours
Makes: 12 servings (about 3 qt.)

- 2 Tbsp. canola oil
- 4 lbs. lean ground beef (90% lean)
- 2 medium onions, chopped
- 1 medium green pepper, chopped
- 4 cans (16 oz. each) kidney beans, rinsed and drained
- 3 cans (14½ oz. each) stewed tomatoes, cut up
- 1 can (14½ oz.) beef broth
- 3 Tbsp. chili powder
- 2 Tbsp. ground coriander
- 2 Tbsp. ground cumin
- 4 garlic cloves, minced
- 1 tsp. dried oregano

In a Dutch oven, heat canola oil over medium heat. Brown beef in batches, crumbling meat, until no longer pink; drain. Add onions and green pepper; cook until tender. Return meat to Dutch oven. Stir in remaining ingredients. Bring to a boil. Reduce heat; simmer, covered, until flavors are blended, about 1½ hours.

1 cup: 444 cal., 16g fat (5g sat. fat), 94mg chol., 703mg sod., 36g carb. (9g sugars, 10g fiber), 41g pro. **Diabetic exchanges:** 5 lean meat, 2½ starch, ½ fat.

SPLIT PEA SOUP WITH HAM

To liven up traditional pea soup, I load mine up with potatoes and veggies. It's peppery rather than smoky, and I pass it around with warm cornbread.

—*Barbara Link, Alta Loma, CA*

Prep: 15 min. • **Cook:** 1¼ hours
Makes: 12 servings (3 qt.)

- 1 pkg. (16 oz.) dried green split peas
- 8 cups water
- ¾ lb. potatoes (about 2 medium), cubed
- 2 large onions, chopped
- 2 medium carrots, chopped
- 2 cups cubed fully cooked ham (about 10 oz.)
- 1 celery rib, chopped
- 5 tsp. reduced-sodium chicken bouillon granules
- 1 tsp. dried marjoram
- 1 tsp. poultry seasoning
- 1 tsp. rubbed sage
- ½ to 1 tsp. pepper
- ½ tsp. dried basil

Place all ingredients in a Dutch oven; bring to a boil. Reduce heat; simmer, covered, 1¼-1½ hours or until peas and vegetables are tender, stirring occasionally.

1 cup: 202 cal., 2g fat (0 sat. fat), 14mg chol., 396mg sod., 33g carb. (5g sugars, 11g fiber), 15g pro. **Diabetic exchanges:** 2 starch, 1 lean meat.

RUBY RASPBERRY SLAW

I enjoy combining fruits and vegetables in fresh salads. This crunchy, colorful combination is always a family favorite.

—*Deborah Biggs, Omaha, NE*

Prep: 15 min. + chilling • **Makes:** 6 servings

- 2 cups shredded red cabbage
- 2 cups shredded cabbage
- 1 cup shredded carrots
- ¼ cup prepared raspberry vinaigrette
- 3 Tbsp. mayonnaise
- ¼ tsp. pepper
- ½ cup fresh raspberries

In a large bowl, combine cabbage and carrots. In a small bowl, whisk vinaigrette, mayonnaise and pepper until blended. Add to cabbage mixture; toss to coat. Refrigerate, covered, for 10 minutes. Top with raspberries.

¾ cup: 122 cal., 11g fat (1g sat. fat), 3mg chol., 144mg sod., 6g carb. (2g sugars, 2g fiber), 1g pro. **Diabetic exchanges:** 2 fat, 1 vegetable.

HEARTY MEATBALL SUB SANDWICHES

The satisfying sandwiches are excellent for casual parties. Making the saucy meatballs in advance and reheating them saves me precious time when I'm expecting company.
—*Deena Hubler, Jasper, IN*

Takes: 30 min. • **Makes:** 12 servings

- 2 large eggs, lightly beaten
- 1 cup dry bread crumbs
- 2 Tbsp. grated Parmesan cheese
- 2 Tbsp. finely chopped onion
- 1 tsp. salt
- ½ tsp. pepper
- ½ tsp. garlic powder
- ¼ tsp. Italian seasoning
- 2 lbs. ground beef
- 1 jar (28 oz.) spaghetti sauce
  Additional Parmesan cheese, and sliced onion and green peppers, optional
- 12 sandwich rolls, split

1. In a large bowl, combine the first eight ingredients. Crumble beef over mixture and mix well. Shape into 1-in. balls. Place the meatballs in a single layer in a 3-qt. microwave-safe dish.

2. Cover and microwave on high for 3-4 minutes. Turn meatballs; cook 3-4 minutes longer or until no longer pink. Drain. Add spaghetti sauce.

3. Cover and microwave on high for 2-4 minutes or until heated through. If desired, top with additional cheese and sliced onion and green peppers. Serve on rolls.

1 sandwich: 464 cal., 18g fat (7g sat. fat), 88mg chol., 1013mg sod., 49g carb. (10g sugars, 3g fiber), 26g pro.

GRILLED FIRECRACKER POTATO SALAD

I never get tired of potato salad, and I love finding variations. A little spice is nice, so I use cayenne and paprika in this grilled salad that comes with its own fireworks.
—*Ashley Armstrong, Kingsland, GA*

Prep: 20 min. • **Grill:** 20 min. + chilling
Makes: 16 servings

- 3 lbs. small red potatoes (about 30), quartered
- 2 Tbsp. olive oil
- 1 tsp. salt
- ½ tsp. pepper

DRESSING
- 1½ cups mayonnaise
- ½ cup finely chopped onion
- ¼ cup Dijon mustard
- 2 Tbsp. sweet pickle relish
- ½ tsp. paprika
- ¼ tsp. cayenne pepper

SALAD
- 6 hard-boiled large eggs, chopped
- 2 celery ribs, finely chopped
  Minced fresh chives, optional

1. Toss the potatoes with oil, salt and pepper; place in a grill wok or basket. Grill, covered, over medium heat for 20-25 minutes or until the potatoes are tender, stirring occasionally. Transfer the potatoes to a large bowl; cool slightly.

2. In a small bowl, mix the dressing ingredients. Add the dressing, eggs and celery to the potatoes; toss to combine. Refrigerate, covered, for 1-2 hours or until cold. If desired, sprinkle with chives.

Note: If you do not have a grill wok or basket, use a large disposable foil pan and poke holes in the bottom of the pan.

1 cup: 265 cal., 20g fat (3g sat. fat), 77mg chol., 398mg sod., 16g carb. (2g sugars, 2g fiber), 4g pro.

VIVA ITALIANO!

If you're out of Italian seasoning— or if your store doesn't carry it— try making your own! Try substituting ¼ teaspoon each of basil, thyme, rosemary and oregano for each teasoon of Italian seasoning called for in a recipe. Other good add-ins: marjoram, savory, and sage. Feel free to mix any or all of the herbs to come up with the blend you like best.

GRANDMA'S SEAFOOD CHOWDER

My grandmother makes this every year to be enjoyed on Christmas morning. But why wait? You can enjoy this satisfying chowder no matter what the season.

—*Melissa Obernesser, Utica, NY*

Prep: 15 min. • **Cook:** 25 min.
Makes: 10 servings (3¼ qt.)

- 3   Tbsp. plus ¼ cup butter, divided
- 1   lb. sliced fresh mushrooms
- ⅓   cup all-purpose flour
- 1   tsp. salt
- ⅛   tsp. pepper
- 4   cups half-and-half cream
- 1½ cups 2% milk
- 1   lb. haddock fillets, skin removed, cut into 1-in. pieces
- 1   lb. uncooked medium shrimp, peeled and deveined
- 2   cups frozen peas (about 10 oz.)
- ¾   cup shredded cheddar cheese
- 1   cup lump crabmeat (about 5 oz.), drained
- 1   jar (4 oz.) diced pimientos, drained
- 1   tsp. paprika
     Biscuits, optional

1. In a 6-qt. stockpot, heat 3 Tbsp. butter over medium-high heat. Add mushrooms; cook and stir until tender, 8-10 minutes. Remove from pot.

2. In the same pot, heat the remaining butter over medium heat. Stir in flour, salt and pepper until smooth; gradually whisk in cream and milk. Bring to a boil, stirring constantly; cook and stir until thickened, 2-3 minutes.

3. Stir in haddock, shrimp, peas and sauteed mushrooms; cook until the fish just begins to flake easily with a fork and the shrimp turn pink, 5-7 minutes. Add cheese, crab and pimientos; stir gently until cheese is melted. If desired, sprinkle individual servings with paprika and top with biscuits.

1¼ cups: 390 cal., 23g fat (14g sat. fat), 176mg chol., 596mg sod., 14g carb. (8g sugars, 2g fiber), 28g pro.

QUINOA TABBOULEH

When my mom and sister developed food allergies, we had to modify many recipes. I substituted quinoa for couscous in this tabbouleh, and now we make it all the time.
—*Jennifer Klann, Corbett, OR*

- -

Prep: 35 min. + chilling • **Makes:** 8 servings

- 2 **cups water**
- 1 **cup quinoa, rinsed**
- 1 **can (15 oz.) black beans, rinsed and drained**
- 1 **small cucumber, peeled and chopped**
- 1 **small sweet red pepper, chopped**
- ⅓ **cup minced fresh parsley**
- ¼ **cup lemon juice**
- 2 **Tbsp. olive oil**
- ½ **tsp. salt**
- ½ **tsp. pepper**

1. In a large saucepan, bring water to a boil. Add quinoa. Reduce heat; cover and simmer until the liquid is absorbed, 12-15 minutes. Remove from the heat; fluff with a fork. Transfer to a bowl; cool quinoa completely.

2. Add the beans, cucumber, red pepper and parsley. In a small bowl, whisk the remaining ingredients; drizzle over salad and toss to coat. Refrigerate until chilled.

Note: Look for quinoa in the cereal, rice or organic food aisle.

¾ cup: 159 cal., 5g fat (1g sat. fat), 0 chol., 255mg sod., 24g carb. (1g sugars, 4g fiber), 6g pro. **Diabetic exchanges:** 1½ starch, 1 fat.

BANDITO CHILI DOGS

These deluxe chili dogs are a surefire hit at family functions. Adults and children alike love the cheesy chili sauce, and the varied toppings are so much fun!
—*Marion Lowery, Medford, OR*

- -

Prep: 15 min. • **Cook:** 4 hours
Makes: 10 servings

- 1 **pkg. (1 lb.) hot dogs**
- 2 **cans (15 oz. each) chili without beans**
- 1 **can (10¾ oz.) condensed cheddar cheese soup, undiluted**
- 1 **can (4 oz.) chopped green chiles**
- 10 **hot dog buns, split**
- 1 **medium onion, chopped**
- 1 **to 2 cups corn chips, coarsely crushed**
- 1 **cup shredded cheddar cheese**

1. Place hot dogs in a 3-qt. slow cooker. In a large bowl, combine chili, soup and green chiles; pour over the hot dogs. Cover and cook on low for 4-5 hours.

2. Serve hot dogs in buns; top with chili mixture, onion, corn chips and cheese.

1 chili dog: 450 cal., 23g fat (10g sat. fat), 53mg chol., 1442mg sod., 43g carb. (6g sugars, 3g fiber), 19g pro.

Breads, Rolls & More

From quick breads and muffins that come together in a snap to yeast breads and rolls that show the care of a risen dough, nothing compares to fresh-baked bread. Sweet coffee cakes, flaky biscuits, savory herb breads and irresistible cinnamon rolls—every recipe in this chapter welcomes you home!

CINNAMON COFFEE CAKE

I love the excellent texture of this old-fashioned streusel-topped coffee cake. Its lovely vanilla flavor enriched by sour cream may remind you of brunch at Grandma's!

—*Eleanor Harris, Cape Coral, FL*

Prep: 20 min. • **Bake:** 1 hour + cooling
Makes: 20 servings

- 1 cup butter, softened
- 2¾ cups sugar, divided
- 4 large eggs, room temperature
- 2 tsp. vanilla extract
- 3 cups all-purpose flour
- 1 tsp. baking soda
- 1 tsp. salt
- 2 cups sour cream
- 2 Tbsp. ground cinnamon
- ½ cup chopped walnuts

1. Preheat oven to 350°. In a large bowl, cream butter and 2 cups of sugar until light and fluffy. Add eggs, one at a time; beat well after each addition. Beat in vanilla. Combine flour, baking soda and salt; add alternately with sour cream, beating just enough after each addition to keep the batter smooth.

2. Spoon a third of the batter into a greased 10-in. tube pan. Combine cinnamon, nuts and the remaining sugar; sprinkle a third over batter in pan. Repeat the layers two more times. Bake until a toothpick inserted in the center comes out clean, 60-65 minutes. Cool 15 minutes before removing from pan to a wire rack to cool completely.

1 piece: 340 cal., 16g fat (9g sat. fat), 83mg chol., 299mg sod., 44g carb. (28g sugars, 1g fiber), 5g pro.

ARIZONA CORNBREAD

Unlike a lot of other cornbreads, this one uses yeast. The oil and sour cream make the loaf tender, and it has a bit of a bite to it from the jalapenos.

—*Margaret Pache, Mesa, AZ*

Prep: 20 min. + rising • **Bake:** 30 min.
Makes: 2 loaves (16 slices each)

- 1 cup cornmeal
- 2 Tbsp. sugar
- 2 pkg. (¼ oz. each) active dry yeast
- 1 tsp. salt
- ½ tsp. baking soda
- ¼ tsp. pepper
- 1 cup sour cream
- ½ cup canola oil
- ½ cup chopped green onions
- 2 large eggs
- 1¼ cups shredded pepper jack cheese
- 1 cup cream-style corn
- 2 jalapeno peppers, seeded and chopped
- 5 to 6 cups all-purpose flour
  Additional cornmeal
  Melted butter

1. In a large bowl, combine the first six ingredients; set aside. In a saucepan, heat the sour cream, oil and onions to 120°-130°. Add to cornmeal mixture; beat until blended. Beat in eggs, cheese, corn and jalapenos. Stir in enough flour to form a stiff dough.

2. Turn onto a floured surface; knead until smooth and elastic, 6-8 minutes. Place in a greased bowl, turning once to grease top. Cover and let rise in a warm place until doubled, about 1 hour.

3. Punch dough down. Turn onto a lightly floured surface; divide in half. Shape into two loaves. Grease two 9x5-in. loaf pans; dust with additional cornmeal. Place loaves seam side down in prepared pans. Cover and let rise until doubled, about 30 minutes. Preheat oven to 375°.

4. Brush butter over loaves. Bake until golden brown, 30-35 minutes; cover loosely with foil if the tops brown too quickly. Remove from pans to wire racks to cool.

Note: Wear disposable gloves when cutting hot peppers; the oils can burn skin. Avoid touching your face.

1 slice: 164 cal., 7g fat (2g sat. fat), 23mg chol., 151mg sod., 21g carb. (2g sugars, 1g fiber), 4g pro.

EASY POTATO ROLLS

After I discovered this recipe, these rolls became a mainstay for me. I make the dough ahead of time when company is coming, and I keep some in the refrigerator to make for the hands on our cattle ranch. Leftover mashed potatoes are almost sure to go into these rolls.

—Jeanette McKinney, Belleview, MO

Prep: 20 min. + rising • **Bake:** 20 min.
Makes: 45 rolls

- 2 pkg. (¼ oz. each) active dry yeast
- 1⅓ cups warm water (110° to 115°), divided
- 1 cup warm mashed potatoes (without added milk and butter)
- ⅔ cup sugar
- ⅔ cup shortening
- 2 large eggs
- 2½ tsp. salt
- 6 to 6½ cups all-purpose flour

1. Dissolve yeast in ⅔ cup warm water. In a large bowl, combine mashed potatoes, sugar, shortening, eggs, salt, remaining ⅔ cup water, the yeast mixture and 2 cups flour; beat until smooth. Stir in enough of the remaining flour to form a soft dough.
2. Do not knead. Shape into a ball; place in a greased bowl, turning once to grease the top. Cover and let rise in a warm place until doubled, about 1 hour.
3. Punch down dough; divide into thirds. Divide; shape one portion into 15 balls. Place in a greased 9-in. round baking pan. Cover with a kitchen towel. Repeat with the remaining dough. Let rise in a warm place until doubled, about 30 minutes. Preheat oven to 375°.
4. Bake the rolls until golden brown, 20-25 minutes. Remove from pans to wire racks. Serve warm.
1 roll: 106 cal., 3g fat (1g sat. fat), 8mg chol., 136mg sod., 17g carb. (3g sugars, 1g fiber), 2g pro.

HERBED BREAD TWISTS

A blend of herbs and a special shape dress up ordinary frozen bread dough in this unbelievably easy recipe.

—Deb Stapert, Comstock Park, MI

Prep: 30 min. + rising • **Bake:** 10 min.
Makes: 2 dozen

- ¼ cup butter, softened
- ¼ tsp. garlic powder
- ¼ tsp. each dried basil, marjoram and oregano
- 1 loaf (1 lb.) frozen bread dough, thawed
- ¾ cup shredded part-skim mozzarella cheese
- 1 large egg
- 1 Tbsp. water
- 4 tsp. sesame seeds

1. In a small bowl, combine butter and seasonings. On a lightly floured surface, roll dough into a 12-in. square. Spread with butter mixture to within ½ in. of edges; sprinkle with cheese.
2. Fold dough into thirds. Cut widthwise into 24 strips. Twist each strip twice; pinch ends to seal. Place 2 in. apart on greased baking sheets. Cover and let rise in a warm place until doubled, about 40 minutes. Preheat oven to 375°.
3. Beat egg and water; brush over the dough. Sprinkle with seeds. Bake until light golden brown, 10-12 minutes. Remove from pans to wire racks.
1 twist: 84 cal., 4g fat (2g sat. fat), 17mg chol., 140mg sod., 10g carb. (1g sugars, 1g fiber), 3g pro.

SWEET POTATO-CRANBERRY DOUGHNUTS

I grew up near Idaho, which is famous for spudnuts, a doughnut made from mashed potatoes. These are my own variation on the regional classic—they use sweet potatoes and tart cranberries!

—Joni Hilton, Rocklin, CA

- -

Prep: 25 min. + rising • **Cook:** 5 min./batch
Makes: 2 dozen

- ¼ cup sugar
- 1½ tsp. active dry yeast
- 1 tsp. ground cinnamon
- ½ tsp. salt
- 4 to 4½ cups all-purpose flour
- 1 cup 2% milk
- ¼ cup shortening
- 2 Tbsp. water
- 2 large eggs
- ½ cup mashed sweet potatoes
- ½ cup finely chopped dried cranberries
  Oil for deep-fat frying
- 1 cup confectioners' sugar
- 2 to 3 Tbsp. apple cider or juice

1. In a large bowl, combine the sugar, yeast, cinnamon, salt and 1½ cups flour. In a small saucepan, heat the milk, shortening and water to 120°-130°; add to dry ingredients. Beat on medium speed for 2 minutes. Add the eggs, mashed potatoes and cranberries; beat 2 minutes longer. Stir in enough of the remaining flour to form a firm dough.

2. Do not knead. Place in a greased bowl, turning once to grease the top. Cover and let rise in a warm place until doubled, about 1 hour.

3. Punch dough down. Turn onto a lightly floured surface; roll out to ½-in. thickness. Cut with a floured 2½-in. doughnut cutter; reroll the scraps. Place 1 in. apart on greased baking sheets. Cover and let rise until doubled, about 30 minutes.

4. In an electric skillet or deep fryer, heat oil to 375°. Fry doughnuts, a few at a time, until golden brown on both sides. Drain on paper towels. Combine confectioners' sugar and apple cider; dip the warm doughnuts in glaze.

1 glazed doughnut: 191 cal., 8g fat (1g sat. fat), 18mg chol., 63mg sod., 27g carb. (10g sugars, 1g fiber), 3g pro.

FLAVORFUL HERB BREAD

Made in a bread machine, this loaf is one of my favorites because it has a wonderful texture and slices beautifully. The flavor of the herbs really comes through.

—Gerri Hamilton, Kingsville, ON

- -

Prep: 15 min. • **Bake:** 3-4 hours
Makes: 1 loaf (16 slices)

- 1 cup warm whole milk (70° to 80°)
- 1 large egg, room temperature
- 2 Tbsp. butter, softened
- ¼ cup dried minced onion
- 2 Tbsp. sugar
- 1½ tsp. salt
- 2 Tbsp. dried parsley flakes
- 1 tsp. dried oregano
- 3½ cups bread flour
- 2 tsp. active dry yeast

Place all ingredients In a bread machine pan in order suggested by manufacturer. Select the basic bread setting. Choose crust color and loaf size if available. Bake according to bread machine directions (check dough after 5 minutes of mixing; add 1 to 2 Tbsp. water or flour if needed).

Note: We recommend that you do not use a bread machine's time-delay feature for this bread recipe.

1 slice: 125 cal., 2g fat (1g sat. fat), 19mg chol., 248mg sod., 23g carb. (3g sugars, 1g fiber), 5g pro.

CRANBERRY PUMPKIN BREAD

Put leftover cranberries and pumpkin to great use in this moist quick bread. It's delicious served with turkey casserole for an after-Thanksgiving meal.
—Dixie Terry, Goreville, IL

Prep: 20 min. • **Bake:** 70 min. + cooling
Makes: 2 loaves (16 slices each)

- 3¾ cups all-purpose flour
- 3 cups sugar
- 4 tsp. pumpkin pie spice
- 2 tsp. baking soda
- 1 tsp. salt
- 4 large eggs
- 1 can (15 oz.) solid-pack pumpkin
- ½ cup canola oil
- 2 cups fresh or frozen cranberries, thawed
- 1 cup chopped walnuts

1. Preheat oven to 350°. In a large bowl, combine the flour, sugar, pumpkin pie spice, baking soda and salt. In another bowl, whisk the eggs, pumpkin and oil; stir into dry ingredients just until moistened. Fold in cranberries and walnuts.
2. Spoon into two greased 9x5-in. loaf pans. Bake for 70-80 minutes or until a toothpick inserted in the center comes out clean. Cool for 10 minutes before removing from pans to wire racks to cool completely.

1 slice: 197 cal., 6g fat (1g sat. fat), 27mg chol., 162mg sod., 32g carb. (19g sugars, 1g fiber), 4g pro.

APPLE STREUSEL MUFFINS

These muffins remind us of coffee cake, and my husband and kids love them as a quick breakfast or snack on the run. The drizzle of glaze makes them pretty enough for company.
—Dulcy Grace, Roaring Spring, PA

Prep: 20 min. • **Bake:** 15 min. + cooling
Makes: 1 dozen

- 2 cups all-purpose flour
- 1 cup sugar
- 1 tsp. baking powder
- ½ tsp. baking soda
- ½ tsp. salt
- 2 large eggs
- ½ cup butter, melted
- 1¼ tsp. vanilla extract
- 1½ cups peeled chopped tart apples

STREUSEL TOPPING
- ⅓ cup packed brown sugar
- 1 Tbsp. all-purpose flour
- ⅛ tsp. ground cinnamon
- 1 Tbsp. cold butter

GLAZE
- ¾ cup confectioners' sugar
- 2 to 3 tsp. 2% milk
- 1 tsp. butter, melted
- ⅛ tsp. vanilla extract
  Dash salt

1. Preheat oven to 375°. Whisk together the first five ingredients. In a second bowl, whisk together the eggs, melted butter and vanilla; add to the flour mixture, stirring just until moistened (batter will be stiff). Fold in apples. Fill 12 greased or paper-lined muffin cups three-fourths full.
2. For topping, mix brown sugar, flour and cinnamon; cut in butter until crumbly. Sprinkle over batter in muffin cups.
3. Bake until a toothpick inserted in center comes out clean, 15-20 minutes. Cool 5 minutes before removing from pan to a wire rack to cool. Mix the glaze ingredients; drizzle over tops.

1 muffin: 295 cal., 10g fat (6g sat. fat), 55mg chol., 398mg sod., 49g carb. (32g sugars, 1g fiber), 3g pro.

LEMON-THYME BREAD

Fresh thyme is best for this bread, but if you have only dried available, reduce the amount to 1 tablespoon and crush it between your fingers before adding it to the batter. As a special touch, dress this bread up further with flavored icing or cream cheese.
—*Cathy Tang, Redmond, WA*

Prep: 25 min. • **Bake:** 40 min. + cooling
Makes: 1 loaf (12 slices)

- ½ cup butter, softened
- ¾ cup sugar
- 1 large egg
- ½ cup buttermilk
- ½ cup sour cream
- 1¾ cups all-purpose flour
- 2 Tbsp. minced fresh thyme
- 1 Tbsp. grated lemon zest
- ½ tsp. baking soda
- ¼ tsp. salt
-   Confectioners' sugar

1. In a large bowl, cream butter and sugar until light and fluffy. Beat in egg. Combine buttermilk and sour cream. Combine the flour, thyme, lemon zest, baking soda and salt; add to creamed mixture alternately with buttermilk mixture, beating well after each addition.

2. Transfer to a greased 8x4-in. loaf pan. Bake at 350° until a toothpick inserted in the center comes out clean, 40-50 minutes or. Cool for 10 minutes before removing from pan to a wire rack. Cool bread completely; sprinkle loaf with confectioners' sugar.

1 slice: 212 cal., 10g fat (6g sat. fat), 45mg chol., 176mg sod., 27g carb. (14g sugars, 1g fiber), 3g pro.

Lemon-Thyme Mini Loaves: Use three greased 5¾ x3x2-in. loaf pans. Bake at 350° until a toothpick inserted in the center comes out clean, 25-30 minutes.

Lemon-Thyme Muffins: Make the batter as directed; fill 12 greased or paper-lined muffin cups two-thirds full. Bake at 400° until a toothpick comes out clean, 16-20 minutes.

Lemon-Thyme Icing: In a small bowl, combine ½ cup confectioners' sugar, ½ tsp. minced fresh thyme and 3-4 tsp. lemon juice, as needed, to achieve a drizzling consistency. **Yield:** 2 Tbsp.

Lemony Cream Cheese: In a small bowl, beat 8 oz. softened cream cheese until fluffy. Add ⅓ cup confectioners' sugar, 4 tsp. lemon juice and 1 tsp. grated lemon zest; beat until smooth. **Yield:** 1 cup.

FEATHER-LIGHT BISCUITS

I always baked extras of these fluffy biscuits to send home with the kids. They split them to fill with cheese or peanut butter and jam.
—*Eleanore Hill, Fresno, CA*

Takes: 30 min. • **Makes:** about 2 dozen

- 6 cups buttermilk baking mix
- ¼ cup sugar
- 1 pkg. (¼ oz.) active dry yeast
- ⅓ cup shortening
- 1 to 1¼ cups warm water (120° to 130°)
- ¼ cup butter, melted

1. In a large bowl, combine the baking mix, sugar and yeast. Cut in shortening until mixture resembles coarse crumbs. Stir in enough warm water to form a soft and slightly sticky dough. Turn onto a floured surface; knead gently 3-4 times.
2. Roll dough to ¾-in. thickness; cut with a 2½-in. round biscuit cutter. Place on ungreased baking sheets. Brush tops with melted butter. Bake at 400° until lightly browned, 10-12 minutes.

1 biscuit: 173 cal., 9g fat (3g sat. fat), 5mg chol., 397mg sod., 21g carb. (3g sugars, 1g fiber), 2g pro.

DEFEAT THE MESS!
Measuring shortening with a spoon can be a mess, so I use an ice cream scoop. The scoop releases the shortening with ease into the measuring cup and eliminates the fuss!
—**Marjorie Dungan** Winnetka, CA

CINNAMON TWISTS

These delightful golden twists are perfect for a spring brunch or lunch. The brown sugar and cinnamon give them a delicate spicy flavor. It's a good thing the recipe makes a big batch, because people can rarely eat just one.
—*Janet Mooberry, Peoria, IL*

Prep: 25 min. + rising • **Bake:** 15 min.
Makes: 4 dozen

- 1 pkg. (¼ oz.) active dry yeast
- ¾ cup warm water (110° to 115°), divided
- 4 to 4½ cups all-purpose flour
- ¼ cup sugar
- 1½ tsp. salt
- ½ cup warm 2% milk (110° to 115°)
- ¼ cup butter, softened
- 1 large egg

FILLING
- ¼ cup butter, melted
- ½ cup packed brown sugar
- 4 tsp. ground cinnamon

1. In a large bowl, dissolve yeast in ¼ cup warm water. Add 2 cups of flour, the sugar, salt, milk, butter, egg and the remaining water; beat on medium speed for 3 minutes. Stir in enough of the remaining flour to form a soft dough.
2. Turn onto a floured surface; knead until smooth and elastic, 6-8 minutes. Place in a greased bowl, turning once to grease top. Cover and let rise in a warm place until doubled, about 1 hour.
3. Punch down dough. Roll into a 16x12-in. rectangle. Brush with butter. Combine brown sugar and cinnamon; sprinkle over butter. Let dough rest for 6 minutes. Cut lengthwise into three 16x4-in. strips. Cut each strip into sixteen 4x1-in. pieces. Twist and place on greased baking sheets. Cover and let rise until doubled, about 30 minutes.
4. Bake at 350° for 15 minutes or until golden brown.

1 twist: 71 cal., 2g fat (1g sat. fat), 10mg chol., 97mg sod., 12g carb. (4g sugars, 0 fiber), 1g pro.

A Twist on Cinnamon Rolls

Nothing lights up faces at the breakfast table like home-baked cinnamon rolls!
These four recipes take the traditional classic out for a spin.
Choose a new one to try—you can't go wrong!

BOURBON-SOAKED BACON & GINGER CINNAMON ROLLS

This recipe is the perfect combination of savory and sweet. The bourbon-soaked bacon adds a smoky, savory, bold taste to normal cinnamon rolls. The ginger and pecan topping makes for a crunchy, spicy finish.
—*Shannen Casey, Berkeley, CA*

- -

Prep: 25 min. + marinating • **Bake:** 10 min.
Makes: 8 rolls

- 8 bacon strips
- ¾ cup bourbon
- 1 tube (12.4 oz.) refrigerated cinnamon rolls with icing
- ½ cup chopped pecans
- 2 Tbsp. maple syrup
- 1 tsp. minced fresh gingerroot

1. Place bacon in a shallow dish; add bourbon. Cover and refrigerate overnight. Remove bacon and pat dry; discard bourbon.
2. In a large skillet over medium heat, cook bacon in batches until nearly crisp but still pliable. Remove to paper towels to drain. Discard all but 1 tsp. drippings.
3. Preheat oven to 375°. Separate dough into eight rolls; reserve icing packet. Unroll spiral rolls into long strips; pat dough to form 6x1-in. strips. Place one bacon strip on each strip of dough, trimming bacon as needed, then reroll into a spiral. Pinch ends to seal. Repeat with the remaining dough. Transfer to a parchment paper-lined baking sheet; bake until golden brown, 9-11 minutes.
4. Meanwhile, combine pecans and maple syrup. In another bowl, stir ginger with contents of icing packet. In same skillet, heat the remaining bacon drippings over medium heat. Add the pecans; cook, stirring frequently, until lightly toasted, 2-3 minutes. Drizzle the icing over warm cinnamon rolls; top with pecans.

1 roll: 267 cal., 14g fat (3g sat. fat), 9mg chol., 490mg sod., 28g carb. (13g sugars, 1g fiber), 5g pro.

RED VELVET CINNAMON ROLLS

Turn a box of red velvet cake mix into this easy breakfast—or dessert! You can also swap in another flavor of cake mix, like spice cake, devil's food or orange.
—*Erin Wright, Wallace, KS*

- -

Prep: 20 min. + rising • **Bake:** 15 min.
Makes: 12 servings

- 1 pkg. red velvet cake mix (regular size)
- 2½ to 3 cups all-purpose flour
- 1 pkg. (¼ oz.) active dry yeast
- 1¼ cups warm water (120° to 130°)
- ½ cup packed brown sugar
- 1 tsp. ground cinnamon
- ¼ cup butter, melted

ICING
- 2 cups confectioners' sugar
- 2 Tbsp. butter, softened
- 1 tsp. vanilla extract
- 3 to 5 Tbsp. 2% milk

1. Combine cake mix, 1 cup flour and yeast. Add water; beat on medium speed 2 minutes. Stir in enough of the remaining flour to form a soft dough (dough will be sticky). Turn onto a lightly floured surface; knead gently 6-8 times. Place in a greased bowl, turning once to grease the top. Cover and let rise in a warm place until doubled, about 2 hours. Meanwhile, in another bowl, mix brown sugar and cinnamon.
2. Punch down dough. Turn onto a lightly floured surface; roll dough into an 18x10-in. rectangle. Brush with melted butter to within ¼ in. of edges; sprinkle with sugar mixture.
3. Roll up jelly-roll style, starting with a long side; pinch seam to seal. Cut crosswise into 12 slices. Place in a greased 13x9-in. baking pan. Cover with a kitchen towel; let rise in a warm place until almost doubled, about 1 hour.
4. Bake in a 350° oven until puffed and light brown, 15-20 minutes. Cool slightly.
5. Beat confectioners' sugar, butter, vanilla and enough milk to reach a drizzling consistency. Drizzle icing over warm rolls.

1 roll: 429 cal., 10g fat (5g sat. fat), 16mg chol., 311mg sod., 81g carb. (48g sugars, 1g fiber), 5g pro.

_____

WANT 'EM EVEN MORE DECADENT?
Spread a fluffy layer of cream cheese frosting over the top!

AUTUMN SWEET ROLLS WITH CIDER GLAZE

I love cooking with pumpkin because it's versatile, colorful and nutritious. Combining it with chopped apple and cider gives these glazed rolls their autumn appeal.
—Jennifer Coduto, Kent, OH

- -

Prep: 30 min. + rising • **Bake:** 25 min.
Makes: 1 dozen

- 2 tsp. active dry yeast
- ⅓ cup warm water (110° to 115°)
- 1 Tbsp. honey
- ¾ cup canned pumpkin
- 2 large eggs
- ¼ cup packed brown sugar
- 2 Tbsp. butter, softened
- 1½ tsp. pumpkin pie spice
- ½ tsp. salt
- 4 to 4½ cups all-purpose flour

FILLING
- ¼ cup sugar
- 1 tsp. ground cinnamon
- 2 Tbsp. butter, melted
- 1 small apple, peeled and finely chopped (about 1 cup)

GLAZE
- 1 cup confectioners' sugar
- 3 Tbsp. apple cider or juice
- ¼ cup finely chopped walnuts, toasted

1. In a small bowl, dissolve yeast in warm water and honey. In a large bowl, combine pumpkin, eggs, brown sugar, butter, pie spice, salt, yeast mixture and 1½ cups of flour; beat on medium speed until smooth. Stir in enough remaining flour to form a soft dough (dough will be sticky).
2. Turn dough onto a floured surface; knead until dough is smooth and elastic, 6-8 minutes. Place in a greased bowl, turning once to grease the top. Cover and let rise in a warm place until doubled, about 1 hour.
3. Punch down dough. Turn onto a lightly floured surface. Press dough into a 14x12-in. rectangle. Brush with melted butter to within ½ in. of edges. Mix sugar and cinnamon. Sprinkle dough with cinnamon-sugar mixture and apple. Roll up jelly-roll style, starting with a long side; pinch seam to seal. Cut into 12 slices.
4. Place in a greased 13x9-in. baking pan, cut side down. Cover with a kitchen towel; let rise in a warm place until doubled, about 30 minutes.
5. Preheat oven to 350°. Bake until golden brown, 25-30 minutes. In a small bowl, mix confectioners' sugar and apple cider; drizzle over warm rolls. Sprinkle with walnuts.

1 roll: 306 cal., 7g fat (3g sat. fat), 41mg chol., 145mg sod., 56g carb. (22g sugars, 2g fiber), 6g pro.

SPECIAL CINNAMON ROLLS

These delicious rolls are a perfect project for the beginning bread baker because the dough doesn't require kneading.
—Brenda Deveau, Cyr, ME

- -

Prep: 25 min. + rising • **Bake:** 25 min.
Makes: 2 dozen

- 2 pkg. (¼ oz. each) active dry yeast
- ½ cup warm water (110° to 115°)
- 8 cups all-purpose flour
- 1 pkg. (3.4 oz.) instant vanilla pudding mix
- 2 cups warm whole milk (110° to 115°)
- 2 large eggs, lightly beaten
- ½ cup sugar
- ½ cup canola oil
- 2 tsp. salt
- ¼ cup butter, melted

FILLING
- 1 cup packed brown sugar
- 2 tsp. ground cinnamon
- 1 cup raisins
- 1 cup chopped walnuts

GLAZE
- 1 cup confectioners' sugar
- 1 to 2 Tbsp. whole milk
- ¼ tsp. vanilla extract

1. In a bowl, dissolve yeast in warm water. Add the next seven ingredients; mix well (do not knead). Place in a greased bowl; turn once to grease top. Cover and let rise in warm place until doubled, about 1 hour.
2. Punch dough down. Turn onto a lightly floured surface; divide in half. Roll each half into a 12x8-in. rectangle; brush with butter. Combine the filling ingredients; spread over dough to within ½ in. of the edges. Roll up dough from long side; seal seam. Cut each roll into 12 slices; place cut side down in two greased 13x9-in. baking pans. Cover and let rise until nearly doubled, 45 minutes.
3. Bake at 350° for 25-30 minutes or until golden brown. Combine the glaze ingredients; drizzle over rolls. Cool in pans on wire racks.

1 roll: 364 cal., 11g fat (3g sat. fat), 26mg chol., 294mg sod., 60g carb. (26g sugars, 2g fiber), 7g pro.

MUSHROOM CHEESE BREAD

This savory grilled bread is delightful with barbecued steak, baked potatoes and corn on the cob. For a variation, we sometimes use half cheddar cheese and half mozzarella.
—*Dolly McDonald, Edmonton, AB*

- -

Takes: 15 min. • **Makes:** 12 servings

- 1 cup shredded part-skim mozzarella cheese
- 1 can (4 oz.) mushroom stems and pieces, drained
- ⅓ cup mayonnaise
- 2 Tbsp. shredded Parmesan cheese
- 2 Tbsp. chopped green onion
- 1 loaf (1 lb.) unsliced French bread

1. In a small bowl, combine mozzarella cheese, mushrooms, mayonnaise, Parmesan cheese and onion. Cut bread in half lengthwise; spread the cheese mixture over cut sides.
2. Grill, covered, over indirect heat or broil 4 in. from heat until lightly browned, 5-10 minutes. Slice bread and serve warm.
1 slice: 180 cal., 8g fat (2g sat. fat), 10mg chol., 347mg sod., 20g carb. (1g sugars, 1g fiber), 6g pro.

HONEY BAGELS

Who has time to make from-scratch bagels? You do, with this easy recipe! The chewy golden bagels offer a hint of honey and will win over even the pickiest eaters.
—*Taste of Home Test Kitchen*

- -

Prep: 1 hour + standing • **Bake:** 20 min.
Makes: 1 dozen

- 1 Tbsp. active dry yeast
- 1¼ cups warm water (110° to 115°)
- 3 Tbsp. canola oil
- 3 Tbsp. sugar
- 3 Tbsp. plus ¼ cup honey, divided
- 1 tsp. brown sugar
- 1½ tsp. salt
- 1 large egg, room temperature
- 4 to 5 cups bread flour
- 1 Tbsp. dried minced onion
- 1 Tbsp. sesame seeds
- 1 Tbsp. poppy seeds

1. In a large bowl, dissolve yeast in warm water. Add the oil, sugar, 3 Tbsp. honey, brown sugar, salt and egg; mix well. Stir in enough flour to form a soft dough.

2. Turn onto a floured surface; knead until a smooth firm dough forms, about 8-10 minutes. Cover and let rest for 10 minutes.
3. Punch dough down. Shape into 12 balls. Push thumb through centers to form a 1½-in. hole. Stretch and shape dough to form an even ring. Place on a floured surface. Cover and let rest for 10 minutes; flatten bagels slightly.
4. Preheat oven to 425°. In a large saucepan or Dutch oven, bring 8 cups water and the remaining honey to a boil. Drop bagels, one at a time, into the boiling water. Cook bagels for 45 seconds; turn and cook 45 seconds longer. Remove with a slotted spoon; drain and sprinkle with minced onion, sesame seeds and poppy seeds.
5. Place bagels 2 in. apart on baking sheets lined with parchment. Bake for 12 minutes. Turn and bake until golden brown, about 5 minutes longer.
1 bagel: 265 cal., 5g fat (1g sat. fat), 16mg chol., 303mg sod., 48g carb. (14g sugars, 2g fiber), 7g pro.

RASPBERRY STREUSEL COFFEE CAKE

One of my mother's friends used to bring this cake over at the holidays, and it never lasted long. With its tangy raspberry filling, tender cake and crunchy topping, it has become a favorite at our house.

—Amy Mitchell, Sabetha, KS

- -

Prep: 25 min. + cooling • **Bake:** 40 min.
Makes: 16 servings

- 3½ cups unsweetened raspberries
- 1 cup water
- 2 Tbsp. lemon juice
- 1¼ cups sugar
- ⅓ cup cornstarch

BATTER
- 3 cups all-purpose flour
- 1 cup sugar
- 1 tsp. baking powder
- 1 tsp. baking soda
- 1 cup cold butter, cubed
- 2 large eggs, lightly beaten
- 1 cup sour cream
- 1 tsp. vanilla extract

TOPPING
- ½ cup all-purpose flour
- ½ cup sugar
- ¼ cup butter, softened
- ½ cup chopped pecans

GLAZE
- ½ cup confectioners' sugar
- 2 tsp. 2% milk
- ½ tsp. vanilla extract

1. In a large saucepan, cook raspberries and water over medium heat 5 minutes. Add lemon juice. Combine sugar and cornstarch; stir into fruit mixture. Bring to a boil; cook and stir 2 minutes or until thickened. Cool.

2. Preheat oven to 350°. In a large bowl, combine flour, sugar, baking powder and baking soda. Cut in butter until mixture resembles coarse crumbs. Stir in eggs, sour cream and vanilla (batter will be stiff).

3. Spread half the batter into a greased 13x9-in. baking dish. Spread the raspberry filling over batter; spoon the remaining batter over the filling. Combine topping ingredients; sprinkle over top.

4. Bake 40-45 minutes or until golden brown. Combine glaze ingredients; drizzle over warm cake.

1 piece: 462 cal., 20g fat (11g sat. fat), 75mg chol., 265mg sod., 65g carb. (39g sugars, 2g fiber), 5g pro.

TRY A FLAVOR CHANGE!

To make a lemon-blueberry variation of this cake, substitute blueberries for the raspberries, and add 1 tsp. grated lemon zest to the batter. The finished cake looks gorgeous served with a dollop of lemon curd.

HONEY CORNBREAD

It's a pleasure to serve this moist cornbread to family and guests. Honey gives it a slightly sweet taste. Most people find it's difficult to eat just one piece.

—Adeline Piscitelli, Sayreville, NJ

Takes: 30 min. • Makes: 9 servings

- 1 cup all-purpose flour
- 1 cup yellow cornmeal
- ¼ cup sugar
- 3 tsp. baking powder
- ½ tsp. salt
- 2 large eggs
- 1 cup heavy whipping cream
- ¼ cup canola oil
- ¼ cup honey

1. Preheat oven to 400°. Combine flour, cornmeal, sugar, baking powder and salt. In a small bowl, beat eggs. Add cream, oil and honey; beat well. stir into the dry ingredients just until moistened. Pour into a greased 9-in. square baking pan.
2. Bake for 20-25 minutes or until a toothpick inserted in the center comes out clean. Serve warm.

1 piece: 318 cal., 17g fat (7g sat. fat), 83mg chol., 290mg sod., 37g carb. (14g sugars, 2g fiber), 5g pro.

WHOLE WHEAT ROLLS

Even though these are whole wheat rolls they have a light texture and are soft and tender. This recipe reminds me of lots of happy meals with my family.

—Wilma Orlano, Carroll, IA

Prep: 40 min. + rising • Bake: 10 min.
Makes: 2 dozen

- 1½ cups boiling water
- ⅓ cup wheat bran
- 3 Tbsp. ground flaxseed
- 1½ tsp. salt
- 1 tsp. ground cinnamon
- ⅓ cup honey
- ¼ cup canola oil
- 2 pkg. (¼ oz. each) active dry yeast
- ¼ cup warm water (110° to 115°)
- 2 tsp. sugar
- 1½ cups whole wheat flour
- 2½ to 3 cups bread flour

1. In a small bowl, pour boiling water over the wheat bran, flaxseed, salt and cinnamon. Add the honey and oil. Let stand until mixture cools to 110°-115°, stirring occasionally.
2. In a large bowl, dissolve yeast in warm water. Add the sugar, whole wheat flour and wheat bran mixture. Beat on medium speed for 3 minutes. Stir in enough bread flour to form a firm dough.
3. Turn onto a floured surface; knead until smooth and elastic, about 6-8 minutes. Place in a greased bowl, turning once to grease the top. Cover and let rise in a warm place until doubled, about 1 hour. Punch dough down.
4. Turn onto a lightly floured surface; divide into 24 pieces. Shape each into a roll. Place 2 in. apart on greased baking sheets. Cover and let rise until doubled, about 30 minutes.
5. Bake at 375° for 10-15 minutes or until golden brown. Remove from pans to wire racks to cool.

1 roll: 120 cal., 3g fat (0 sat. fat), 0 chol., 149mg sod., 22g carb. (4g sugars, 2g fiber), 4g pro.
Diabetic exchanges: 1½ starch, ½ fat.

CAPPUCCINO MUFFINS

These are my favorite muffins to serve with a cup of coffee or a tall glass of cold milk. Not only are they great for breakfast, they make a tasty dessert or midnight snack. I get lots of recipe requests whenever I serve them. The espresso spread is also super on a bagel.
—Janice Schulz, Racine, WI

Prep: 15 min. • **Bake:** 20 min.
Makes: about 14 muffins (¾ cup spread)

ESPRESSO SPREAD
- 4 oz. cream cheese, cubed
- 1 Tbsp. sugar
- ½ tsp. instant coffee granules
- ½ tsp. vanilla extract
- ¼ cup miniature semisweet chocolate chips

MUFFINS
- 2 cups all-purpose flour
- ¾ cup sugar
- 2½ tsp. baking powder
- 1 tsp. ground cinnamon
- ½ tsp. salt
- 1 cup 2% milk
- 2 Tbsp. instant coffee granules
- ½ cup butter, melted
- 1 large egg
- 1 tsp. vanilla extract
- ¾ cup miniature semisweet chocolate chips

1. Preheat oven to 375°. In a food processor, combine spread ingredients; cover and process until well blended. Transfer to a small bowl; cover and refrigerate until serving.
2. In a large bowl, combine the flour, sugar, baking powder, cinnamon and salt. In another bowl, combine milk and coffee granules until the coffee is dissolved. Add the butter, egg and vanilla. Stir into the dry ingredients just until moistened. Fold in chocolate chips.
3. Fill greased or paper-lined muffin cups two-thirds full. Bake 17-20 minutes or until a toothpick inserted in the center comes out clean. Cool for 5 minutes before removing from pans to wire racks. Serve warm with espresso spread.
1 muffin with 1 Tbsp. spread: 273 cal., 14g fat (9g sat. fat), 44mg chol., 261mg sod., 34g carb. (20g sugars, 1g fiber), 4g pro.

FRESH PEAR BREAD

When our tree branches are loaded with ripe, juicy pears, I treat my family and friends to loaves of this cinnamony bread richly studded with walnuts and pears. I always receive raves and requests for the recipe.
—Linda Patrick, Houston, TX

Prep: 15 min. • **Bake:** 55 min. + cooling
Makes: 2 loaves (16 slices each)

- 3 large eggs
- 1½ cups sugar
- ¾ cup vegetable oil
- 1 tsp. vanilla extract
- 3 cups all-purpose flour
- 2 tsp. baking powder
- 2 tsp. ground cinnamon
- 1 tsp. baking soda
- 1 tsp. salt
- 4 cups finely chopped peeled ripe pears (about 4 medium)
- 1 tsp. lemon juice
- 1 cup chopped walnuts

1. Preheat oven to 350°. In a bowl, combine the eggs, sugar, oil and vanilla; mix well. Combine flour, baking powder, cinnamon, baking soda and salt; stir into the egg mixture just until moistened. Toss pears with lemon juice. Stir pears and walnuts into batter (batter will be thick).
2. Spoon into two greased 9x5-in. loaf pans. Bake for 55-60 minutes or until a toothpick inserted in the center comes out clean. Cool for 10 minutes before removing from pans to wire racks.
1 slice: 168 cal., 8g fat (1g sat. fat), 20mg chol., 144mg sod., 22g carb. (12g sugars, 1g fiber), 3g pro.

Contest Winner

MORNING MUFFINS

I like to grab one of these muffins with coffee on days when I get a late start to work. It's a quick and tasty hand-held breakfast. If you want, dress them up with some sweet icing!

—Sandy Szerensci, Masontown, PA

- -

Prep: 20 min. • **Bake:** 20 min. • **Makes:** 1 dozen

¼ cup butter, softened
½ cup packed brown sugar
2 large eggs
1 cup sour cream
1 cup shredded carrots
½ cup sweetened shredded coconut
½ cup raisins
1½ cups all-purpose flour
1 tsp. baking soda
1 tsp. ground cinnamon
½ cup chopped nuts

1. Preheat oven to 375°. In a small bowl, cream butter and brown sugar. Add the eggs and sour cream; beat well. Stir in the carrots, coconut and raisins.
2. Combine the flour, baking soda and cinnamon; stir into creamed mixture just until moistened. Fold in nuts.
3. Fill greased or paper-lined muffin cups three-fourths full. Bake for 20-25 minutes or until a toothpick inserted in muffin comes out clean. Cool for 5 minutes before removing from pan to a wire rack.

1 muffin: 250 cal., 13g fat (6g sat. fat), 46mg chol., 174mg sod., 30g carb. (15g sugars, 2g fiber), 5g pro.

Confectioners' Sugar Icing: Mix ¼ cup confectioners' sugar and 1-2 tsp. half-and-half cream. Drizzle over cooled muffins.

DELICIOUS ALMOND BRAIDS

Similar to an almond crescent, this coffee cake is light and flaky, with a rich almond center. It's so versatile you can serve it for dessert, breakfast or brunch. It tastes like it came from a high-end bakery, but puff pastry dough makes it easy.

—Gina Idone, Staten Island, NY

- -

Prep: 25 min. • **Bake:** 30 min. + cooling
Makes: 2 braids (6 slices each)

1 pkg. (7 oz.) almond paste
½ cup butter
½ cup sugar
1 large egg
2 Tbsp. all-purpose flour
1 pkg. (17.3 oz.) frozen puff pastry, thawed
GLAZE
¾ cup plus 1 Tbsp. confectioners' sugar
2 Tbsp. 2% milk
½ tsp. almond extract
¼ cup sliced almonds, toasted

1. Preheat oven to 375°. Place the almond paste, butter and sugar in a food processor; cover and pulse until chopped. Add egg and flour; process until smooth.
2. Place puff pastry sheets onto a greased baking sheet. Spread half of the filling mixture down the center third of one pastry sheet. On each side, cut eight strips about 3½ in. into the center. Starting at one end, fold alternating strips at an angle across the filling. Pinch the ends to seal. Repeat with the remaining pastry and filling. Bake until golden brown, 30-35 minutes. Remove to a wire rack.
3. Combine the confectioners' sugar, milk and almond extract. Drizzle over braids; sprinkle with almonds. Cut into slices to serve.

1 slice: 430 cal., 25g fat (8g sat. fat), 38mg chol., 197mg sod., 49g carb. (22g sugars, 4g fiber), 6g pro.

NO-KNEAD KNOT ROLLS

My mom loved to serve these light, golden rolls when I was growing up on our Iowa farm. They're extra nice since they require no kneading. The dough rises in the refrigerator overnight, so there's little last-minute fuss to serve fresh hot rolls with any meal.
—*Toni Hilscher, Omaha, NE*

Prep: 25 min. + rising • **Bake:** 10 min.
Makes: 4 dozen

- 2 pkg. (¼ oz. each) active dry yeast
- 2 cups warm water (110° to 115°)
- ½ cup sugar
- 2 tsp. salt
- 6 to 6½ cups all-purpose flour
- 1 large egg
- ½ cup shortening
- ½ cup butter, softened

1. In a large bowl, dissolve yeast in warm water. Add the sugar, salt and 2 cups of flour. Beat on medium speed for 2 minutes. Beat in egg and shortening. Stir in enough of the remaining flour to form a soft dough (do not knead). Cover and refrigerate overnight.
2. Punch dough down and divide into four portions. Roll one portion into a 14x12-in. rectangle. Spread 2 Tbsp. butter over dough. Fold in half lengthwise; cut into 12 strips. Tie each strip into a knot; tuck and pinch ends under. Place 2 in. apart on greased baking sheets. Repeat with the three remaining dough portions. Cover rolls and let rise until doubled, about 1 hour.
3. Bake at 400° until golden brown, 10-12 minutes. Remove to wire rack to cool.

1 roll: 102 cal., 4g fat (2g sat. fat), 10mg chol., 119mg sod., 14g carb. (2g sugars, 0 fiber), 2g pro.

FREEZE IT
CHERRY CHIP SCONES

These buttery scones, dotted with dried cherries and white chips, are so sweet and flaky that sometimes I serve them for dessert. For a change, try using dried blueberries, or dried cranberries with semisweet chocolate chips.
—*Pam Brooks, South Berwick, ME*

Prep: 15 min. • **Bake:** 20 min.
Makes: 8 servings

- 3 cups all-purpose flour
- ½ cup sugar
- 2½ tsp. baking powder
- ½ tsp. baking soda
- 6 Tbsp. cold butter
- 1 cup (8 oz.) vanilla yogurt
- ¼ cup plus 2 Tbsp. whole milk, divided
- 1⅓ cups dried cherries
- ⅔ cup white baking chips
  Coarse sugar, optional

1. Preheat oven to 400°. In a large bowl, combine the flour, sugar, baking powder and baking soda. Cut in cold butter until the mixture resembles coarse crumbs. Combine yogurt and ¼ cup milk; stir into crumb mixture just until moistened. Knead in cherries and chips.
2. On a greased baking sheet, pat dough into a 9-in. circle. Cut into eight wedges; separate the wedges. Brush with the remaining milk. If desired, sprinkle with sugar. Bake until golden brown, 20-25 minutes. Serve scones warm.
Freeze option: Freeze cooled scones in freezer containers. To use, thaw at room temperature. Or, microwave each scone on high until heated through, 20-30 seconds.

1 scone: 543 cal., 23 g fat (14 g sat. fat), 52 mg chol., 410 mg sod., 77 g carb., 2 g fiber, 8 g pro.

CARDAMOM BRAID BREAD

I came across this recipe in 1983 and have been making it for the holidays ever since, and it's only grown more well-loved. One year I gave away 20 loaves!
—Rita Bergman, Olympia, WA

Prep: 30 min. + rising • **Bake:** 20 min. + cooling
Makes: 2 loaves (20 slices each)

- 6 cups all-purpose flour
- 2 pkg. (¼ oz. each) active dry yeast
- 1½ tsp. ground cardamom
- 1 tsp. salt
- 1½ cups plus 2 Tbsp. milk, divided
- ½ cup butter, cubed
- ½ cup honey
- 2 large eggs
- 2 Tbsp. sugar

1. In a large bowl, combine 2 cups flour, yeast, cardamom and salt. In a small saucepan, heat 1½ cups milk, butter and honey to 120°-130°. Add to the dry ingredients; beat just until moistened. Add eggs; beat until smooth. Stir in enough of the remaining flour to form a firm dough (dough will be sticky).
2. Turn dough onto a floured surface; knead until smooth and elastic, about 6-8 minutes. Place in a greased bowl, turning once to grease top. Cover and let rise in a warm place until doubled, about 45 minutes.
3. Punch dough down. Turn onto a lightly floured surface; divide in half. Divide each portion into thirds. Shape each into a 14-in. rope. Place three ropes on a greased baking sheet; braid, then pinch the ends to seal and tuck under. Repeat with the remaining dough. Cover and let rise until doubled, about 30 minutes.
4. Brush loaves with the remaining milk and sprinkle with sugar. Bake at 375° for 20-25 minutes or until golden brown. Remove from pans to wire racks to cool.
1 slice: 114 cal., 3g fat (2g sat. fat), 18mg chol., 91mg sod., 19g carb. (5g sugars, 1g fiber), 3g pro.

RHUBARB NUT MUFFINS

Muffins are my weakness. And I'm not alone! When I make these to take to a gathering, I always come home with an empty plate.
—*Mary Kay Morris, Cokato, MN*

Prep: 15 min. • **Bake:** 20 min. + cooling
Makes: about 10 muffins

1½ cups all-purpose flour
¾ cup packed brown sugar
½ tsp. baking soda
½ tsp. salt
1 large egg
⅓ cup canola oil
½ cup buttermilk
1 tsp. vanilla extract
1 cup diced fresh or frozen rhubarb
½ cup chopped walnuts
TOPPING
¼ cup packed brown sugar
½ cup chopped walnuts
½ tsp. ground cinnamon

1. Preheat oven to 375°. In a large bowl, combine flour, brown sugar, baking soda and salt. In a small bowl, whisk the egg, oil, buttermilk and vanilla. Stir into dry ingredients just until moistened. Fold in rhubarb and walnuts.
2. Fill greased or paper-lined muffin cups two-thirds full. Combine topping ingredients; sprinkle over muffins. Bake 20-25 minutes or until a toothpick comes out clean. Cool for 5 minutes before removing from pan to a wire rack.
1 muffin: 307 cal., 15g fat (2g sat. fat), 22mg chol., 210mg sod., 39g carb. (23g sugars, 1g fiber), 6g pro.

CHIVE PINWHEEL ROLLS

My light, pleasant-tasting rolls complement almost any entree. With the chive filling swirled through the golden bread, they're attractive enough for special occasions.
—*Ann Niemela, Ely, MN*

Prep: 25 min. + rising • **Bake:** 30 min.
Makes: 15 rolls

3½ cups all-purpose flour
3 Tbsp. sugar
1 pkg. (¼ oz.) active dry yeast
1½ tsp. salt
1 cup whole milk
⅓ cup canola oil
¼ cup water
¼ cup mashed potatoes (without added milk and butter)
1 large egg
CHIVE FILLING
1 cup sour cream
1 cup minced chives
1 large egg yolk
  Butter, melted

1. In a large bowl, combine 2½ cups flour, sugar, yeast and salt. In a small saucepan, heat milk, oil, water and mashed potatoes to 120°-130°. Add to dry ingredients; beat just until moistened. Add egg; beat until smooth. Stir in enough of the remaining flour to form a soft dough.
2. Turn onto a floured surface; knead until smooth and elastic, 6-8 minutes. Place in a greased bowl; turn once to grease top. Cover and let rise in a warm place until doubled, about 1 hour.
3. Turn dough onto a floured surface. Roll into a 15x10-in. rectangle. In a bowl, combine sour cream, chives and egg yolk. Spread sour cream mixture over the dough to within ½ in. of the edges.
4. Roll up jelly-roll style, starting with a long side; pinch seam to seal. Cut into 1-in. slices. Place cut side down in a 13x9-in. baking pan. Cover and let rise until doubled, about 1 hour.
5. Bake at 350° for 30-35 minutes or until golden brown. Brush with butter. Cool on a wire rack. Refrigerate leftovers.
1 roll: 214 cal., 9g fat (3g sat. fat), 41mg chol., 258mg sod., 27g carb. (4g sugars, 1g fiber), 5g pro.

Main Dishes

Welcome them home with meals they'll remember forever! One-dish skillet meals, savory casseroles, grilled meats—plus four ways to make roast chicken!—the 36 recipes in this chapter are down-home cooking at its finest. Every dish will make your family eagerly look forward to dinnertime!

SUGAR-GLAZED HAM

This old-fashioned sugar glaze gives your ham a pretty, golden brown coating just like the holiday hams Grandma used to make. The mustard and vinegar complement the brown sugar and add tangy flavor. Be ready to dish up lots of second helpings, because everyone will want more!
—*Carol Strong Battle, Heathsville, VA*

Prep: 5 min. • **Bake:** 1¾ hours
Makes: 14 servings

- 1   fully cooked bone-in ham (5 to 7 lbs.)
- 1   cup packed brown sugar
- 2   tsp. prepared mustard
- 1   to 2 Tbsp. cider vinegar

1. Preheat oven to 325°. Place ham on a rack in a shallow roasting pan. Using a sharp knife, score the surface of the ham with ¼-in.-deep cuts in a diamond pattern. Cover; bake until a thermometer reads 130°, 1½-2 hours.
2. Meanwhile, in a small bowl, combine the brown sugar, mustard and enough vinegar to make a thick paste. Remove ham from oven. Spread the sugar mixture over the ham. Bake, uncovered, until a thermometer reads 140°, 15-30 minutes.
4 oz. ham: 284 cal., 16g fat (6g sat. fat), 57mg chol., 1110mg sod., 15g carb. (15g sugars, 0 fiber), 20g pro.

MEATBALL CHILI WITH DUMPLINGS

My family enjoys this delicious recipe—it's like a spicy meatball stew with dumplings!
—*Sarah Yoder, Middlebury, IN*

Prep: 20 min. • **Cook:** 50 min.
Makes: 6 servings

- 1   large egg, beaten
- ¾   cup finely chopped onion, divided
- ¼   cup dry bread crumbs or rolled oats
- 5   tsp. beef bouillon granules, divided
- 3   tsp. chili powder, divided
- 1   lb. ground beef
- 3   Tbsp. all-purpose flour
- 1   Tbsp. canola oil
- 1   can (28 oz.) diced tomatoes, undrained
- 1   garlic clove, minced
- ½   tsp. ground cumin
- 1   can (16 oz.) kidney beans, rinsed and drained

CORNMEAL DUMPLINGS
- 1½   cups biscuit/baking mix
- ½   cup yellow cornmeal
- ⅔   cup whole milk
       Minced chives, optional

1. In a large bowl, combine egg, ¼ cup onion, the bread crumbs, 3 tsp. bouillon and 1 tsp. chili powder; crumble beef over the bread crumb mixture and mix well. Shape into twelve 1½-in. meatballs. Roll meatballs in flour.
2. Heat oil in a 12-in. cast-iron or other ovenproof skillet; brown meatballs. Drain on paper towels. Meanwhile, in a large saucepan, combine the tomatoes, garlic and cumin with the remaining onion, bouillon and chili powder. Add meatballs. Cover and cook over low heat for about 20 minutes. Stir in beans.
3. Combine the dumpling ingredients. Drop by spoonfuls onto chili; cook on low, uncovered, for 10 minutes. Cover and cook until a toothpick inserted in one of the dumplings comes out clean, 10-12 minutes longer. If desired, sprinkle with minced chives.
1 serving: 475 cal., 16g fat (6g sat. fat), 76mg chol., 1523mg sod., 56g carb. (8g sugars, 7g fiber), 26g pro.

SHORT RIB POUTINE

This dish combines the hearty, spicy flavors of my beloved slow-cooker short ribs with my favorite comfort food: fries and gravy. With a little prep in the morning, it's just about ready when I come home from work (plus, the kitchen smells amazing!). If you're sensitive to spice, reduce the amount of Sriracha sauce.
—*Erin DeWitt, Long Beach, CA*

- -

Prep: 45 min. • **Cook:** 6 hours
Makes: 4 servings

- 1 lb. well-trimmed boneless beef short ribs
- 3 Tbsp. all-purpose flour
- ½ tsp. pepper
- 2 Tbsp. olive oil
- 1 medium onion, coarsely chopped
- 4 garlic cloves, minced
- 1½ cups beef stock, divided

- ¼ cup Sriracha Asian hot chili sauce
- 3 Tbsp. ketchup
- 2 Tbsp. Worcestershire sauce
- 1 Tbsp. packed brown sugar
- 3 cups frozen french-fried potatoes (about 11 oz.)
- 1 cup cheese curds or 4 oz. white cheddar cheese, broken into small chunks

1. Toss short ribs with flour and pepper, shaking off excess; reserve the remaining flour mixture. In a large skillet, heat oil over medium-high heat; brown ribs on all sides. Transfer to a 3-qt. slow cooker, reserving drippings.

2. In the same skillet, saute the onion in drippings over medium heat until tender, 2-3 minutes. Add minced garlic; cook and stir 1 minute. Stir in 1 cup stock; bring to a boil, stirring to loosen browned bits from pan.

3. In a small bowl, whisk the reserved flour mixture, chili sauce, ketchup, Worcestershire sauce, brown sugar and remaining stock until smooth; stir into onion mixture. Pour over ribs.

4. Cook, covered, on low until ribs are tender, 6-8 hours. Remove ribs; shred with two forks and keep warm. Skim fat from onion mixture; puree using an immersion blender. (Or, cool slightly and puree in a blender; return to slow cooker to heat through.)

5. Cook potatoes according to package directions. Serve beef over potatoes; top with gravy and cheese.

1 serving: 560 cal., 31g fat (12g sat. fat), 80mg chol., 1453mg sod., 39g carb. (15g sugars, 3g fiber), 28g pro.

OVEN-BAKED SHRIMP & GRITS

On chilly days, I doctor up grits and top them with shrimp for a comfy meal. If you're not a seafood lover, use chicken, ham or both.
—*Jerri Gradert, Lincoln, NE*

Prep: 20 min. • **Bake:** 45 min.
Makes: 6 servings

- 1 carton (32 oz.) chicken broth
- 1 cup quick-cooking grits
- 1 can (10 oz.) diced tomatoes and green chiles, drained
- 1 cup shredded Monterey Jack cheese
- 1 cup shredded cheddar cheese, divided
  Freshly ground pepper
- 2 Tbsp. butter
- 1 medium green pepper, chopped
- 1 medium onion, chopped
- 1 lb. uncooked shrimp (31-40 per lb.), peeled and deveined
- 2 garlic cloves, minced

1. Preheat oven to 350°. In a 13x9-in. or 2½-qt. baking dish, combine broth and grits. Bake, uncovered, until liquid is absorbed and the grits are tender, 30-35 minutes.
2. Stir in tomatoes, Monterey Jack cheese and ½ cup of the cheddar cheese. Bake, uncovered, until heated through, about 10 minutes. Sprinkle with pepper and the remaining cheese; let stand 5 minutes.
3. In a large skillet, heat butter over medium-high heat; saute green pepper and onion until tender, 6-8 minutes. Add shrimp and garlic; cook and stir until shrimp turn pink, 2-3 minutes. Spoon over grits.
1⅔ cups: 360 cal., 18g fat (10g sat. fat), 141mg chol., 1199mg sod., 26g carb. (2g sugars, 2g fiber), 25g pro.
Note: A switch to reduced-sodium broth will save almost 300mg sodium per serving.

COMPANY STUFFED PORK CHOPS

These comforting pork chops bake to a perfect golden brown, and the stuffing is incredibly moist. It's one of my favorite dishes to serve guests; I always know they'll love it.
—*Lorraine Darocha, Mountain City, TN*

Prep: 40 min. • **Bake:** 30 min.
Makes: 6 servings

- 2 celery ribs, diced
- 1 small onion, chopped
- 1 tsp. olive oil
- 9 slices white bread, cubed
- ¼ cup minced fresh parsley
- ¼ tsp. salt
- ¼ tsp. rubbed sage
- ⅛ tsp. white pepper
- ⅛ tsp. dried marjoram
- ⅛ tsp. dried thyme
- ¾ cup reduced-sodium chicken broth

PORK CHOPS

- 6 pork rib chops (7 oz. each)
- 2 tsp. olive oil
- ¼ tsp. salt
- ¼ tsp. pepper

1. Preheat oven to 350°. In a large skillet coated with cooking spray, saute celery and onion in 1 tsp. oil until tender; remove from heat. In a large bowl, combine bread and seasonings. Add the celery mixture and broth; toss to coat. Set aside.
2. Cut a pocket in each pork chop by making a horizontal slice almost to the bone. Coat the same skillet with cooking spray. Cook the chops in oil in batches over medium-high heat until browned, 1-2 minutes on each side. Fill chops with the bread mixture; secure with toothpicks if necessary.
3. Transfer to a 13x9-in. baking dish coated with cooking spray. Sprinkle with salt and pepper. Cover and bake for 15 minutes. Uncover; bake or until a thermometer reads 145° when inserted in the center of the stuffing and the pork is tender, 15-20 minutes longer. Discard toothpicks and let pork chops stand 5 minutes before serving.
1 serving: 314 cal., 12g fat (4g sat. fat), 64mg chol., 526mg sod., 20g carb. (3g sugars, 1g fiber), 29g pro. **Diabetic exchanges:** 4 lean meat, 1 starch.

ITALIAN PASTA BAKE

I love to make this whenever I need to bring a dish to pass. Fresh tomatoes rather than canned add a nice touch that's missing from most other meat and pasta casseroles.
—*Karla Johnson, East Helena, MT*

Prep: 40 min. • **Bake:** 25 min.
Makes: 8 servings

- 2 lbs. ground beef
- 1 large onion, chopped
- 2 garlic cloves, minced
- 1 jar (24 oz.) spaghetti sauce
- 1 can (14½ oz.) diced tomatoes, undrained
- 1 can (4 oz.) mushroom stems and pieces, drained
- 1 tsp. Italian seasoning
- 3 cups uncooked medium pasta shells
- 3 plum tomatoes, sliced
- ¾ cup shredded provolone cheese
- ¾ cup shredded part-skim mozzarella cheese

1. In a large skillet, cook beef and onion over medium heat until meat is no longer pink. Add garlic; cook 1 minute longer. Drain. Stir in the spaghetti sauce, diced tomatoes, mushrooms and the Italian seasoning. Bring to a boil. Reduce heat; simmer, uncovered, 20 minutes.
2. Meanwhile, preheat oven to 350°. Cook pasta according to the package directions; drain. Add to beef mixture and gently stir in tomatoes.
3. Transfer to an ungreased 13x9-in. baking dish. Sprinkle with cheeses. Bake 25-30 minutes or until bubbly and heated through.
1½ cups: 489 cal., 20g fat (8g sat. fat), 80mg chol., 702mg sod., 45g carb. (10g sugars, 5g fiber), 32g pro.

BARBECUED PICNIC CHICKEN

I like to serve this savory chicken at family picnics. Cooked on a covered grill, the poultry stays so tender and juicy. Everyone loves the zesty, slightly sweet homemade barbecue sauce—and it's so easy to make.
—*Priscilla Weaver, Hagerstown, MD*

Prep: 15 min. • **Grill:** 45 min.
Makes: 8 servings

- 2 garlic cloves, minced
- 2 tsp. butter
- 1 cup ketchup
- ¼ cup packed brown sugar
- ¼ cup chili sauce
- 2 Tbsp. Worcestershire sauce
- 1 Tbsp. celery seed
- 1 Tbsp. prepared mustard
- ½ tsp. salt
- 2 dashes hot pepper sauce
- 2 broiler/fryer chickens (3½ to 4 lbs. each), cut up

1. In a large saucepan, saute garlic in butter until tender. Add the next eight ingredients. Bring to a boil, stirring constantly. Remove from the heat; set aside.
2. On a lightly greased grill rack, grill the chicken, covered, over medium heat for 30 minutes, turning occasionally. Baste with sauce. Grill 15 minutes longer or until a thermometer reaches 170°, basting and turning several times.
3 oz. cooked chicken: 296 cal., 14g fat (4g sat. fat), 79mg chol., 761mg sod., 18g carb. (12g sugars, 1g fiber), 25g pro.

SAUCE SUGGESTIONS
This sauce is best when made a day or two in advance, giving the flavors time to come together. If you don't have chili sauce on hand, you can use ¼ cup extra ketchup or ¼ cup cocktail sauce.

TANGY CRANBERRY CHICKEN

My husband loves chicken when it's nice and moist, as in this autumn recipe. I serve it over hot rice with a salad and warm rolls. The ruby red sauce has a wonderful sweet-tart flavor.
—*Dorothy Bateman, Carver, MA*

Prep: 20 min. • **Cook:** 20 min.
Makes: 6 servings

- ½ cup all-purpose flour
- ½ tsp. salt
- ¼ tsp. pepper
- 6 boneless skinless chicken breast halves (4 oz. each)
- 3 Tbsp. butter
- 1 cup water
- 1 cup fresh or frozen cranberries
- ½ cup packed brown sugar
    Dash ground nutmeg
- 1 Tbsp. red wine vinegar, optional
    Hot cooked rice

1. In a shallow dish, combine flour, salt and pepper; dredge chicken in the flour mixture. In a skillet, melt butter over medium heat. Brown the chicken on both sides. Remove and keep warm.
2. Add water, cranberries, brown sugar, nutmeg and, if desired, vinegar to the pan; cook and stir until the berries burst, about 5 minutes. Return chicken to skillet. Cover and simmer for 20-30 minutes or until chicken is tender, basting occasionally with the sauce. Serve with rice.

Freeze option: Place the chicken in freezer containers; top with sauce. If desired, place rice in separate freezer containers. Cool and freeze. To use, partially thaw in refrigerator overnight. Microwave, covered, on high in a microwave-safe dish until heated through, gently stirring and adding a little water to chicken if necessary.

1 serving: 284 cal., 9g fat (1g sat. fat), 73mg chol., 122mg sod., 22g carb. (0 sugars, 0 fiber), 28g pro.

BEEF BRISKET ON BUNS

With its slightly smoky flavor, this beef turns out tender and delicious every time. Plus, it slices well, so it looks great on a buffet!

—Debra Waggoner, Grand Island, NE

- -

Prep: 25 min. + standing • **Bake:** 5 hours
Makes: 16 servings

½ tsp. ground ginger
½ tsp. ground mustard
1 fresh beef brisket (4 to 5 lbs.)
2 cups water
1 cup ketchup
½ cup Worcestershire sauce
2 Tbsp. brown sugar
2 tsp. Liquid Smoke, optional
1 tsp. chili powder
16 to 20 sandwich buns, split, optional

1. Combine the ginger and mustard; rub over brisket. Place on a rack in a shallow roasting pan. Bake, uncovered, at 325° for 2 hours.

2. Let stand for 20 minutes. Thinly slice across the grain. Place in a foil-lined 13x9-in. baking dish. Combine the water, ketchup, Worcestershire sauce, brown sugar, Liquid Smoke (if desired) and chili powder; pour over meat. Cover tightly with foil; bake 3 hours longer or until tender. Serve on buns if desired.

Note: This is a fresh brisket, not corned beef.

3 oz. cooked brisket: 171 cal., 5g fat (2g sat. fat), 48mg chol., 313mg sod., 7g carb. (7g sugars, 0 fiber), 23g pro. **Diabetic exchanges:** 3 lean meat.

CHICKEN & DUMPLING CASSEROLE

This savory casserole is one of my husband's favorites. He loves the fluffy dumplings with plenty of gravy poured over them. The basil adds just the right touch of flavor and makes the whole house smell so good while this dish cooks.

—Sue Mackey, Jackson, WI

- -

Prep: 30 min. • **Bake:** 40 min.
Makes: 8 servings

½ cup chopped onion
½ cup chopped celery
¼ cup butter, cubed
2 garlic cloves, minced
½ cup all-purpose flour
2 tsp. sugar
1 tsp. salt
1 tsp. dried basil
½ tsp. pepper
4 cups chicken broth
1 pkg. (10 oz.) frozen green peas
4 cups cubed cooked chicken
DUMPLINGS
2 cups biscuit/baking mix
2 tsp. dried basil
⅔ cup 2% milk

1. Preheat oven to 350°. In a large saucepan, saute onion and celery in butter until tender. Add garlic; cook 1 minute longer. Stir in flour, sugar, salt, basil and pepper until blended. Gradually add broth; bring to a boil. Cook and stir 1 minute or until thickened; reduce heat. Add peas and cook 5 minutes, stirring constantly. Stir in chicken. Pour into a greased 13x9-in. baking dish.

2. For the dumplings: In a small bowl, combine baking mix and basil. Stir in milk with a fork until moistened. Drop by tablespoonfuls into mounds over chicken mixture.

3. Bake, uncovered, for 30 minutes. Cover and bake 10 minutes longer or until a toothpick inserted in a dumpling comes out clean.

1 serving: 393 cal., 17g fat (7g sat. fat), 80mg chol., 1313mg sod., 33g carb. (6g sugars, 3g fiber), 27g pro.

GREEK TILAPIA

While on a trip through the Greek islands, my husband and I had a dish that we loved. I tried to duplicate it by combining several different recipes and came up with this delicious meal.
—*Sally Jean Burrell, ID Falls, ID*

- -

Prep: 30 min. • **Bake:** 10 min.
Makes: 4 servings

  4   tilapia fillets (4 oz. each)
  4   tsp. butter
  1   large egg
  ¾   cup (3 oz.) crumbled tomato
       and basil feta cheese
  ¼   cup fat-free milk
  ¼   tsp. cayenne pepper
  1   large tomato, seeded and chopped
  ¼   cup chopped ripe olives
  ¼   cup pine nuts, toasted
  1   Tbsp. minced fresh parsley
  1   Tbsp. lemon juice
  ⅛   tsp. pepper

1. In a large cast-iron or other ovenproof skillet, brown fish in butter.
2. In a small bowl, combine egg, cheese, milk and cayenne; spoon over the fish. Sprinkle with tomato, olives and pine nuts. Bake, uncovered, at 425° until fish just begins to flake easily with a fork, 10-15 minutes.
3. In a small bowl, combine the parsley, lemon juice and pepper; drizzle over fish.
1 fillet: 279 cal., 16g fat (6g sat. fat), 123mg chol., 362mg sod., 5g carb. (2g sugars, 2g fiber), 29g pro.

PASTA FAGIOLI AL FORNO

The name of this Italian-inspired dish means "baked pasta with beans." But my busy family translates it as a super satisfying dinner.
—*Cindy Preller, Grayslake, IL*

- -

Prep: 35 min. • **Bake:** 30 min. + standing
Makes: 8 servings

  3   cups uncooked penne pasta
       (about 12 oz.)
  1   can (28 oz.) whole plum tomatoes
  1   lb. bulk Italian sausage
  1   medium onion, chopped
  1   medium carrot, chopped
  1   celery rib, chopped
  4   garlic cloves, minced
  2   Tbsp. tomato paste
  1   tsp. dried oregano
  ½   tsp. salt
  ½   tsp. dried basil
  ¼   tsp. crushed red pepper flakes
  ¼   tsp. pepper
  1   can (15 oz.) cannellini beans,
       rinsed and drained
  ½   cup grated Parmesan cheese, divided
  ½   cup minced fresh parsley, divided
  2   cups shredded fontina or
       provolone cheese

1. Preheat oven to 350°. Cook pasta according to package directions for al dente; drain.
2. Meanwhile, drain tomatoes, reserving juices; coarsely chop tomatoes. In a 6-qt. stockpot, cook and crumble sausage with onion, carrot, celery and garlic over medium-high heat until meat is no longer pink, 6-8 minutes; drain. Stir in tomato paste, seasonings, chopped tomatoes and the reserved juices; bring to a boil. Reduce heat; simmer, uncovered, 10 minutes.
3. Stir in beans and ¼ cup Parmesan cheese and ¼ cup parsley. Stir in pasta. Transfer to a greased 13x9-in. baking dish; sprinkle with fontina cheese and the remaining Parmesan cheese.
4. Bake, covered, 20 minutes. Uncover; bake until cheese melts, 10-15 minutes. Sprinkle with remaining parsley.
Freeze option: Cool unbaked casserole; cover and freeze. To use, partially thaw in refrigerator overnight. Remove casserole from refrigerator 30 minutes before baking. Preheat oven to 350°. Bake as directed, increasing time as necessary to heat through and for a thermometer inserted in center to read 165°.
1 serving: 440 cal., 23g fat (10g sat. fat), 66mg chol., 1029mg sod., 37g carb. (5g sugars, 6g fiber), 22g pro.

CITRUS & HERB ROASTED TURKEY BREAST

This recipe will make you love turkey in a whole new way. Brining with lemon, rosemary and orange juice makes it so flavorful. It's the star attraction at our Thanksgiving table.
—*Fay Moreland, Wichita Falls, TX*

- -

Prep: 1 hour + chilling
Bake: 2 hours + standing • **Makes:** 10 servings

4	**cups water**
¾	**cup kosher salt**
¾	**cup sugar**
2	**medium lemons, quartered**
6	**fresh rosemary sprigs**
6	**fresh thyme sprigs**
8	**garlic cloves, halved**
1	**Tbsp. coarsely ground pepper**
2	**cups cold apple juice**
2	**cups cold orange juice**
2	**large oven roasting bags**
1	**bone-in turkey breast (5 to 6 lbs.)**

HERB BUTTER

⅓	**cup butter, softened**
4	**tsp. grated lemon zest**
1	**Tbsp. minced fresh rosemary**
1	**Tbsp. minced fresh thyme**
1½	**tsp. coarsely ground pepper**

SEASONED SALT BUTTER

¼	**cup butter, melted**
1½	**tsp. seasoned salt**

1. In a 6-qt. stockpot, combine the first eight ingredients. Bring to a boil. Remove from heat. Add cold juices to brine; cool to room temperature.

2. Place one oven roasting bag inside the other. Place turkey breast inside both bags; pour in cooled brine. Seal bags, pressing out as much air as possible, and turn to coat. Place in a roasting pan. Refrigerate for 8 hours or overnight, turning occasionally.

3. In a small bowl, beat the herb butter ingredients until blended. Remove turkey from brine; rinse and pat dry. Discard brine. Place turkey breast on a rack in a 15x10x1-in. baking pan. With fingers, carefully loosen skin from turkey breast; rub herb butter under the skin. Secure skin to the underside of breast with toothpicks. Refrigerate, covered, for 18-24 hours.

4. Preheat oven to 425°. In a small bowl, mix butter and seasoned salt; brush over outside of turkey. Roast 15 minutes.

5. Reduce oven setting to 325°. Roast turkey until a thermometer reads 170°, 1¾-2¼ hours longer. (Cover loosely with foil if turkey browns too quickly.) Remove turkey from oven; tent with foil. Let stand 15 minutes before carving.

6 oz. cooked turkey: 411 cal., 23g fat (10g sat. fat), 151mg chol., 482mg sod., 1g carb. (0 sugars, 0 fiber), 48g pro.

Contest Winner

FREEZE IT
TACO-FILLED PASTA SHELLS

I've been stuffing shells with different fillings for years, but my family enjoys this version the most. The frozen shells are so convenient. You can take out only the number you need for a single-serving lunch or family dinner.
—*Marge Hodel, Roanoke, IL*

- -

Prep: 20 min. + chilling • **Bake:** 45 min.
Makes: 2 casseroles (6 servings each)

- 2 lbs. ground beef
- 2 envelopes taco seasoning
- 1½ cups water
- 1 pkg. (8 oz.) cream cheese, cubed
- 24 uncooked jumbo pasta shells
- ¼ cup butter, melted

ADDITIONAL INGREDIENTS (FOR EACH CASSEROLE)

- 1 cup salsa
- 1 cup taco sauce
- 1 cup shredded cheddar cheese
- 1 cup shredded Monterey Jack cheese
- 1½ cups crushed tortilla chips
- 1 cup sour cream
- 3 green onions, chopped

1. In a Dutch oven, cook beef over medium heat until no longer pink; drain. Stir in taco seasoning and water. Bring to a boil. Reduce heat; simmer, uncovered, for 5 minutes. Stir in cream cheese until melted. Transfer to a bowl; cool. Chill for 1 hour.

2. Cook pasta according to package directions; drain. Gently toss with butter. Fill each shell with about 3 Tbsp. of meat mixture. Place 12 shells in a freezer container. Cover and freeze for up to 3 months.

3. To prepare the remaining shells, spoon salsa into a greased 9-in. square baking dish. Top with stuffed shells and taco sauce. Cover and bake at 350° for 30 minutes. Uncover; sprinkle with cheeses and chips. Bake 15 minutes longer or until heated through. Serve with sour cream and onions.

To use frozen shells: Thaw in the refrigerator for 24 hours (shells will be partially frozen). Remove from dish. Add salsa to dish; top with shells and taco sauce. Cover and bake at 350° for 40 minutes. Uncover; sprinkle with cheeses and chips; continue as above.

2 shells: 492 cal., 31g fat (16g sat. fat), 98mg chol., 982mg sod., 29g carb. (4g sugars, 1g fiber), 23g pro.

ROAST PORK LOIN WITH ROSEMARY APPLESAUCE

I made this for a family get-together on my husband's birthday. The homemade rosemary applesauce adds an extra layer of comfort to the tender pork.
—*Angela Lemoine, Howell, NJ*

- -

Prep: 15 min. + marinating
Bake: 55 min. + standing
Makes: 8 servings (3 cups applesauce)

- ¼ cup olive oil
- 2 Tbsp. salt
- 4 tsp. garlic powder
- 4 tsp. minced fresh rosemary or 1½ tsp. dried rosemary, crushed
- 2 tsp. pepper
- 1 boneless pork loin roast (2 to 3 lbs.), halved

APPLESAUCE
- ¼ cup butter, cubed
- 6 medium Golden Delicious apples, peeled and chopped (about 5 cups)
- 1 to 2 tsp. ground cinnamon
- 2 tsp. brown sugar
- 1½ tsp. minced fresh rosemary or ½ tsp. dried rosemary, crushed
- ½ tsp. salt
- 1 cup water

1. In a large bowl, combine the first five ingredients. Add the pork; turn to coat. Cover; refrigerate 8 hours or overnight.
2. Preheat oven to 350°. Place pork roast on a rack in a shallow roasting pan, fat side up. Roast until a thermometer reads 145°, 55-65 minutes.
3. Meanwhile, in a large skillet, heat butter over medium heat. Add apples, cinnamon, brown sugar, rosemary and salt; cook until the apples are tender, 8-10 minutes, stirring occasionally.
4. Stir in water; bring to a boil. Reduce heat; simmer, uncovered, until apples are very soft, about 10 minutes. Remove from heat; mash the apples to desired consistency.
5. Remove roast from oven; tent with foil. Let stand 10 minutes before slicing. Serve with warm applesauce.

3 oz. cooked pork with ⅓ cup applesauce: 287 cal., 16g fat (6g sat. fat), 72mg chol., 1418mg sod., 15g carb. (11g sugars, 2g fiber), 22g pro.

GRILLED SOUTHWESTERN STEAK SALAD

Pasta salad loaded with steak, peppers and onions makes both my boyfriend and me happy. Plus, it's versatile! We serve it hot, room temperature or cold.
—*Yvonne Starlin, Westmoreland, TN*

- -

Prep: 25 min. • **Grill:** 20 min.
Makes: 4 servings

- 1 beef top sirloin steak (1 in. thick and ¾ lb.)
- ¼ tsp. salt
- ¼ tsp. ground cumin
- ¼ tsp. pepper
- 3 poblano peppers, halved and seeded
- 2 large ears sweet corn, husks removed
- 1 large sweet onion, cut into ½-in. rings
- 1 Tbsp. olive oil
- 2 cups uncooked multigrain bow tie pasta
- 2 large tomatoes

DRESSING
- ¼ cup lime juice
- 1 Tbsp. olive oil
- ¼ tsp. salt
- ¼ tsp. ground cumin
- ¼ tsp. pepper
- ⅓ cup chopped fresh cilantro

1. Rub steak with salt, cumin and pepper. Brush poblano peppers, corn and onion with oil. Grill steak, covered, over medium heat or broil 4 in. from heat 6-8 minutes on each side or until the meat reaches desired doneness (for medium-rare, a thermometer should read 135°; medium, 140°; medium-well, 145°). Grill the vegetables, covered, 8-10 minutes or until crisp-tender, turning occasionally.
2. Cook pasta according to package directions. Meanwhile, cut the corn from the cob; coarsely chop peppers, onion and tomatoes. Transfer vegetables to a large bowl. In a small bowl, whisk lime juice, oil, salt, cumin and pepper until blended; stir in cilantro.
3. Drain pasta; add to vegetable mixture. Drizzle with dressing; toss to coat. Cut steak into thin slices; add to salad.

2 cups pasta mixture with 2 oz. cooked beef: 456 cal., 13g fat (3g sat. fat), 34mg chol., 378mg sod., 58g carb. (15g sugars, 8g fiber), 30g pro.

Four Ways to Roast a Chicken

Simple yet elegant, hearty and delicious, roast chicken is one of our favorite foods. Here are four ways to go about it: as a whole bird, as a sheet-pan supper, in a slow cooker or on the grill. Choose your favorite—they're all comfort food perfection!

ROASTED CHICKEN & RED POTATOES

Pop this homey dinner in the oven for about an hour, then enjoy! It's got plenty of flavor—the meat juices help cook the veggies just perfectly.

—*Sherri Melotik, Oak Creek, WI*

Prep: 15 min. • **Bake:** 55 min.
Makes: 6 servings

- 2 lbs. red potatoes, cut into 1-in. pieces
- 1 pkg. (9 oz.) fresh spinach
- 1 large onion, cut into 1-in. pieces
- 2 Tbsp. olive oil
- 4 garlic cloves, minced
- 1 tsp. salt, divided
- 1 tsp. dried thyme
- ¾ tsp. pepper, divided
- 6 chicken leg quarters
- ¾ tsp. paprika

1. Preheat oven to 375°. Place potatoes, spinach and onion in a greased shallow roasting pan. Add the oil, minced garlic, ¾ tsp. salt, thyme and ½ tsp. pepper; toss to combine.
2. Arrange chicken over vegetables; sprinkle with paprika and remaining salt and pepper. Roast on an upper oven rack 55-60 minutes or until a thermometer inserted in chicken reads 180° and the potatoes are tender.
1 chicken leg quarter with 1 cup vegetable mixture: 449 cal., 21g fat (5g sat. fat), 105mg chol., 529mg sod., 29g carb. (3g sugars, 4g fiber), 35g pro.

CITRUS-MUSTARD ROASTED CHICKEN

Tender roast chicken is a snap to make and elegant to serve. We love the tang of orange and lemon slices and subtle heat from mustard.

—*Debra Keil, Owasso, OK*

Prep: 20 min. + chilling
Bake: 1¼ hours + standing • **Makes:** 4 servings

- 3 Tbsp. mustard seed
- ¼ cup olive oil
- 1 Tbsp. minced fresh chervil or 1 tsp. dried chervil
- 1 Tbsp. champagne vinegar
- 1 Tbsp. Worcestershire sauce
- ½ tsp. pepper
- 1 broiler/fryer chicken (3 to 4 lbs.)
- 2 orange slices
- 2 lemon slices
- 2 onion slices
- 3 sprigs fresh parsley, stems removed

1. In a spice grinder or with a mortar and pestle, grind mustard seed to a powder; transfer to a small bowl. Stir in oil, chervil, vinegar, Worcestershire sauce and pepper. Rub over outside and inside of chicken; place chicken on a large plate. Refrigerate, covered, overnight.
2. Preheat oven to 350°. Place chicken in a shallow roasting pan, breast side up. Loosely stuff with orange, lemon, onion and parsley. Tuck wings under chicken; tie drumsticks together.
3. Roast until a thermometer inserted in thickest part of a thigh reads 170°-175°, 1¼-1¾ hours. (Cover loosely with foil if chicken browns too quickly.) Remove chicken from oven; tent with foil. Let stand 15 minutes before carving.
1 serving: 537 cal., 37g fat (8g sat. fat), 131mg chol., 156mg sod., 6g carb. (2g sugars, 2g fiber), 44g pro.

SLOW-COOKER ROAST CHICKEN

It's easy to make roast chicken in a slow cooker. We save the shredded chicken to use throughout the week.
—Courtney Stultz, Weir, KS

Prep: 20 min. • **Cook:** 4 hours + standing
Makes: 6 servings

- 2 medium carrots, cut into 1-in. pieces
- 1 medium onion, cut into 1-in. pieces
- 2 garlic cloves, minced
- 2 tsp. olive oil
- 1 tsp. dried parsley flakes
- 1 tsp. pepper
- ¾ tsp. salt
- ½ tsp. dried oregano
- ½ tsp. rubbed sage
- ½ tsp. chili powder
- 1 broiler/fryer chicken (4 to 5 lbs.)

1. Place carrots and onion in a 6-qt. slow cooker. In a small bowl, mix garlic and oil. In another bowl, mix dry seasonings.

2. Tuck wings under chicken; tie the drumsticks together. With your fingers, carefully loosen the skin from the chicken breast; rub garlic mixture under the skin. Secure skin to the underside of breast with toothpicks.

3. Place chicken in slow cooker over carrots and onions, breast side up; sprinkle with the seasoning mixture. Cook chicken, covered, on low until a thermometer inserted in a thigh reads at least 170°, 4-5 hours.

4. Remove chicken from slow cooker; tent with foil. Discard vegetables. Let chicken stand 15 minutes before carving.

Freeze option: Cool chicken pieces and any juices. Freeze in freezer containers. To use, partially thaw in refrigerator overnight. Heat through slowly in a covered skillet until a thermometer inserted in the chicken reads 165°, stirring occasionally and adding a little broth or water if necessary.

5 oz. cooked chicken: 408 cal., 24g fat (6g sat. fat), 139mg chol., 422mg sod., 1g carb. (0 sugars, 0 fiber), 44g pro.

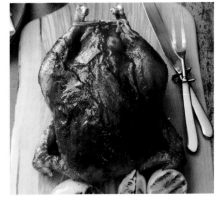

APPLE-BUTTER BARBECUED ROASTED CHICKEN

I love cooking so much I sometimes think of recipes in my sleep and wake up to write them down! This dream-inspired dish is my family's most-requested chicken recipe.
—Holly Kilbel, Akron, OH

Prep: 15 min. • **Grill:** 1½ hours + standing
Makes: 8 servings

- 1 tsp. salt
- ¾ tsp. garlic powder
- ¼ tsp. pepper
- ⅛ tsp. cayenne pepper
- 1 roasting chicken (6 to 7 lbs.)
- 1 can (11½ oz.) unsweetened apple juice
- ½ cup apple butter
- ¼ cup barbecue sauce

1. Combine salt, garlic powder, pepper and cayenne; sprinkle over chicken.

2. Prepare grill for indirect heat, using a drip pan. Pour half of the apple juice into another container; save for another use.

3. With a can opener, poke additional holes in the top of the apple-juice can. Holding the chicken with legs pointed down, lower chicken over the can so it fills the body cavity. Place chicken on grill rack over drip pan.

4. Grill, covered, over indirect medium heat 1½-2 hours or until a thermometer reads 180°. Combine the apple butter and barbecue sauce; baste the chicken occasionally during the last 30 minutes. Remove chicken from grill; cover and let stand for 10 minutes. Remove can from chicken before carving.

8 oz. cooked chicken: 441 cal., 24g fat (7g sat. fat), 134mg chol., 489mg sod., 11g carb. (10g sugars, 0 fiber), 43g pro.

CREAMY TUNA-NOODLE CASSEROLE

When you need supper fast, this casserole makes a super one-dish meal. Cooked chicken breast also works well in place of the tuna.
—*Edie DeSpain, Logan, UT*

Prep: 20 min. • **Bake:** 25 min.
Makes: 6 servings

- 5 cups uncooked egg noodles
- 1 cup frozen peas
- 1 can (10¾ oz.) reduced-fat reduced-sodium condensed cream of mushroom soup, undiluted
- 1 cup fat-free sour cream
- ⅔ cup grated Parmesan cheese
- ⅓ cup 2% milk
- ¼ tsp. salt
- 2 cans (5 oz. each) light tuna in water, drained and flaked
- ¼ cup finely chopped onion
- ¼ cup finely chopped green pepper

TOPPING
- ½ cup soft bread crumbs
- 1 Tbsp. butter, melted

1. Preheat oven to 350°. Cook noodles according to package directions for al dente, adding peas during the last minute of cooking; drain.
2. Meanwhile, in a large bowl, combine soup, sour cream, cheese, milk and salt; stir in tuna, onion and pepper. Add the noodles and peas; toss to combine.
3. Transfer to an 11x7-in. baking dish coated with cooking spray. In a small bowl, toss bread crumbs with melted butter; sprinkle over top. Bake casserole, uncovered, 25-30 minutes or until bubbly.

Note: To make soft bread crumbs, tear bread into pieces and place in a food processor or blender. Cover and pulse until crumbs form. One slice of bread yields ½-¾ cup of crumbs.

1⅓ cups: 340 cal., 8g fat (4g sat. fat), 63mg chol., 699mg sod., 41g carb. (7g sugars, 3g fiber), 25g pro. **Diabetic exchanges:** 3 starch, 2 lean meat, ½ fat.

ARTICHOKE & LEMON PASTA

While sailing in the Mediterranean, we tasted a scrumptious lemony pasta. I developed my own version of it that our guests love. Try it with shrimp and kalamata olives.
—*Peter Halferty, Corpus Christi, TX*

Prep: 20 min. • **Cook:** 20 min.
Makes: 6 servings

- 2½ tsp. salt, divided
- ½ lb. fresh asparagus, trimmed and cut into 1½-in. pieces
- 4 cups uncooked bow tie pasta (about 12 oz.)
- 3 Tbsp. olive oil, divided
- 1 can (14 oz.) water-packed quartered artichoke hearts, well drained
- 2 garlic cloves, minced
- 1 cup crumbled goat cheese
- 2 Tbsp. minced fresh parsley
- 1 Tbsp. grated lemon zest
- 2 to 3 Tbsp. lemon juice
- ⅓ cup grated Parmesan cheese

1. Fill a 6-qt. stockpot three-fourths full with water; add 2 tsp. salt and bring to a boil. Add asparagus; cook, uncovered, just until crisp-tender, 1-2 minutes. Remove asparagus and immediately drop into ice water. Drain and pat dry.
2. In the same pot of water, cook the pasta according to package directions for al dente. Drain, reserving 1 cup of the pasta water. Return pasta to pot.
3. Meanwhile, in a large skillet, heat 1 Tbsp. oil over medium-high heat. Add artichoke hearts; cook and stir until lightly browned, 3-4 minutes. Add garlic; cook 1 minute longer. Add to pasta.
4. Add asparagus, goat cheese, parsley, lemon zest, lemon juice and the remaining salt and oil; toss to combine, adding enough of the reserved pasta water to coat. Heat through. Sprinkle with Parmesan cheese.

1¼ cups: 343 cal., 14g fat (5g sat. fat), 27mg chol., 919mg sod., 43g carb. (2g sugars, 3g fiber), 14g pro.

FREEZE IT

MOROCCAN APPLE BEEF STEW

I love the mix of sweet and savory in this stew. It's the perfect blend of adventurous and comforting, and makes a fun dish to share with guests.
—*Trisha Kruse, Eagle, ID*

- -

Prep: 20 min. • **Cook:** 2 hours
Makes: 8 servings (2 qt.)

1¼ tsp. salt
½ tsp. ground cinnamon
½ tsp. pepper
¼ tsp. ground allspice
2½ lbs. beef stew meat,
    cut into 1-in. pieces
2 to 3 Tbsp. olive oil

1 large onion, chopped (about 2 cups)
3 garlic cloves, minced
1 can (15 oz.) tomato sauce
1 can (14½ oz.) beef broth
1 cup pitted dried plums,
    coarsely chopped
1 Tbsp. honey
2 medium Fuji or Gala apples, peeled
    and cut into 1½-in. pieces
    Hot cooked rice or couscous,
    optional

1. Mix salt, cinnamon, pepper and allspice; sprinkle over the beef and toss to coat. In a Dutch oven, heat 2 Tbsp. oil over medium heat. Brown the beef in batches, adding additional oil as necessary. Remove the beef with a slotted spoon.

2. Add onion to the same pan; cook and stir until tender, 6-8 minutes. Add garlic; cook 1 minute longer. Stir in tomato sauce, broth, dried plums and honey. Return beef to pan; bring to a boil. Reduce heat; simmer, covered, 1½ hours.

3. Add apples; cook, covered, until the beef and apples are tender, 30-45 minutes longer. Skim fat. If desired, serve stew with rice.

Freeze option: Freeze cooled stew in freezer containers. To use, partially thaw in refrigerator overnight. Heat through in a saucepan, stirring occasionally and adding a little broth if necessary.

1 cup: 339 cal., 13g fat (4g sat. fat), 88mg chol., 905mg sod., 24g carb. (14g sugars, 2g fiber), 29g pro.

Contest Winner

WHITE SEAFOOD LASAGNA

We make lasagna with shrimp and scallops as part of the traditional Italian Feast of the Seven Fishes each holiday season. Every bite delivers a tasty jewel from the sea.
—*Joe Colamonico, North Charleston, SC*

- -

Prep: 1 hour • **Bake:** 40 min. + standing
Makes: 12 servings

- 9   uncooked lasagna noodles
- 1   Tbsp. butter
- 1   lb. uncooked shrimp (31 to 40 per lb.), peeled and deveined
- 1   lb. bay scallops
- 5   garlic cloves, minced
- ¼   cup white wine
- 1   Tbsp. lemon juice
- 1   lb. fresh crabmeat

CHEESE SAUCE
- ¼   cup butter, cubed
- ¼   cup all-purpose flour
- 3   cups 2% milk
- 1   cup shredded part-skim mozzarella cheese
- ½   cup grated Parmesan cheese
- ½   tsp. salt
- ¼   tsp. pepper
-     Dash ground nutmeg

RICOTTA MIXTURE
- 1   carton (15 oz.) part-skim ricotta cheese
- 1   pkg. (10 oz.) frozen chopped spinach, thawed and squeezed dry
- 1   cup shredded part-skim mozzarella cheese
- ½   cup grated Parmesan cheese
- ½   cup seasoned bread crumbs
- 1   large egg, lightly beaten

TOPPING
- 1   cup shredded part-skim mozzarella cheese
- ¼   cup grated Parmesan cheese
-     Minced fresh parsley

1. Preheat oven to 350°. Cook noodles according to package directions; drain.
2. Meanwhile, in a large skillet, heat butter over medium heat. Add shrimp and scallops in batches; cook 2-4 minutes or until shrimp turn pink and scallops are firm and opaque. Remove from pan.
3. Add garlic to same pan; cook 1 minute. Add wine and lemon juice, stirring to loosen browned bits from pan. Bring to a boil; cook 1-2 minutes or until liquid is reduced by half. Add crab; heat through. Stir in shrimp and scallops.

4. For cheese sauce, melt butter over medium heat in a large saucepan. Stir in flour until smooth; gradually whisk in milk. Bring to a boil, stirring constantly; cook and stir 1-2 minutes or until thickened. Remove from heat; stir in remaining cheese sauce ingredients. In a large bowl, combine the ricotta mixture ingredients; stir in 1 cup cheese sauce.
5. Spread ½ cup of the cheese sauce into a greased 13x9-in. baking dish. Layer with three noodles, half of the ricotta mixture, half of the seafood mixture and ⅔ cup of the cheese sauce. Repeat layers. Top with the remaining noodles and cheese sauce. Sprinkle with the remaining mozzarella cheese and Parmesan cheese.
6. Bake, uncovered, for 40-50 minutes or until bubbly and top is golden brown. Let stand 10 minutes before serving. Sprinkle with parsley.
1 piece: 448 cal., 19g fat (11g sat. fat), 158mg chol., 957mg sod., 29g carb. (5g sugars, 2g fiber), 39g pro.

CHICKEN ORZO SKILLET

Here's a great one-skillet supper that's colorful, healthy, satisfying and definitely special! The blend of spices, the touch of heat and the sophisticated flavor make this dish a must-try.
—*Kellie Mulleavy, Lambertville, MI*

Prep: 15 min. • **Cook:** 20 min.
Makes: 4 servings

- 1 lb. boneless skinless chicken breasts, cut into ½-in. strips
- 2 tsp. salt-free garlic seasoning blend
- 1 small onion, chopped
- 1 Tbsp. olive oil
- 1 garlic clove, minced
- 1 can (14½ oz.) diced tomatoes, undrained
- 1 pkg. (10 oz.) frozen chopped spinach, thawed and squeezed dry
- 1 cup reduced-sodium chicken broth
- ¾ cup uncooked orzo pasta
- 1 tsp. Italian seasoning
- ⅛ tsp. crushed red pepper flakes, optional
- ¼ cup grated Parmesan cheese, optional

1. Sprinkle chicken with garlic seasoning blend. In a large cast-iron or other heavy skillet, saute chicken and onion in oil until chicken is no longer pink, 5-6 minutes. Add garlic; cook 1 minute longer.
2. Stir in the tomatoes, spinach, broth, orzo, Italian seasoning and, if desired, pepper flakes. Bring to a boil; reduce heat. Cover and simmer until the orzo is tender and liquid is absorbed, 15-20 minutes. If desired, sprinkle with cheese.
1¼ cups: 339 cal., 7g fat (1g sat. fat), 63mg chol., 384mg sod., 38g carb. (6g sugars, 5g fiber), 32g pro. **Diabetic exchanges:** 3 lean meat, 2 starch, 2 vegetable, ½ fat.

Contest Winner

JIM'S SECRET FAMILY RECIPE RIBS

For more than 30 years, my brother-in-law Jim kept his famous rib recipe a secret, much to the chagrin of my husband, Dennis. When he finally came around to sharing it, we loved it so much we just had to pass it along. This one's for you, Jim!
—*Vicki Young, Brighton, CO*

Prep: 20 min. + chilling • **Cook:** 3 hours 10 min.
Makes: 8 servings

- 2 racks pork baby back ribs (about 5 lbs.)
- ¼ cup soy sauce
- ¼ cup dried oregano
- 2 Tbsp. onion powder
- 2 tsp. garlic powder
- 1 liter lemon-lime soda
- ½ cup unsweetened pineapple or orange juice, optional

BARBECUE SAUCE
- ½ cup sugar or packed brown sugar
- ½ cup hot water
- 1 cup ketchup
- ¼ cup honey mustard
- ¼ cup barbecue sauce of choice
- 3 Tbsp. lemon juice
- 1½ tsp. white vinegar

1. Brush ribs with soy sauce. Combine oregano, onion powder and garlic powder; rub over both sides of the ribs. Transfer to a large shallow roasting pan; refrigerate, covered, overnight.
2. Preheat oven to 225°. Add lemon-lime soda and, if desired, juice to the roasting pan (do not pour over ribs). Bake, covered, until tender, about 3 hours.
3. Meanwhile, make barbecue sauce by dissolving sugar in hot water; combine with the remaining ingredients, thinning with additional lemon-lime soda or juice if necessary. Reserve 1 cup for serving.
4. Remove ribs from oven; discard juices. Brush both sides with barbecue sauce. Grill, covered, on a greased grill rack over low direct heat, turning and brushing occasionally with the remaining sauce, until heated through, about 10 minutes. Cut into serving-size pieces; serve with the reserved sauce.
1 serving: 483 cal., 27g fat (10g sat. fat), 102mg chol., 1107mg sod., 31g carb. (26g sugars, 1g fiber), 30g pro.

CHICKEN PICCATA

Once you've tried this tangy yet delicate entree, you won't hesitate to make it for company. Seasoned with Parmesan and parsley, the chicken cooks up golden brown, then is drizzled with a light lemon sauce.
—Susan Pursell, Fountain Valley, CA

- -

Prep: 25 min. • **Cook:** 25 min.
Makes: 8 servings

- 8 boneless skinless chicken breast halves (4 oz. each)
- ½ cup egg substitute
- 2 Tbsp. plus ¼ cup dry white wine or chicken broth, divided
- 5 Tbsp. lemon juice, divided
- 3 garlic cloves, minced
- ⅛ tsp. hot pepper sauce
- ½ cup all-purpose flour
- ½ cup grated Parmesan cheese
- ¼ cup minced fresh parsley
- ½ tsp. salt
- 3 tsp. olive oil, divided
- 2 Tbsp. butter

1. Flatten chicken to ¼-in. thickness. In a shallow dish, combine the egg substitute, 2 Tbsp. wine, 2 Tbsp. lemon juice, the garlic and hot pepper sauce. In another shallow dish, combine the flour, Parmesan cheese, parsley and salt. Coat chicken with the flour mixture, dip in the egg substitute mixture, then coat again with the flour mixture.

2. In a large nonstick skillet, brown four of the chicken breast halves in 1½ tsp. oil for 3-5 minutes on each side or until juices run clear. Remove and keep warm. Drain drippings. Repeat with the remaining chicken and oil. Remove and keep warm.

3. In the same pan, melt butter. Add the remaining wine and lemon juice. Bring to a boil. Boil, uncovered, until the sauce is reduced by a fourth. Drizzle sauce over the chicken.

1 chicken breast half: 232 cal., 9g fat (4g sat. fat), 75mg chol., 346mg sod., 8g carb. (1g sugars, 0 fiber), 27g pro. **Diabetic exchanges:** 3 lean meat, 1 fat, ½ starch.

FREEZE IT
SPINACH-BASIL LASAGNA

In the kitchen, my husband and I like to use classic ingredients in new ways. I came up with this lasagna one day and haven't made another type since. We love it!
—Charlotte Gehle, Brownstown, MI

- -

Prep: 20 min. • **Bake:** 45 min.
Makes: 9 servings

- 1 large egg, lightly beaten
- 2 cups reduced-fat ricotta cheese
- 4 oz. crumbled feta cheese
- ¼ cup grated Parmesan cheese
- ¼ cup chopped fresh basil
- 2 garlic cloves, minced
- ¼ tsp. pepper
- 1 jar (24 oz.) pasta sauce
- 9 no-cook lasagna noodles
- 3 cups fresh baby spinach
- 2 cups shredded part-skim mozzarella cheese

1. Preheat oven to 350°. Mix first seven ingredients.

2. Spread ½ cup of the pasta sauce into a greased 13x9-in. baking dish. Layer with three lasagna noodles, ¾ cup ricotta mixture, 1 cup spinach, ½ cup mozzarella cheese and ⅔ cup sauce. Repeat layers twice. Sprinkle with the remaining mozzarella cheese.

3. Bake, covered, 35 minutes. Uncover; bake until heated through and the cheese is melted, 10-15 minutes. Let stand for 5 minutes before serving.

Freeze option: Cover and freeze unbaked lasagna. To use, partially thaw in refrigerator overnight. Remove from the refrigerator 30 minutes before baking. Preheat oven to 350°. Bake lasagna as directed, increasing time as necessary to heat through and for a thermometer inserted in center to read 165°.

1 piece: 292 cal., 12g fat (6g sat. fat), 59mg chol., 677mg sod., 27g carb. (10g sugars, 3g fiber), 18g pro. **Diabetic exchanges:** 2 starch, 2 medium-fat meat.

PRIME RIB WITH FRESH HERB SAUCE

Nothing says special occasion like a perfectly seasoned prime rib. Savory, succulent, tender, it's the perfect choice when you want to share something truly divine.
—*Tonya Burkhard, Palm Coast, FL*

- -

Prep: 40 min. • **Bake:** 3¼ hours + standing
Makes: 10 servings (1½ cups sauce)

- 1 bone-in beef rib roast (6 to 8 lbs.)
- 1 tsp. kosher salt
- 1 tsp. freshly ground pepper
- 3 cups water
- 2 small onions, halved
- 7 garlic cloves, crushed
- 5 fresh sage sprigs
- 5 fresh thyme sprigs
- 2 bay leaves

SAUCE
- 2 Tbsp. butter
- 2 shallots, thinly sliced
- 4 garlic cloves, thinly sliced
- 5 fresh sage sprigs
- 5 fresh thyme sprigs
- 2 bay leaves
- 1 Tbsp. all-purpose flour
- 2 Tbsp. cracked black pepper
- ¼ tsp. kosher salt
- 1½ to 2½ cups beef stock, divided
- ½ cup dry red wine or beef stock
- ½ tsp. red wine vinegar
  Fresh thyme sprigs, optional

1. Preheat oven to 450°. Place roast in a shallow roasting pan, fat side up; rub with salt and pepper. Add 1 cup water, onions, garlic and herbs to roasting pan. Roast 15 minutes.

2. Reduce oven setting to 325°. Roast 3-3½ hours longer or until the meat reaches desired doneness (for medium-rare, a thermometer should read 135°; medium, 140°; medium-well, 145°), adding 1 cup water every hour.

3. For the sauce, in a large saucepan, heat butter over medium-high heat. Add shallots; cook and stir 5-6 minutes or until tender. Add garlic and herbs; cook 1 minute longer. Stir in the flour, pepper and salt until blended. Gradually stir in 1½ cups stock. Remove from heat.

4. Remove the roast to a serving platter; tent with foil. Let stand 15 minutes before carving. Meanwhile, strain any pan juices through a sieve into a measuring cup;

discard onions and herbs. Skim fat from pan juices. If necessary, add additional stock to pan juices to measure 1 cup. Add to the shallot mixture.

5. Place the roasting pan over two burners; add wine. Bring to a boil; cook 2-3 minutes, stirring to loosen browned bits from pan. Add to the sauce. Bring to a boil, stirring occasionally; cook until mixture is reduced to about 1½ cups, 10-15 minutes.

6. Stir in vinegar; strain, discarding the shallots and herbs. Serve with roast. If desired, garnish with thyme.

5 oz. cooked beef with 2 Tbsp. sauce: 353 cal., 20g fat (9g sat. fat), 6mg chol., 430mg sod., 2g carb. (1g sugars, 0g fiber), 37g pro.

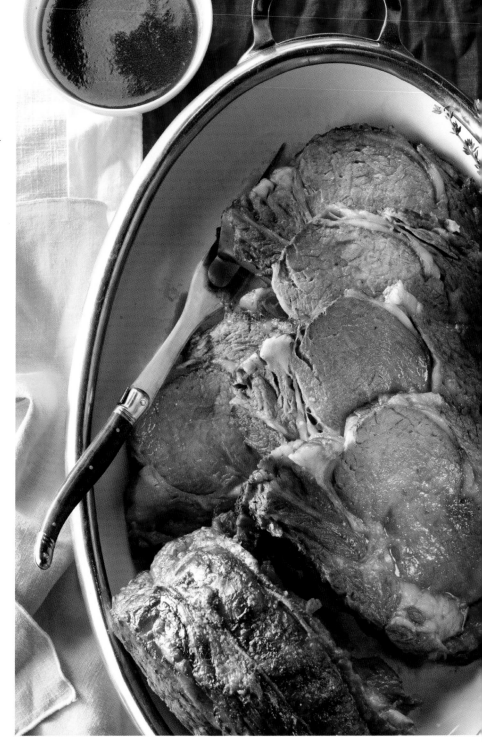

COD WITH HEARTY TOMATO SAUCE

My father made up this sweet, flavorful recipe for my mother when he took over the cooking. We serve it with whole wheat pasta or brown rice.
—*Ann Marie Eberhart, Gig Harbor, WA*

- -

Takes: 30 min. • **Makes:** 4 servings

2 cans (14½ oz. each) diced tomatoes with basil, oregano and garlic, undrained
4 cod fillets (6 oz. each)
2 Tbsp. olive oil, divided
2 medium onions, halved and thinly sliced (about 1½ cups)
½ tsp. dried oregano
¼ tsp. pepper
¼ tsp. crushed red pepper flakes
 Hot cooked whole wheat pasta
 Minced fresh parsley, optional

1. Place tomatoes in a blender. Cover and process until pureed.
2. Pat fish dry with paper towels. In a large skillet, heat 1 Tbsp. oil over medium-high heat. Add cod; cook until surface of fish begins to color, 2-4 minutes on each side. Remove from pan.
3. In the same skillet, heat remaining oil over medium-high heat. Add onions; cook and stir until tender, 2-4 minutes. Stir in seasonings and pureed tomatoes; bring to a boil. Add cod fillets; return just to a boil, spooning sauce over top. Reduce heat; simmer, uncovered, until fish just begins to flake easily with a fork, 5-7 minutes. Serve with pasta. If desired, sprinkle with fresh parsley.

1 fillet with ¾ cup sauce: 271 cal., 8g fat (1g sat. fat), 65mg chol., 746mg sod., 17g carb. (9g sugars, 4g fiber), 29g pro. **Diabetic exchanges:** 3 lean meat, 2 vegetable, 1½ fat.

STOUT & SHIITAKE POT ROAST

A bit of stout beer, mushrooms and onions add excellent flavor to my pot roast. I find that this one-dish wonder often tastes even better the next day.
—*Madeleine Bessette, Coeur d Alene, ID*

- -

Prep: 30 min. • **Cook:** 1¾ hours
Makes: 6 servings

3 Tbsp. olive oil, divided
1 boneless beef chuck roast (2 to 3 lbs.)
2 medium onions, sliced
1 garlic clove, minced
1 bottle (12 oz.) stout or nonalcoholic beer
½ oz. dried shiitake mushrooms (about ½ cup)
1 Tbsp. brown sugar
1 tsp. Worcestershire sauce
½ tsp. dried savory
1 lb. red potatoes (about 8 small), cut into 1-in. pieces
2 medium carrots, sliced
½ cup water
½ tsp. salt
¼ tsp. pepper

1. In a Dutch oven, heat 1 Tbsp. oil over medium heat. Brown roast on all sides; remove from pan.
2. In the same pan, heat the remaining oil. Add the onions and garlic; cook and stir until tender. Add the beer, stirring to loosen any browned bits from pan. Stir in the mushrooms, brown sugar, Worcestershire sauce and savory. Return the roast to pan. Bring to a boil. Reduce heat; simmer, covered, 1½ hours.
3. Stir in the remaining ingredients. Return to a boil. Reduce heat; simmer, covered, 15-25 minutes longer or until the meat and vegetables are tender. If desired, skim fat and thicken cooking juices for gravy.

4 oz. cooked beef with 1 cup vegetables: 441 cal., 21g fat (7g sat. fat), 98mg chol., 293mg sod., 24g carb. (9g sugars, 3g fiber), 33g pro.

SPANISH MARSALA TURKEY BREAST

Every home cook has a go-to party dish; this one is mine. The only prep is popping everything in to marinate before roasting. It's a lifesaver during the holidays!
—*Johnna Johnson, Scottsdale, AZ*

Prep: 15 min. + marinating • **Bake:** 35 min.
Makes: 8 servings

- 2 skin-on boneless turkey breast halves (about 2 lbs. each)
- 1 cup pitted dates, quartered
- ½ cup pitted green olives, halved
- ½ cup red wine vinegar
- ½ cup olive oil
- 1 jar (3½ oz.) capers, drained
- 1 whole garlic bulb, cloves separated, peeled and minced (about ¼ cup)
- ¼ cup dried oregano
- 6 bay leaves
- ½ tsp. salt
- 1 cup packed brown sugar
- 1 cup Marsala wine

1. Cut each turkey breast half crosswise in half; place in a bowl or shallow dish. Add dates, olives, vinegar, oil, capers, garlic, oregano, bay leaves and salt. Turn turkey to coat; cover and refrigerate 3-4 hours.
2. Preheat oven to 350°. Place turkey in a single layer in a large shallow roasting pan; top with the marinade mixture. Sprinkle brown sugar over the turkey. Pour wine around turkey. Bake, uncovered, until a thermometer inserted in turkey reads 165°, basting occasionally with pan juices, 35-45 minutes.
3. Remove turkey from oven; let stand 5 minutes before slicing. Discard bay leaves. Serve turkey with date-olive mixture and pan juices.

Note: If skin-on boneless turkey breast halves are not available, you may ask your butcher to debone a 5-pound bone-in turkey breast, leaving the skin attached.

8 oz. cooked turkey with 2 Tbsp. olive mixture and ¼ cup pan juices: 661 cal., 29g fat (6g sat. fat), 132mg chol., 793mg sod., 47g carb. (39g sugars, 3g fiber), 52g pro.

CREAMY SPINACH & RIGATONI BAKE

Italian ingredients give mac and cheese—the ultimate comfort food—a whole new twist.
—*Tammy Rex, New Tripoli, PA*

Prep: 25 min. • **Bake:** 20 min.
Makes: 10 servings

- 1 pkg. (16 oz.) rigatoni
- 8 oz. sliced pancetta, chopped
- ¾ cup butter, cubed
- ½ cup chopped onion
- ¾ cup all-purpose flour
- 1½ tsp. salt
- ¾ tsp. pepper
- 5¼ cups 2% milk
- 4 cups shredded Italian cheese blend
- 1 can (14 oz.) water-packed artichoke hearts, rinsed, drained and chopped
- 1 pkg. (10 oz.) frozen chopped spinach, thawed and squeezed dry
- ¼ cup shredded Parmesan cheese

1. Preheat oven to 375°. Cook rigatoni according to package directions.
2. In a large skillet, cook pancetta over medium heat until crisp. Remove with a slotted spoon; drain on paper towels. Discard drippings; wipe skillet clean.
3. In same pan, heat butter over medium-high heat. Add onion; cook and stir until tender. Stir in flour, salt and pepper; gradually whisk in milk. Bring to a boil, stirring constantly; cook and stir until thickened, 2-3 minutes. Remove from heat. Stir in cheese blend until melted.
4. Stir in artichokes, spinach and pancetta. Drain rigatoni; add to cheese sauce. Transfer to a greased 13x9-in. baking dish; sprinkle with Parmesan cheese. Bake, uncovered, until golden brown and bubbly, 20-25 minutes.

¼ cup: 643 cal., 35g fat (20g sat. fat), 99mg chol., 1438mg sod., 53g carb. (8g sugars, 3g fiber), 28g pro.

Contest Winner

SPICY BEAN & BEEF PIE

My daughter helped me come up with this recipe when we wanted a one-dish meal that was different than our regular casseroles. This pie slices nicely and is a fun and filing dish.

—*Debra Dohy, Newcomerstown, OH*

- -

Prep: 20 min. • **Bake:** 30 min.
Makes: 8 servings

1   lb. ground beef
2   to 3 garlic cloves, minced
1   can (11½ oz.) condensed bean with bacon soup, undiluted
1   jar (16 oz.) thick and chunky picante sauce, divided
¼   cup cornstarch
1   Tbsp. chopped fresh parsley
1   tsp. paprika
1   tsp. salt
¼   tsp. pepper

1   can (16 oz.) kidney beans, rinsed and drained
1   can (15 oz.) black beans, rinsed and drained
2   cups shredded cheddar cheese, divided
¾   cup sliced green onions, divided
    Pastry for double-crust pie (10 in.)
1   cup sour cream
1   can (2¼ oz.) sliced ripe olives, drained

Contest Winner

1. Preheat oven to 425°. In a large skillet, cook the beef over medium heat until meat is no longer pink. Add garlic; cook 1 minute longer. Drain.

2. In a large bowl, combine the soup, 1 cup of picante sauce, the cornstarch, parsley, paprika, salt and pepper. Fold in the beans, 1½ cups of cheese, ½ cup onions and the beef mixture.

3. Line a 9-in. deep-dish pie plate with bottom pastry; fill with the bean mixture. Top with the remaining pastry; seal and flute the edges. Cut slits in the top crust.

4. Bake for 30-35 minutes or until lightly browned. Let stand for 5 minutes before cutting. Garnish with the sour cream, olives and remaining picante sauce, cheese and onions.

Freeze option: Cover and freeze unbaked pie for up to 3 months. To use, remove from the freezer 30 minutes before baking. Cover edges of crust loosely with foil; place on a baking sheet. Bake at 425° for 30 minutes. Reduce heat to 350°; remove foil. Bake 55-60 minutes longer or until golden brown. Garnish pie as recipe directs, with sour cream, olives, picante sauce, cheese and onions.

1 piece: 682 cal., 34g fat (18g sat. fat), 88mg chol., 1509mg sod., 61g carb. (8g sugars, 8g fiber), 28g pro.

PENNE & SMOKED SAUSAGE

My sausage-pasta dish is a must-try. It just tastes so good when it's hot and bubbly from the oven. The cheddar french-fried onions lend a cheesy, crunchy touch.
—*Margaret Wilson, San Bernardino, CA*

- -

Prep: 15 min. • **Bake:** 30 min.
Makes: 6 servings

- **2** cups uncooked penne pasta
- **1** lb. smoked sausage, cut into ¼-in. slices
- **1½** cups 2% milk
- **1** can (10¾ oz.) condensed cream of celery soup, undiluted
- **1½** cups cheddar french-fried onions, divided
- **1** cup shredded part-skim mozzarella cheese, divided
- **1** cup frozen peas

1. Preheat oven to 375°. Cook pasta according to the package directions.
2. Meanwhile, in a large skillet, brown sausage over medium heat 5 minutes; drain. In a large bowl, combine milk and soup. Stir in ½ cup onions, ½ cup cheese, peas and sausage. Drain pasta; stir into the sausage mixture.
3. Transfer to a greased 13x9-in. baking dish. Cover dish and bake until bubbly, 25-30 minutes. Sprinkle with remaining onions and cheese. Bake, uncovered, until cheese is melted, 3-5 minutes longer.
Freeze option: Sprinkle remaining onions and cheese over unbaked casserole. Cover; freeze. To use, partially thaw in refrigerator overnight. Remove from refrigerator 30 minutes before baking. Preheat oven to 375°. Bake as directed, increasing time as necessary to heat through and for a thermometer inserted in center to read 165°.
1½ cups: 553 cal., 35g fat (14g sat. fat), 70mg chol., 1425mg sod., 36g carb. (7g sugars, 3g fiber), 22g pro.

SKIP THE OIL
Many home cooks add oil to the cooking water to keep pasta from clumping together—but that can make sauce slide right off the pasta. Skip the oil, drain pasta right before adding it to the sauce mixture, and your pasta won't clump.

GRILLED JERK SHRIMP ORZO SALAD

It doesn't matter what the temperature is outside—you'll feel as if you're in the Caribbean when you take your first bite of this salad.
—*Eileen Budnyk, Palm Beach Gardens, FL*

- -

Prep: 25 min. • **Grill:** 10 min.
Makes: 2 servings

- **⅓** cup uncooked whole wheat orzo pasta
- **½** lb. uncooked shrimp (31-40 per lb.), peeled and deveined
- **1** Tbsp. Caribbean jerk seasoning
- **1** medium ear sweet corn
- **1** tsp. olive oil
- **6** fresh asparagus spears, trimmed
- **1** small sweet red pepper, chopped

DRESSING
- **3** Tbsp. lime juice
- **1** Tbsp. water
- **1** Tbsp. olive oil
- **⅛** tsp. salt
- **⅛** tsp. pepper

1. Cook orzo according to the package directions. Drain and rinse with cold water; drain well. Meanwhile, toss the shrimp with jerk seasoning; thread onto metal or soaked wooden skewers. Brush corn with oil.
2. On a covered grill over medium heat, cook corn until tender and lightly browned, 10-12 minutes; cook asparagus until crisp-tender, 5-7 minutes, turning both the corn and asparagus occasionally. Grill shrimp until it turns pink, 1-2 minutes per side.
3. Cut corn from the cob; cut asparagus into 1-in. pieces. Remove shrimp from skewers. In a large bowl, combine orzo, grilled vegetables, shrimp and red pepper. Whisk together the dressing ingredients; toss with salad.
2 cups: 340 cal., 12g fat (2g sat. fat), 138mg chol., 716mg sod., 35g carb. (6g sugars, 7g fiber), 25g pro. **Diabetic exchanges:** 2 starch, 3 lean meat, 1 vegetable, 1 fat.

Meals in Minutes

When time is tight, turn to these quick and easy recipes to get a satisying, delicious meal on the table fast. Each of the 29 dishes clocks in at 30 minutes or less, beginning to end. Skillet and one-dish meals, pizzas, soups, stir fry and pasta— they're all here!

HAY & STRAW

This dish is not only easy to prepare, but it's colorful, too. Start cooking the ham about five minutes before the linguine is due to be done, and all the ingredients will be ready at the same time.

—Priscilla Weaver, Hagerstown, MD

Takes: 20 min. • **Makes:** 8 servings

- 1 pkg. (16 oz.) linguine
- 2 cups julienned fully cooked ham
- 1 Tbsp. butter
- 3 cups frozen peas
- 1½ cups shredded Parmesan cheese
- ⅓ cup heavy whipping cream

Cook linguine according to package directions. Meanwhile, in a large skillet, saute ham in butter for 3 minutes. Add peas; heat through. Drain linguine; toss with the ham mixture, Parmesan cheese and cream. Serve immediately.

1 serving: 410 cal., 14g fat (7g sat. fat), 47mg chol., 783mg sod., 50g carb. (6g sugars, 4g fiber), 23g pro.

Contest Winner

LOADED FLANK STEAK

I wanted to do something a little different with flank steak, so I stuffed it with bacon, green onions and ranch dressing. The recipe is fast, but it's a little bit fancy, too.

—Tammy Thomas, Mustang, OK

Takes: 25 min. • **Makes:** 6 servings

- ½ cup butter, softened
- 6 bacon strips, cooked and crumbled
- 3 green onions, chopped
- 2 Tbsp. ranch salad dressing mix
- ½ tsp. pepper
- 1 beef flank steak (1½ to 2 lbs.)

1. In a small bowl, beat the first five ingredients. Cut a pocket horizontally in steak; fill the pocket with the butter mixture.

2. Grill steak, covered, over medium heat or broil 4 in. from heat for 5-7 minutes on each side or until meat reaches the desired doneness (for medium-rare, a thermometer should read 135°; medium, 140°; medium-well, 145°). Let steak stand for 5 minutes before serving. To serve, slice across the grain.

4 oz. cooked beef: 267 cal., 20g fat (10g sat. fat), 76mg chol., 714mg sod., 4g carb. (0 sugars, 0 fiber), 18g pro.

SAUSAGE PIZZA PASTA

It's pizza in a bowl! Here's a terrific (and tasty) way to make sure your kids get the whole grains and vegetables they need to grow up big and strong.
—*Danna Holt, Shoals, IN*

- -

Takes: 30 min. • **Makes:** 6 servings

- 1 lb. Italian turkey sausage links, casings removed
- 2 cups sliced fresh mushrooms
- 1 medium green pepper, chopped
- 1 medium onion, chopped
- 3 cups uncooked whole grain spiral pasta
- 1 can (15 oz.) pizza sauce
- 1½ cups water
- 1½ tsp. Italian seasoning
- ¼ tsp. salt
- ¾ cup shredded part-skim mozzarella cheese

1. In a Dutch oven, cook the sausage, mushrooms, green pepper and onion over medium heat for 5-6 minutes or until the sausage is no longer pink and the vegetables are tender, breaking up the sausage into crumbles; drain.

2. Stir in pasta, pizza sauce, water, Italian seasoning and salt; bring to a boil. Reduce heat; simmer, covered, 10-15 minutes or until pasta is tender. Remove from heat; sprinkle with cheese. Let stand, covered, 5 minutes or until the cheese is melted.

1¼ cups: 358 cal., 8g fat (3g sat. fat), 36mg chol., 577mg sod., 52g carb. (7g sugars, 4g fiber), 21g pro.

SOUPY CHICKEN NOODLE SUPPER

At least once a week my 6-year-old son (also known as Doctor John!) hands me a prescription for this chicken noodle soup. I'm always happy to fill it.
—*Heidi Hall, North Saint Paul, MN*

- -

Takes: 30 min. • **Makes:** 4 servings

- 1 Tbsp. butter
- 1 medium carrot, sliced
- 1 celery rib, sliced
- 1 small onion, chopped
- 4 cups water
- 4 tsp. chicken bouillon granules
- 1½ tsp. dried parsley flakes
- ¼ tsp. Italian seasoning
- ⅛ tsp. celery seed
- ⅛ tsp. pepper
- 3 cups uncooked wide egg noodles
- 1½ cups cubed rotisserie chicken
- 1 can (10¾ oz.) condensed cream of chicken soup, undiluted
- ½ cup sour cream
  Hot cooked stuffing, optional

1. In a large saucepan, heat butter over medium-high heat. Add carrot, celery and onion; cook and stir for 6-8 minutes or until tender.

2. Stir in water, bouillon and seasonings; bring to a boil. Add noodles; cook, uncovered, 5-7 minutes or until tender. Stir in chicken, soup and sour cream; heat through. If desired, serve with stuffing.

1⅔ cups: 392 cal., 19g fat (8g sat. fat), 92mg chol., 1497mg sod., 32g carb. (4g sugars, 3g fiber), 22g pro.

REUBEN PIZZA

Fridays are pizza nights at our house. We do a lot of experimenting so we don't have the same old thing every week. With only five ingredients, this pizza is a snap to whip up, and it tastes just like a Reuben sandwich.
—*Nicole German, Hutchinson, MN*

- -

Takes: 25 min. • **Makes:** 6 servings

- 1 prebaked 12-in. pizza crust
- ⅔ cup Thousand Island salad dressing
- ½ lb. sliced deli corned beef, cut into strips
- 1 can (14 oz.) sauerkraut, rinsed and well drained
- 2 cups shredded Swiss cheese

Preheat oven to 400°. Place the pizza crust on an ungreased or parchment-lined baking sheet. Spread with salad dressing. Top with corned beef, sauerkraut and cheese. Bake until the cheese is melted, 12-15 minutes.

1 slice: 480 cal., 27g fat (10g sat. fat), 57mg chol., 1527mg sod., 36g carb. (6g sugars, 3g fiber), 23g pro.

SKILLET BEEF & MACARONI

I found this recipe about 30 years ago on a can label. My family loved it, and I always received compliments when I took the dish to potluck suppers. Since it's so easy to put together, it'a a real timesaver for anyone who's juggling a busy schedule.
—*Maxine Neuhauser, Arcadia, CA*

- -

Takes: 30 min. • **Makes:** 6 servings

- 1½ lb. ground beef
- ½ cup chopped onion
- 2 cans (8 oz. each) tomato sauce
- 1 cup water
- 1 pkg. (7 oz.) macaroni
- ½ cup chopped green pepper
- 2 Tbsp. Worcestershire sauce
- 1 tsp. salt
- ¼ tsp. pepper

In a large skillet over medium-high heat, cook beef and onion until the meat is no longer pink; drain. Stir in the remaining ingredients; bring to a boil. Reduce heat; simmer, covered, until macaroni is tender, stirring occasionally, 20-25 minutes. Add more water if needed.

1 cup: 317 cal., 11g fat (5g sat. fat), 56mg chol., 700mg sod., 29g carb. (3g sugars, 2g fiber), 25g pro.

APPLE BARBECUE CHICKEN

My husband and I had just moved to Dallas when I first made this recipe. Everything was different—new home, big city—but this dish felt familiar and comforting.
—*Darla Andrews, Schertz, TX*

- -

Takes: 30 min. • **Makes:** 6 servings

 12 **chicken drumsticks**
 ¼ **tsp. pepper**
  1 **Tbsp. olive oil**
  1 **bottle (18 oz.) sweet and spicy barbecue sauce**
  2 **cups applesauce**
 ⅓ **cup packed brown sugar**
  1 **Tbsp. chili powder**

1. Sprinkle drumsticks with pepper. In a Dutch oven, heat oil over medium heat. Brown the drumsticks in batches; drain. Remove from pan.

2. Add the remaining ingredients to pan, stirring to combine. Return chicken to pan; bring to a boil. Reduce heat; simmer, covered, 20-25 minutes or until the chicken is tender.

2 chicken drumsticks with ½ cup sauce: 501 cal., 15g fat (4g sat. fat), 95mg chol., 949mg sod., 58g carb. (50g sugars, 1g fiber), 29g pro.

SALMON WITH SPINACH & WHITE BEANS

My husband is a Southerner at heart. This salmon with garlicky beans and spinach won him over at first bite.
—*Mary Ellen Hofstetter, Brentwood, TN*

- -

Takes: 15 min. • **Makes:** 4 servings

  4 **salmon fillets (4 oz. each)**
  2 **tsp. plus 1 Tbsp. olive oil, divided**
  1 **tsp. seafood seasoning**
  1 **garlic clove, minced**
  1 **can (15 oz.) cannellini beans, rinsed and drained**
 ¼ **tsp. salt**
 ¼ **tsp. pepper**
  1 **pkg. (8 oz.) fresh spinach**
     Lemon wedges

1. Preheat broiler. Rub fillets with 2 tsp. oil; sprinkle with seafood seasoning. Place on the greased rack of a broiler pan. Broil 5-6 in. from heat 6-8 minutes or until the fish just begins to flake easily with a fork.

2. Meanwhile, in a large skillet, heat the remaining oil over medium heat. Add the garlic; cook 15-30 seconds or until fragrant. Add beans, salt and pepper, stirring to coat the beans with garlic oil. Stir in spinach until wilted. Serve the salmon with the spinach mixture and lemon wedges.

1 fillet with ½ cup spinach mixture : 317 cal., 17g fat (3g sat. fat), 57mg chol., 577mg sod., 16g carb. (0 sugars, 5g fiber), 24g pro.
Diabetic exchanges: 3 lean meat, 2 vegetable, 1 fat, ½ starch.

SAUSAGE & VEGETABLE SKILLET DINNER

I dashed this together one night while trying to use up produce before going out of town. Who knew it was going to be such a hit? Now it's a go-to when I don't have much time to cook or wash dishes.

—Elizabeth Kelley, Chicago, IL

Takes: 30 min. • **Makes:** 4 servings

1   Tbsp. olive oil
1   pkg. (12 oz.) fully cooked
     Italian chicken sausage links,
     cut into 1-in. pieces

1   large onion, chopped
3   garlic cloves, minced
¼   tsp. crushed red pepper flakes
1½   lbs. red potatoes (about
     5 medium), thinly sliced
1   pkg. (10 oz.) frozen corn
¼   tsp. pepper
1¼   cups vegetable broth
2   cups fresh baby spinach

1. In a 12-in. skillet, heat oil over medium-high heat; saute sausage and onion until the onion is tender. Add garlic and pepper flakes; cook and stir 1 minute.
2. Add potatoes, corn, pepper and broth; bring to a boil. Reduce heat to medium; cook, covered, until potatoes are tender, 15-20 minutes. Stir in spinach until wilted.

1½ cups: 371 cal., 11g fat (3g sat. fat), 65mg chol., 715mg sod., 48g carb. (6g sugars, 5g fiber), 22g pro. **Diabetic exchanges:** 3 starch, 3 lean meat, 1 fat.

Health Tip: Italian chicken sausage has less than half the fat of regular. It's lean, but adds a lot of flavor.

BARBECUED ONION MEAT LOAVES

Onion soup mix and stuffing are the surprise ingredients in these incredibly simple mini meat loaves. They're definite family-pleasers.
—*Nicole Russman, Lincoln, NE*

Takes: 25 min. • **Makes:** 5 servings

- 1 large egg, lightly beaten
- ⅓ cup whole milk
- 2 Tbsp. plus ¼ cup barbecue sauce, divided
- ½ cup crushed seasoned stuffing
- 1 Tbsp. onion soup mix
- 1¼ lbs. lean ground beef (90% lean)
  Minced fresh parsley, optional

1. In a large bowl, combine the egg, milk, 2 Tbsp. barbecue sauce, stuffing and onion soup mix. Crumble beef over mixture and mix well. Shape into five loaves; arrange around the edge of a microwave-safe dish.
2. Microwave, uncovered, on high for 4½ to 5½ minutes or until no pink remains and a thermometer reads 160°. Cover and let stand for 5-10 minutes. Top with the remaining barbecue sauce. If desired, sprinkle with minced parsley.
1 meat loaf: 234 cal., 10g fat (4g sat. fat), 100mg chol., 451mg sod., 9g carb. (3g sugars, 1g fiber), 25g pro. **Diabetic exchanges:** 3 lean meat, ½ starch.

CHICKEN-FRIED STEAK & GRAVY

As a child, I learned from my grandmother how to make these chicken-fried steaks. I taught my daughters, and when my granddaughters are bigger, I'll show them, too.
—*Donna Cater, Fort Ann, NY*

Takes: 30 min. • **Makes:** 4 servings

- 1¼ cups all-purpose flour, divided
- 2 large eggs
- 1½ cups 2% milk, divided
- 4 beef cube steaks (6 oz. each)
- 1¼ tsp. salt, divided
- 1 tsp. pepper, divided
  Oil for frying
- 1 cup water

1. Place 1 cup flour in a shallow bowl. In a separate shallow bowl, whisk eggs and ½ cup milk until blended. Sprinkle steaks with ¾ tsp. each salt and pepper. Dip in flour to coat both sides; shake off excess. Dip in egg mixture, then again in the flour.
2. In a large skillet, heat ¼ in. of oil over medium heat. Add the steaks; cook for 4-6 minutes on each side or until golden brown and a thermometer reads 160°. Remove from pan; drain on paper towels. Keep warm.
3. Remove all but 2 Tbsp. oil from pan. Stir in the remaining ¼ cup flour, ½ tsp. salt and ¼ tsp. pepper until smooth; cook and stir over medium heat 3-4 minutes or until golden brown. Gradually whisk in water and the remaining milk. Bring to a boil, stirring constantly; cook and stir for 1-2 minutes or until thickened. Serve with steaks.
1 steak with ⅓ cup gravy: 563 cal., 28g fat (5g sat. fat), 148mg chol., 839mg sod., 29g carb. (4g sugars, 1g fiber), 46g pro.

Frittatas in a Flash

The rustic cousin of the omelet, a frittata can be dressed up or down depending on the ingredients you use. Start them on the stove, finish them in the oven, and make the most of the freshest eggs you can find to create these hearty one-pan meals!

WHAT'S IN THE FRIDGE FRITTATA

Great for a last-minute breakfast, brunch or lunch, guests rave about the crab and Swiss combination in this frittata. I also like to use sausage and cheddar with asparagus or whatever vegetable is in season.
—*Deborah Posey, Virginia Beach, VA*

- -

Takes: 25 min. • **Makes:** 4 servings

- 6 large eggs
- ⅓ cup chopped onion
- ⅓ cup chopped sweet red pepper
- ⅓ cup chopped fresh mushrooms
- 1 Tbsp. olive oil
- 1 can (6 oz.) lump crabmeat, drained
- ¼ cup shredded Swiss cheese
- 1 Tbsp. minced fresh parsley, optional

1. In a small bowl, whisk eggs; set aside. In an 8-in. ovenproof skillet, saute the onion, pepper and mushrooms in oil until tender. Reduce heat; sprinkle with crab. Top with eggs. Cover and cook for 5-7 minutes or until nearly set.

2. Uncover skillet; sprinkle with cheese. Broil 3-4 in. from the heat for 2-3 minutes or until eggs are completely set. Let stand for 5 minutes. Cut into wedges.

1 wedge: 215 cal., 13g fat (4g sat. fat), 361mg chol., 265mg sod., 3g carb. (2g sugars, 1g fiber), 21g pro. **Diabetic exchanges:** 3 lean meat, 1½ fat.

ASPARAGUS & CHEESE FRITTATA

This rich and creamy frittata begins in the skillet and ends in the oven. We like this melty, cheesy dish with salad on the side.
—*Gilda Lester, Millsboro, DE*

- -

Takes: 30 min. • **Makes:** 4 servings

- 5 large eggs
- ½ cup grated Romano cheese
- ½ cup vegetable broth
- ¼ tsp. salt
- ¼ tsp. pepper
- 2 slices Italian bread (½ in. thick), cubed
- 2 Tbsp. olive oil
- 2 cups cut fresh asparagus (½-in. pieces)
- 1 medium onion, finely chopped
- ½ cup shredded Gruyere cheese

1. Preheat broiler. In a small bowl, whisk the first five ingredients until blended; stir in bread cubes.

2. In an 8-in. ovenproof skillet, heat oil over medium-high heat. Add asparagus and onion; cook and stir 8-10 minutes or until the onion is tender.

3. Reduce heat to medium-low; pour in the egg mixture. Cook, uncovered, for 4-6 minutes or until nearly set. Sprinkle with Gruyere cheese.

4. Broil 3-4 in. from heat 5-7 minutes or until the cheese is melted and the eggs are completely set. Let stand 5 minutes. Cut into wedges.

1 wedge: 325 cal., 22g fat (9g sat. fat), 263mg chol., 779mg sod., 12g carb. (3g sugars, 2g fiber), 21g pro.

FRITTATA FLORENTINE

My family is all about brunchy meals like this gorgeous Italian omelet. Lucky for us, it's loaded with ingredients we tend to have at the ready, so we have it often.
—*Jenny Flake, Newport Beach, CA*

- -

Takes: 30 min. • **Makes:** 4 servings

6	large egg whites
3	large eggs
½ tsp.	dried oregano
¼ tsp.	garlic powder
¼ tsp.	salt
¼ tsp.	pepper
1 Tbsp.	olive oil
1	small onion, finely chopped
¼ cup	finely chopped sweet red pepper
2	turkey bacon strips, chopped
1 cup	fresh baby spinach
3 Tbsp.	thinly sliced fresh basil leaves
½ cup	shredded part-skim mozzarella cheese

1. Preheat broiler. In a small bowl, whisk the first six ingredients.

2. In an 8-in. ovenproof skillet, heat the oil over medium-high heat. Add onion, red pepper and bacon; cook and stir for 4-5 minutes or until the onion is tender. Reduce the heat to medium-low; top with spinach.

3. Pour in the egg mixture. As the eggs set, push cooked portions toward the center, letting the uncooked eggs flow underneath; cook until eggs are nearly thickened. Remove from heat; sprinkle with basil, then cheese.

4. Broil 3-4 in. from heat 2-3 minutes or until eggs are completely set. Let stand 5 minutes. Cut into wedges.

1 wedge: 176 cal., 11g fat (4g sat. fat), 174mg chol., 451mg sod., 4g carb. (2g sugars, 1g fiber), 15g pro. **Diabetic exchanges:** 2 medium-fat meat, ½ fat.

EGG-WHITE OPTION

Want to be super healthy? Substitute 6 egg whites for the 3 whole eggs listed in the ingredients, for a total of 12 egg whites used to complete the recipe.

SAUSAGE & MUSHROOM PIZZA FRITTATA

The combination of fresh flavors make this frittata truly special. It's the perfect sunny South Florida breakfast.
—*Wolfgang Hanau, West Palm Beach, FL*

- -

Takes: 30 min. • **Makes:** 4 servings

4 oz.	bulk Italian sausage
2 cups	sliced fresh mushrooms
2 Tbsp.	finely chopped red onion
2 Tbsp.	finely chopped green pepper
¼ cup	finely chopped fresh pineapple
6	large eggs, beaten
6 Tbsp.	marinara sauce
2 Tbsp.	shredded part-skim mozzarella cheese
2 Tbsp.	grated Parmigiano-Reggiano cheese
2 Tbsp.	minced fresh parsley

1. Preheat broiler. In a 10-in. ovenproof skillet, cook sausage, mushrooms, onion and pepper over medium heat until the sausage is no longer pink and vegetables are tender, 6-8 minutes, breaking sausage into crumbles; drain.

2. Return sausage mixture to skillet; stir in pineapple. Pour in beaten eggs. Cook, covered, until nearly set, 4-6 minutes. Spread marinara sauce over top; sprinkle with cheeses.

3. Broil 3-4 in. from heat until the eggs are completely set and cheese is melted, 2-3 minutes. Let stand 5 minutes. Sprinkle with parsley; cut into wedges.

1 wedge: 226 cal., 15g fat (5g sat. fat), 299mg chol., 459mg sod., 7g carb. (4g sugars, 1g fiber), 16g pro.

CAJUN SHRIMP SKILLET

There's plenty of sauce with these shrimp—I always serve some bread on the side to soak it up. Make it your own by using your favorite amber beer or flavorful broth.
—*Mark Oppe, North Pole, AK*

- -

Takes: 25 min. • **Makes:** 4 servings

  3 Tbsp. butter
  2 garlic cloves, minced
  ½ cup amber beer or beef broth
  1 tsp. Worcestershire sauce
  1 tsp. pepper
  ½ tsp. salt
  ½ tsp. dried thyme
  ½ tsp. dried rosemary, crushed
  ½ tsp. crushed red pepper flakes
  ¼ tsp. cayenne pepper
  ⅛ tsp. dried oregano
  1 lb. uncooked large shrimp, peeled and deveined
     Hot cooked grits, optional

In a large cast-iron or other heavy skillet, heat butter over medium-high heat. Add garlic; cook and stir 1 minute. Stir in beer, Worcestershire sauce and seasonings; bring to a boil. Add shrimp; cook until shrimp turn pink, 3-4 minutes, stirring occasionally. If desired, serve over grits.
½ cup: 186 cal., 10g fat (6g sat. fat), 160mg chol., 505mg sod., 3g carb. (1g sugars, 0 fiber), 19g pro. **Diabetic exchanges:** 3 lean meat, 2 fat.

ASPARAGUS BEEF LO MEIN

This springtime beef stir-fry is as easy as it gets. Ramen noodles make it extra crunchy and fun.
—*Dottie Wanat, Modesto, CA*

- -

Takes: 20 min. • **Makes:** 4 servings

  1 beef top sirloin steak (1 lb.), cut into thin strips
  2 pkg. (3 oz. each) beef ramen noodles
  ⅔ cup hoisin sauce
  2¼ cups water, divided
  2 Tbsp. olive oil, divided
  1 lb. fresh asparagus, trimmed and cut into 2½-in. pieces
  1 small garlic clove, minced

1. Toss beef with ½ tsp. seasoning from a ramen seasoning packet (discard the remaining opened packet). In a small bowl, mix hoisin sauce and ¼ cup water.
2. In a saucepan, bring the remaining water to a boil. Add noodles and the contents of the unopened seasoning packet; cook, uncovered, 3 minutes. Remove from heat; let stand, covered, until noodles are tender.
3. Meanwhile, in a large skillet, heat 1 Tbsp. oil over medium-high heat; stir-fry beef until browned, 3-4 minutes. Remove from pan.
4. In the same pan, heat the remaining oil over medium-high heat; stir-fry asparagus with garlic until crisp-tender, 1-3 minutes. Stir in the hoisin sauce mixture; bring to a boil. Cook until slightly thickened. Stir in beef; heat through. Serve over noodles.
1 serving: 511 cal., 21g fat (7g sat. fat), 47mg chol., 1367mg sod., 48g carb. (13g sugars, 3g fiber), 31g pro.

CHICKEN THIGHS WITH SHALLOTS & SPINACH

What could be better than an entree that comes with its own creamy vegetable side? It makes an eye-catching presentation and goes together in no time flat for a healthy supper.
—*Genna Johannes, Wrightstown, WI*

Takes: 30 min. • **Makes:** 6 servings

- 6 boneless skinless chicken thighs (about 1½ lbs.)
- ½ tsp. seasoned salt
- ½ tsp. pepper
- 1½ tsp. olive oil
- 4 shallots, thinly sliced
- ⅓ cup white wine or reduced-sodium chicken broth
- 1 pkg. (10 oz.) fresh spinach, trimmed
- ¼ tsp. salt
- ¼ cup fat-free sour cream

1. Sprinkle chicken with seasoned salt and pepper. In a large nonstick skillet coated with cooking spray, heat oil over medium heat. Add the chicken; cook until a thermometer reads 170°, about 6 minutes on each side. Remove from pan; keep warm.

2. In same pan, cook and stir shallots until tender. Add wine; bring to a boil. Cook until the wine is reduced by half. Add spinach and salt; cook and stir just until the spinach is wilted. Stir in sour cream; serve with chicken.

Freeze option: Before adding sour cream, cool the chicken and spinach mixture. Freeze in freezer containers. To use, partially thaw in refrigerator overnight. Heat through slowly in a covered skillet until a thermometer inserted in chicken reads 165°, stirring occasionally. Stir in sour cream.

1 chicken thigh with ¼ cup spinach mixture: 225 cal., 10g fat (2g sat. fat), 77mg chol., 338mg sod., 8g carb. (2g sugars, 1g fiber), 24g pro. **Diabetic exchanges:** 3 lean meat, 1½ fat, 1 vegetable.

BLACK BEAN CHICKEN WITH RICE

This family favorite requires only a few ingredients, so it's easy to fix on a weeknight.
—*Molly Andersen, Portland, OR*

Takes: 25 min. • **Makes:** 4 servings

- 3 tsp. chili powder
- 1 tsp. ground cumin
- 1 tsp. pepper
- ¼ tsp. salt
- 4 boneless skinless chicken breast halves (4 oz. each)
- 2 tsp. canola oil
- 1 can (15 oz.) black beans, rinsed and drained
- 1 cup frozen corn
- 1 cup salsa
- 2 cups hot cooked brown rice

1. In a small bowl, mix seasonings; sprinkle over both sides of the chicken. In a large nonstick skillet, heat the oil over medium heat. Brown chicken on both sides.

2. Add beans, corn and salsa to skillet; cook, covered, 10-15 minutes or until a thermometer inserted in chicken reads 165°. Remove chicken from pan; cut into slices. Serve with bean mixture and rice.

1 chicken breast half with ¾ cup bean mixture and ½ cup cooked rice: 400 cal., 7g fat (1g sat. fat), 63mg chol., 670mg sod., 52g carb. (4g sugars, 8g fiber), 32g pro.

HONEY WALLEYE

In a state known as the Land of 10,000 Lakes, it's not surprising that fishing is one of the favorite recreational activities. This recipe is a quick way to prepare the fresh walleye hooked by the anglers in our family.
—*Kitty McCue, St. Louis Park, MN*

Takes: 20 min. • **Makes:** 6 servings

- 1 large egg
- 2 tsp. honey
- 2 cups crushed Ritz crackers (about 45 to 50)
- ½ tsp. salt
- 1½ lbs. walleye fillets
- ⅓ to ½ cup canola oil
  Lemon wedge and minced fresh parsley

1. In a shallow bowl, beat egg; add honey. In a shallow dish, combine crackers and salt. Dip fish in egg mixture, then in the cracker mixture until coated.

2. In a cast-iron or other heavy skillet, cook fillets in oil over medium heat until golden and fish flakes easily with a fork, 3-5 minutes on each side. Top with parsley and serve with lemon wedges.

3 oz. cooked fish: 389 cal., 22g fat (3g sat. fat), 133mg chol., 514mg sod., 23g carb. (5g sugars, 1g fiber), 25g pro.

JUST PEACHY PORK TENDERLOIN

I had a pork tenderloin and ripe peaches and decided to put them together. The results couldn't have been more irresistible! Here's a fresh entree that tastes like summer.
—*Julia Gosliga, Addison, VT*

Takes: 20 min. • **Makes:** 4 servings

- 1   lb. pork tenderloin, cut into 12 slices
- ½   tsp. salt
- ¼   tsp. pepper
- 2   tsp. olive oil
- 4   medium peaches, peeled and sliced
- 1   Tbsp. lemon juice
- ¼   cup peach preserves

1. Flatten each tenderloin slice to ¼-in. thickness. Sprinkle with salt and pepper. In a large nonstick skillet over medium heat, cook the pork in oil until tender. Remove from skillet and keep warm.

2. To the same skillet, add peaches and lemon juice, stirring to loosen browned bits from pan. Cook and stir until the peaches are tender, 3-4 minutes. Stir in the pork and preserves; heat through.

1 serving: 241 cal., 6g fat (2g sat. fat), 63mg chol., 340mg sod., 23g carb. (20g sugars, 2g fiber), 23g pro. **Diabetic exchanges:** 3 lean meat, 1 fruit, ½ starch, ½ fat.

SMOKY ESPRESSO STEAK

This juicy steak rubbed with espresso, cocoa and pumpkin pie spice is one of my husband's favorites. We love making it on the grill, too.
—*Deborah Biggs, Omaha, NE*

Takes: 30 min. • **Makes:** 4 servings

- 3   tsp. instant espresso powder
- 2   tsp. brown sugar
- 1½ tsp. smoked or regular paprika
- 1   tsp. salt
- 1   tsp. baking cocoa
- ¼   tsp. pumpkin pie spice
- ¼   tsp. pepper
- 1   lb. beef flat iron or top sirloin steak (¾ in. thick)

1. Preheat broiler. Mix the first seven ingredients; rub over both sides of steak. Place the steak on a broiler pan; let stand for 10 minutes.

2. Broil the steak 3-4 in. from heat for 4-6 minutes on each side or until the meat reaches desired doneness (for medium-rare, a thermometer should read 135°; medium, 140°; medium-well, 145°). Let stand 5 minutes before slicing.

3 oz. cooked beef: 216 cal., 12g fat (5g sat. fat), 73mg chol., 661mg sod., 4g carb. (2g sugars, 0 fiber), 22g pro. **Diabetic exchanges:** 3 lean meat.

SMOTHERED CHICKEN BREASTS

After trying a similar dish in a restaurant, I decided to re-create it at home. Topped with bacon, caramelized onions and shredded cheese, this savory dish comes together in no time, and uses ingredients that I usually have on hand. And since it cooks in one skillet, it's a cinch to clean up!

—Brenda Carpenter, Warrensburg, MO

Takes: 30 min. • **Makes:** 4 servings

    4   boneless skinless chicken
        breast halves (6 oz. each)
    ¼   tsp. salt
    ¼   tsp. lemon-pepper seasoning
    1   Tbsp. canola oil
    8   bacon strips
    1   medium onion, sliced
    ¼   cup packed brown sugar
    ½   cup shredded Colby-Monterey
        Jack cheese

1. Sprinkle chicken with salt and lemon pepper. In a large skillet, heat oil over medium heat; cook the chicken until a thermometer reads 165°, 6-8 minutes per side. Remove from pan; keep warm.
2. In same skillet, cook the bacon strips over medium heat until crisp. Remove bacon to paper towels; pour off all but 2 Tbsp. drippings.
3. In the remaining drippings, saute onion with brown sugar over medium heat until tender and golden brown. Top chicken with bacon, onion mixture and cheese.

1 serving: 560 cal., 34g fat (12g sat. fat), 143mg chol., 710mg sod., 17g carb. (15g sugars, 0 fiber), 45g pro.

TENDERLOIN WITH HORSERADISH CREAM CHEESE

My husband and I both love the classic combination of beef and horseradish. Baked potatoes make a great side dish.

—Mary Lou Cook, Welches, OR

Takes: 20 min. • **Makes:** 4 servings

    4   beef tenderloin steaks (4 oz. each)
    ¼   tsp. salt
    ¼   tsp. pepper
    1   tsp. olive oil
    1   pkg. (8 oz.) cream cheese, softened
    2   Tbsp. grated Parmesan cheese
    2   Tbsp. prepared horseradish
    2   Tbsp. minced fresh parsley

1. Sprinkle steaks with salt and pepper. In a large skillet, heat oil over medium heat. Add the steaks; cook 4-6 minutes on each side or until the meat reaches desired doneness (for medium-rare, a thermometer should read 135°; medium, 140°; medium-well, 145°).
2. Meanwhile, in a small bowl, mix the cream cheese, Parmesan cheese and horseradish until blended. Serve with steaks. Sprinkle with parsley.

1 steak with ¼ cup topping: 387 cal., 28g fat (16g sat. fat), 114mg chol., 378mg sod., 3g carb. (1g sugars, 0 fiber), 30g pro.

GRILLED RIBEYES WITH BROWNED GARLIC BUTTER

Use the grill's smoke to flavor the ribeyes, then slather them with garlicky butter for a standout entree your friends and family will always remember.

—Arge Salvatori, Waldwick, NJ

- -

Takes: 25 min. • **Makes:** 8 servings

- 6 Tbsp. unsalted butter, cubed
- 2 garlic cloves, minced
- 4 beef ribeye steaks (about 1 in. thick and 12 oz. each)
- 1½ tsp. salt
- 1½ tsp. pepper

1. In a small heavy saucepan, melt butter with garlic over medium heat. Heat until the butter is golden brown, 4-6 minutes, stirring constantly. Remove from heat.
2. Season steaks with salt and pepper. Grill, covered, over medium heat or broil 4 in. from heat 5-7 minutes on each side or until meat reaches desired doneness (for medium-rare, a thermometer should read 135°; for medium, 140°; for medium-well, 170°).
3. Gently warm the garlic butter over low heat. Serve with steaks.

4 oz. cooked beef with 2 tsp. butter: 449 cal., 36g fat (16g sat. fat), 123mg chol., 521mg sod., 1g carb. (0 sugars, 0 fiber), 30g pro.

CONFETTI KIELBASA SKILLET

Here's one of my husband's favorite dishes. When corn is in season, substitute fresh for frozen. Add a dash of cayenne pepper if you like a little heat.

—Sheila Gomez, Shawnee, KS

- -

Takes: 30 min. • **Makes:** 4 servings

- 1 Tbsp. canola oil
- 7 oz. smoked turkey kielbasa, cut into ¼-in. slices
- 1 medium onion, halved and sliced
- ½ cup sliced baby portobello mushrooms
- 2 garlic cloves, minced
- ½ cup reduced-sodium chicken broth
- ¾ tsp. Mrs. Dash Garlic & Herb seasoning blend
- 1 can (15 oz.) no-salt-added black beans, rinsed and drained
- 1 pkg. (8.8 oz.) ready-to-serve brown rice
- 1 cup frozen corn
- ½ cup chopped roasted sweet red peppers
- 4 tsp. minced fresh cilantro

1. In a large skillet, heat oil over medium-high heat. Add the kielbasa, onion and mushrooms; cook and stir 4-6 minutes or until the vegetables are tender. Add garlic; cook 1 minute longer.
2. Add the broth and seasoning blend, stirring to loosen browned bits from pan. Bring to a boil; cook 2-3 minutes or until liquid is almost evaporated. Stir in the remaining ingredients; heat through.

1¼ cups: 347 cal., 9g fat (1g sat. fat), 31mg chol., 692mg sod., 45g carb. (4g sugars, 7g fiber), 18g pro. **Diabetic exchanges:** 3 starch, 2 lean meat, ½ fat.

EASY BEEF PIES

We make a lot of French dips and always have leftover roast beef—I put it to good use in these pies. Use any veggies you like. They're extra awesome drenched in cheese sauce.
—Jennie Weber, Palmer, AK

- -

Takes: 30 min. • **Makes:** 4 servings

- 1 pkg. (15 oz.) refrigerated beef roast au jus
- 1 Tbsp. canola oil
- ¼ cup finely chopped onion
- ¼ cup finely chopped green pepper
- 1 garlic clove, minced
- 1 pkg. (14.1 oz.) refrigerated pie pastry
- 1 cup shredded Mexican cheese blend
Salsa con queso dip, optional

1. Preheat oven to 425°. Drain beef, reserving ¼ cup juices; shred meat with two forks. In a large skillet, heat oil over medium-high heat. Add the onion and pepper; cook and stir for 1-2 minutes or until tender. Add garlic; cook 30 seconds longer. Remove from heat; stir in beef and the reserved juices.

2. Unroll one pastry sheet; cut in half. Layer ¼ of the cup shredded cheese and about ⅓ cup of the beef mixture over half of each pastry to within ½ in. of edge. Fold pastry over the filling; press edges with a fork to seal. Place on a greased baking sheet. Repeat with the remaining pastry and filling.

3. Bake 15-18 minutes or until golden brown. If desired, serve with queso dip.

Freeze option: Freeze cooled pastries in a freezer container. To use, reheat pastries on a greased baking sheet in a preheated 350° oven until heated through.

1 pie: 752 cal., 46g fat (19g sat. fat), 108mg chol., 921mg sod., 53g carb. (7g sugars, 0 fiber), 31g pro.

FLAVORFUL GRILLED PORK TENDERLOIN

Folks can always find me grilling, no matter the weather. This moist pork tenderloin has loads of flavor thanks to its special spice blend, and it doesn't get much easier to make. My wife especially likes that she doesn't have to do the cooking!
—*Steve Ehrhart, Villa Park, IL*

Takes: 30 min. • **Makes:** 8 servings

- ¾ tsp. salt
- ¾ tsp. seasoned salt
- ¾ tsp. poultry seasoning
- ¾ tsp. onion powder
- ¾ tsp. garlic powder
- ¾ tsp. chili powder
- ⅛ tsp. cayenne pepper
- 2 pork tenderloins (1 lb. each)

Mix seasonings; sprinkle over tenderloins. Grill, covered, over medium heat until a thermometer reads 145°, 20-25 minutes, turning occasionally. Let stand 5 minutes before slicing.

3 oz. cooked pork: 135 cal., 4g fat (1g sat. fat), 64mg chol., 416mg sod., 1g carb. (0 sugars, 0 fiber), 23g pro. **Diabetic exchanges:** 3 lean meat.

ASPARAGUS HAM DINNER

I've been making this light meal for my family for years, and it's always well received. With asparagus, tomato, pasta and chunks of ham, it's a tempting blend of tastes and textures.
—*Rhonda Zavodny, David City, NE*

Takes: 25 min. • **Makes:** 6 servings

- 2 cups uncooked corkscrew or spiral pasta
- ¾ lb. fresh asparagus, cut into 1-in. pieces
- 1 medium sweet yellow pepper, julienned
- 1 Tbsp. olive oil
- 6 medium tomatoes, diced
- 6 oz. boneless fully cooked ham, cubed
- ¼ cup minced fresh parsley
- ½ tsp. salt
- ½ tsp. dried oregano
- ½ tsp. dried basil
- ⅛ to ¼ tsp. cayenne pepper
- ¼ cup shredded Parmesan cheese

Cook pasta according to the package directions. Meanwhile, in a large cast-iron or other heavy skillet, saute asparagus and yellow pepper in oil until crisp-tender. Add tomatoes and ham; heat through. Drain pasta; add to the vegetable mixture. Stir in parsley and seasonings. Sprinkle with cheese.

1⅓ cups: 204 cal., 5g fat (1g sat. fat), 17mg chol., 561mg sod., 29g carb. (5g sugars, 3g fiber), 12g pro. **Diabetic exchanges:** 1½ starch, 1 lean meat, 1 vegetable, ½ fat.

Cooking for Two

Cooking for two means scaled-down recipes— but only in size! Smaller dinners don't have to be plain. Main courses, sides, desserts, appetizers— here are 26 recipes just right for two, without breaking the budget or leaving you with a week's worth of leftovers.

SPINACH RICE

I like to serve this Greek-style rice dish alongside steak with mushrooms. It makes an elegant meal that easily can be doubled for guests.

—*Jeanette Cakouros, Brunswick, ME*

Takes: 20 min. • **Makes:** 2 servings

- 2   Tbsp. olive oil
- ½   cup chopped onion
- ¾   cup water
- 1   Tbsp. dried parsley flakes
- ¼   to ½ tsp. salt
- ⅛   tsp. pepper
- ½   cup uncooked instant rice
- 2   cups fresh baby spinach

1. In a saucepan, heat oil over medium-high heat; saute onion until tender. Stir in water, parsley, salt and pepper; bring to a boil. Stir in rice; top with spinach.
2. Cover; remove from heat. Let stand until the rice is tender, 7-10 minutes. Stir to combine.

¾ cup: 235 cal., 14g fat (2g sat. fat), 0 chol., 326mg sod., 25g carb. (2g sugars, 2g fiber), 3g pro. **Diabetic exchanges:** 3 fat, 1½ starch, 1 vegetable.

MIXED FRUIT SHORTCAKES

This delightful downsized recipe makes just two biscuit-like shortcakes. Fill them with the fresh fruit of your choice and top with whipped cream for an impressive finale to your dinner.

—*Sue Ross, Casa Grande, AZ*

Takes: 30 min. • **Makes:** 2 servings

- 1   cup mixed fresh berries
- ½   cup sliced fresh peaches or nectarines
- 4   tsp. sugar, divided
- ½   cup all-purpose flour
- ¾   tsp. baking powder
- ⅛   tsp. salt
- 2   Tbsp. shortening
- 3   Tbsp. 2% milk
      Whipped cream

1. Preheat oven to 425°. In a small bowl, combine the berries, peaches and 2 tsp. sugar; set aside. In another bowl, combine the flour, baking powder and salt; cut in shortening until the mixture is crumbly. Stir in milk just until moistened. Drop by lightly packed ⅓ cupfuls 2 in. apart onto an ungreased baking sheet. Gently flatten into 2½-in. circles. Sprinkle dough with the remaining sugar.
2. Bake shortcakes 10-12 minutes or until golden brown. Remove to a wire rack to cool. Split in half horizontally. Spoon fruit onto bottoms; spread whipped cream over the fruit or on the shortcake tops.

1 serving: 329 cal., 13g fat (3g sat. fat), 2mg chol., 311mg sod., 48g carb. (20g sugars, 5g fiber), 5g pro.

GARLIC-BUTTER STEAK

This entree is a wonder—it's quick and easy to make, and the results are positively restaurant quality. It's sure to become a staple at your house, too!
—*Lily Julow, Lawrenceville, GA*

- -

Takes: 20 min. • **Makes:** 2 servings

- 2 **Tbsp. butter, softened, divided**
- 1 **tsp. minced fresh parsley**
- ½ **tsp. minced garlic**
- ¼ **tsp. reduced-sodium soy sauce**
- 1 **beef flat iron steak or boneless top sirloin steak (¾ lb.)**
- ⅛ **tsp. salt**
- ⅛ **tsp. pepper**

1. Mix 1 Tbsp. butter, parsley, garlic and soy sauce; set aside.
2. Sprinkle steak with salt and pepper. In a large skillet, heat remaining butter over medium heat. Add steak; cook until meat reaches desired doneness (for medium-rare, a thermometer should read 135°; medium, 140°; medium-well, 145°), 4-7 minutes per side. Serve with garlic butter.
1 serving: 316 cal., 20g fat (10g sat. fat), 124mg chol., 337mg sod., 0 carb. (0 sugars, 0 fiber), 32g pro.

BREADED SEA SCALLOPS

I never liked seafood until my husband urged me to try scallops, and now I love them. He says my crispy breaded version is the best he's ever had.
—*Martina Preston, Willow Grove, PA*

- -

Takes: 15 min. • **Makes:** 2 servings

- 1 **large egg**
- ⅓ **cup mashed potato flakes**
- ⅓ **cup seasoned bread crumbs**
- ⅛ **tsp. salt**
- ⅛ **tsp. pepper**
- 6 **sea scallops (about ¾ lb.)**
- 2 **Tbsp. all-purpose flour**
- 2 **Tbsp. butter**
- 1 **Tbsp. canola oil**

1. In a shallow bowl, lightly beat egg. In another bowl, toss potato flakes and bread crumbs with salt and pepper. In a third bowl, toss scallops with flour to coat lightly. Dip in egg, then in potato mixture, patting to adhere.
2. In a large skillet, heat butter and oil over medium heat. Add scallops; cook until they are golden brown, firm and opaque, 2-3 minutes per side.
3 scallops: 454 cal., 23g fat (9g sat. fat), 164mg chol., 1262mg sod., 33g carb. (2g sugars, 2g fiber), 28g pro.
Almond-Crusted Sea Scallops: Substitute ⅓ cup ground almonds for the potato flakes. Add ½ tsp. grated lemon zest to the bread crumb mixture. Proceed as directed.

BRAVO ITALIAN CHICKEN

With a handful of Italian-style pantry staples, you're on your way to a quick, hearty chicken entree that both of you will love. Just add a salad and breadsticks!

—*Kristin Miller, Carmel, IN*

- -

Prep: 20 min. + standing • **Bake:** 35 min.
Makes: 2 servings

- 1 small eggplant, peeled and cut into 1-in. cubes
- ½ tsp. salt
- 2 boneless skinless chicken breast halves (5 oz. each)
- ⅛ tsp. Italian seasoning
- ⅛ tsp. pepper
- 2 cups tomato basil pasta sauce
- ¾ cup shredded part-skim mozzarella cheese

1. Place eggplant in a colander over a plate; sprinkle with salt and toss. Let stand for 30 minutes.
2. Meanwhile, sprinkle the chicken with Italian seasoning and pepper. In a large skillet coated with cooking spray, brown chicken on both sides. Transfer chicken to a greased 13x9-in. baking dish; sprinkle with ⅓ cup of the mozzarella cheese.
3. Preheat oven to 350°. Rinse the eggplant; pat dry with paper towels. Transfer to a large bowl; add the pasta sauce and toss to coat. Spoon over chicken; top with the remaining cheese.
4. Cover and bake for 35-40 minutes or until a thermometer reads 170°.
1 serving: 468 cal., 14g fat (5g sat. fat), 103mg chol., 1459mg sod., 38g carb. (25g sugars, 11g fiber), 45g pro.

CHOCOLATE CAYENNE SOUFFLES

This rich, chocolaty souffle has a surprise ending...a little kick of heat from the cayenne pepper. It's yummy.

—*Diane Halferty, Corpus Christi, TX*

- -

Prep: 25 min. • **Bake:** 15 min.
Makes: 2 servings

- 1 large egg
- 1 tsp. plus 1 Tbsp. butter, divided
- 2 tsp. plus 4 Tbsp. sugar, divided
- 2 Tbsp. all-purpose flour
- ½ cup 2% milk
- 2 oz. semisweet chocolate, chopped
- ⅛ tsp. cayenne pepper
- Dash salt

1. Separate egg; let stand at room temperature for 30 minutes. Coat two 6-oz. ramekins with 1 tsp. butter and sprinkle with 2 tsp. sugar. Place the ramekins on a baking sheet; set aside.
2. Preheat oven to 400°. In a small saucepan over medium heat, melt the remaining butter. Stir in 2 Tbsp. sugar and the flour until smooth. Gradually whisk in milk. Bring to a boil, stirring constantly. Cook and stir 1-2 minutes longer or until thickened. Whisk in chocolate, cayenne and salt until the chocolate is melted. Transfer to a small bowl.
3. Stir a small amount of the hot mixture into the egg yolk; return all to the bowl, stirring constantly. Cool slightly.
4. In another bowl, with clean beaters, beat egg white on medium speed until soft peaks form. Gradually beat in the remaining sugar on high until stiff peaks form. With a spatula, stir a fourth of the egg white into the chocolate mixture until no white streaks remain. Fold in the remaining egg white until combined. Transfer to prepared ramekins.
5. Bake for 12-15 minutes or until the tops are puffed and centers appear set. Serve immediately.
1 souffle: 384 cal., 19g fat (10g sat. fat), 125mg chol., 179mg sod., 50g carb. (42g sugars, 2g fiber), 8g pro.

SKILLET SHEPHERD'S PIE

Leftover mashed potatoes? Add them to a few pantry staples and you'll have warm comfort food in no time!
—*Sharon Tipton, Casselberry, FL*

Takes: 20 min. • **Makes:** 2 servings

- ¾ lb. ground beef
- ½ cup chopped onion
- 1 garlic clove, minced
- ¼ cup water
- 2 Tbsp. taco seasoning
- 1 cup shredded cheddar cheese, divided
- 1½ cups leftover or refrigerated mashed potatoes, warmed

1. In an ovenproof skillet, cook beef and onion over medium heat until the meat is no longer pink; drain. Add garlic; cook 1 minute longer. Stir in water and taco seasoning; heat through. Stir in ½ cup of the cheese.
2. Combine potatoes and the remaining cheese; spread over beef. Broil 4-6 in. from the heat for 5-6 minutes or until golden brown.
1 serving: 783 cal., 45g fat (24g sat. fat), 206mg chol., 1780mg sod., 40g carb. (4g sugars, 3g fiber), 51g pro.

PORK CHOPS WITH MUSHROOM BOURBON SAUCE

Golden crusted pork chops accompanied by a rich mushroom sauce—this scrumptious entree is loved by my family and also makes a terrific company dish. It's wonderful served with mashed potatoes!
—*Nadine Mesch, Mount Healthy, OH*

Prep: 20 min. • **Cook:** 30 min.
Makes: 2 servings

- ½ lb. sliced fresh mushrooms
- 2 Tbsp. chopped onion
- 2 Tbsp. olive oil, divided
- 1 Tbsp. butter
- 1 garlic clove, minced
- ¼ cup white wine or reduced-sodium chicken broth
- 2 Tbsp. bourbon
- ½ cup reduced-sodium chicken broth
- ¼ cup heavy whipping cream
- 2 boneless pork loin chops (6 oz. each)
- ¼ tsp. salt
- ¼ tsp. paprika
- ⅛ tsp. pepper
- 1 large egg
- 2 Tbsp. water
- 3 Tbsp. all-purpose flour
- ½ cup panko (Japanese) bread crumbs
- 4 tsp. minced fresh basil

1. In a large skillet, saute mushrooms and onion in 1 Tbsp. oil and butter until tender. Add garlic; cook 1 minute longer. Remove from the heat. Add wine and bourbon; cook over medium heat until liquid is evaporated. Add chicken broth and cream; bring to a boil. Reduce heat and simmer until sauce is thickened, stirring occasionally; keep warm.
2. Sprinkle chops with salt, paprika and pepper. In a shallow bowl, whisk egg and water. Place flour and bread crumbs in separate shallow bowls. Dip pork in the flour, egg mixture, then bread crumbs.
3. In a large skillet, cook pork chops over medium heat in remaining oil until crisp and juices run clear, 4-5 minutes on each side. Stir basil into the mushroom sauce; serve over pork.
1 pork chop with ⅓ cup sauce: 646 cal., 42g fat (16g sat. fat), 202mg chol., 601mg sod., 20g carb. (3g sugars, 2g fiber), 42g pro.

STEAK & FRIES SALAD

This is a very popular dish at restaurants in central Pennsylvania—one taste will show you why! Prepared sweet-and-sour dressing is good on this salad, too.
—Nancy Collins, Clearfield, PA

- -

Takes: 30 min. • **Makes:** 2 servings

- 3 Tbsp. sugar
- 2 Tbsp. canola oil
- 1 to 2 Tbsp. malt vinegar
- 1½ tsp. water

- 1 cup frozen french-fried potatoes
- ½ lb. beef top sirloin steak
- 3 cups torn iceberg lettuce
- ⅓ cup chopped tomato
- ¼ cup chopped red onion
- ½ cup shredded part-skim mozzarella cheese

1. For the dressing, whisk the first four ingredients until sugar is dissolved. Cook potatoes according to package directions.
2. Meanwhile, place a skillet coated with cooking spray over medium heat. Add steak; cook until the meat reaches the desired doneness (for medium-rare, a thermometer should read 135°; medium, 140°), 5-6 minutes per side. Remove from the heat; let stand for 5 minutes before slicing.
3. To serve, divide lettuce, tomato and onion between two plates; top with potatoes, steak and cheese. Drizzle with dressing.

1 serving: 525 cal., 28g fat (6g sat. fat), 80mg chol., 206mg sod., 39g carb. (24g sugars, 4g fiber), 31g pro.

SOUTHERN FRIED OKRA

Golden brown with a little fresh green showing through, these okra nuggets are crunchy and addicting! My sons like to dip them in ketchup.

—*Pam Duncan, Summers, AR*

Takes: 30 min. • **Makes:** 2 servings

- 1½ **cups sliced fresh or frozen okra, thawed**
- 3 **Tbsp. buttermilk**
- 2 **Tbsp. all-purpose flour**
- 2 **Tbsp. cornmeal**
- ¼ **tsp. salt**
- ¼ **tsp. garlic herb seasoning blend**
- ⅛ **tsp. pepper**
  Oil for deep-fat frying
  Additional salt and pepper, optional

1. Pat okra dry with paper towels. Place buttermilk in a shallow bowl. In another shallow bowl, combine flour, cornmeal, salt, seasoning blend and pepper. Dip the okra in the buttermilk, then roll in the cornmeal mixture.

2. In an electric skillet or deep-fat fryer, heat 1 in. of oil to 375°. Fry okra, a few pieces at a time, 1½-2½ minutes on each side or until golden brown. Drain okra on paper towels. Season with additional salt and pepper if desired.

¾ cup: 368 cal., 31g fat (2g sat. fat), 1mg chol., 410mg sod., 19g carb. (4g sugars, 4g fiber), 5g pro.

RUSTIC FRUIT TART

My husband and I love pie, but we can't eat a whole 9-inch pie by ourselves! So I make these easy tarts using raspberries and rhubarb picked at home. Sometimes I'll substitute apples, peaches or our garden blueberries for the rhubarb.

—*Naomi Olson, Hamilton, MI*

Prep: 20 min. + standing • **Bake:** 25 min.
Makes: 2 servings

- 1 **cup all-purpose flour**
- ½ **tsp. salt**
- ¼ **cup canola oil**
- 2 **Tbsp. whole milk**
- 1 **cup diced fresh or frozen rhubarb, thawed**
- 1 **cup fresh or frozen raspberries, thawed**
- ½ **cup sugar**
- 2 **Tbsp. quick-cooking tapioca**

GLAZE

- 6 **Tbsp. confectioners' sugar**
- 1 **tsp. water**
- ⅛ **tsp. almond extract**

1. In a large bowl, combine flour and salt. Add oil and milk, tossing with a fork until the mixture forms a ball. Shape the dough into a disk; wrap in plastic. Refrigerate for at least 1 hour.

2. In another bowl, combine the rhubarb, raspberries, sugar and tapioca; let stand for 15 minutes. Unwrap dough and place on a parchment-lined baking sheet. Cover with waxed paper and roll the dough into an 11-in. circle. Discard the waxed paper.

3. Preheat oven to 400°. Spoon the fruit mixture into the center of dough to within 2 in. of the edges. Fold the edges of the dough over the fruit, leaving the center uncovered. Bake 25-30 minutes or until crust is golden brown and filling is bubbly. Remove to a wire rack. Combine glaze ingredients until smooth. Drizzle over warm tart.

Note: If using frozen rhubarb, measure it while it's still frozen, then thaw completely. Drain in a colander, but do not press liquid out.

½ tart: 852 cal., 30g fat (2g sat. fat), 2mg chol., 602mg sod., 141g carb. (77g sugars, 7g fiber), 8g pro.

Romantic Night In

For Valentine's Day, an anniversary dinner or a weekend date night, step up your game with these delicious, sophisticated dishes perfect for evenings meant just for two.

SMOKY GRILLED SHRIMP APPETIZERS

Grill up these bacon-wrapped hors d'oeuvres and watch them disappear! The reserved sauce is wonderful for dipping.

—Debbie Taylor, White Bluff, TN

Takes: 20 min.
Makes: 1 dozen (⅓ cup sauce)

- ½ lb. bacon strips
- ⅔ cup honey Dijon salad dressing
- 2 tsp. prepared horseradish
- 1 small garlic clove, minced
- 12 uncooked large shrimp, peeled and deveined

1. Cut bacon strips in half widthwise. In a large skillet, cook bacon over medium heat until partially cooked but not crisp. Remove to paper towels to drain.
2. In a small bowl, combine the salad dressing, horseradish and garlic; set aside ⅓ cup. Brush the remaining mixture over both sides of shrimp. Wrap a piece of bacon around each shrimp; thread onto two metal or soaked wooden skewers.
3. Grill, covered, on an oiled rack over medium heat or broil 4 in. from the heat for 5-8 minutes or until shrimp turn pink, turning once. Serve with reserved sauce.
1 piece: 133 cal., 10g fat (3g sat. fat), 32mg chol., 268mg sod., 4g carb. (3g sugars, 0 fiber), 5g pro.

BEEF TENDERLOIN IN MUSHROOM SAUCE

Just a skillet, a couple juicy steaks, fresh mushrooms and a few simple ingredients prove it doesn't take much fuss to fix a special meal for two.

—Denise McNab, Warminster, PA

Takes: 25 min. • **Makes:** 2 servings

- 4 Tbsp. butter, divided
- 1 tsp. canola oil
- 2 beef tenderloin steaks (1 in. thick and 4 oz. each)
- 1 cup sliced fresh mushrooms
- 1 Tbsp. chopped green onion
- 1 Tbsp. all-purpose flour
- ⅛ tsp. salt
  Dash pepper
- ⅔ cup chicken or beef broth
- ⅛ tsp. browning sauce, optional

1. In a large skillet, heat 2 Tbsp. of butter and the oil over medium-high heat; cook steaks to desired doneness (for medium-rare, a thermometer should read 135°; medium, 140°), 5-6 minutes per side. Remove from pan, reserving drippings; keep warm.
2. In the same pan, heat the drippings and the remaining butter over medium-high heat; saute mushrooms and green onion until tender. Stir in flour, salt and pepper until blended; gradually stir in broth and, if desired, browning sauce. Bring to a boil, stirring constantly; cook and stir until thickened, 1-2 minutes. Serve with steaks.
1 serving: 417 cal., 32g fat (17g sat. fat), 112mg chol., 659mg sod., 5g carb. (1g sugars, 1g fiber), 26g pro.

PEAR PERFECTION

This great dessert can be made in advance and year-round. I use raspberry sherbet for Valentine's Day, lime for St. Patrick's Day and pineapple for Easter. For a yuletide touch, add a sprinkle of pomegranate seeds.
—*Pat Neaves, Lees Summit, MO*

Prep: 20 min. • **Cook:** 30 min. + chilling
Makes: 2 servings

- ½ cup pomegranate juice
- ¼ cup orange juice
- 1½ tsp. lemon juice
- ¼ cup sugar
- 1 tsp. grated lemon zest
- 1 large pear, peeled, halved and cored
- 1 Tbsp. semisweet chocolate chips
- 1 Tbsp. white baking chips
- ⅔ cup raspberry sherbet
- 2 Tbsp. sliced almonds

1. In a small saucepan, bring the juices, sugar and lemon zest to a boil. Reduce heat; carefully add pear halves. Cover and simmer for 8-10 minutes or until tender. Remove the pears with a slotted spoon; refrigerate for 1 hour.

2. Bring the poaching liquid to a boil; cook until liquid is reduced to about 2 Tbsp.; cool.

3. In a microwave, melt chocolate and baking chips in separate bowls; stir until smooth. Drizzle chocolate on a plate. Place pear halves on plate; top with sherbet. Drizzle with the poaching liquid and the melted baking chips. Sprinkle with almonds. Serve immediately.

1 serving: 379 cal., 7g fat (3g sat. fat), 1mg chol., 37mg sod., 79g carb. (68g sugars, 6g fiber), 3g pro.

SCENTED RICE IN BAKED PUMPKIN

This easy, delicious and healthy side is a showpiece that always delights. You can use grain, squash, fruits and nuts to suit your taste—it's impossible to go wrong!
—*Lynn Heisel, Jackson, MO*

Prep: 30 min. • **Bake:** 35 min.
Makes: 2 servings

- 1 small pie pumpkin (about 2 lbs.)
- 1 Tbsp. olive oil
- ½ cup uncooked brown rice
- 1 cup water
- ¼ cup coarsely chopped pecans, toasted
- 3 dried apricots, chopped
- 2 Tbsp. raisins
- ¼ tsp. salt
- ¼ tsp. curry powder
- ⅛ tsp. ground cinnamon
- ⅛ tsp. ground cardamom, optional
- ⅛ tsp. ground cumin

1. Preheat oven to 400°. Wash pumpkin; cut into six wedges. Remove loose fibers and seeds from the inside; discard or save seeds for toasting. Brush wedges with oil. Place onto an ungreased 15x10x1-in. baking sheet. Bake for 35-40 minutes or until tender.

2. Meanwhile, in a small saucepan, bring rice and water to a boil. Reduce heat; cover and simmer 20-25 minutes or until the liquid is absorbed and rice is tender. Stir in pecans, apricots, raisins, salt, curry, cinnamon and, if desired, cardamom.

3. Set four of the pumpkin wedges aside for another use. Sprinkle cumin onto the remaining wedges; top with the rice mixture and serve.

1 serving: 389 cal., 15g fat (2g sat. fat), 0 chol., 309mg sod., 62g carb. (13g sugars, 5g fiber), 7g pro.

ROSEMARY CITRUS SORBET

This pretty pink dessert bursts with the fresh flavors of grapefruit, lime and rosemary.
—*Rebecca Baird, Salt Lake City, UT*

- -

Prep: 10 min. **Freeze:** 1¾ hours
Makes: 2 servings

- ½ cup sugar
- ½ cup water
- 1½ tsp. packed fresh rosemary leaves
- ½ cup pink grapefruit juice
- 1 tsp. lime juice

1. In a small saucepan, bring the sugar, water and rosemary to a boil. Remove from the heat; let stand for 2 minutes. Strain and discard the rosemary. Stir in the grapefruit juice and lime juice.
2. Pour into a shallow 1-qt. dish; cover and freeze for 45 minutes or until edges begin to firm. Stir and return to freezer. Repeat every 30 minutes or until slushy, about 1 hour.
1 cup: 219 cal., 0 fat (0 sat. fat), 0 chol., 1mg sod., 56g carb. (54g sugars, 0 fiber), 0 pro.

PUMPKIN & SAUSAGE PENNE

I once made this dish for my Italian father-in-law, who swears he'll eat pasta only with red sauce. He loved it!
—*Karen Cambiotti, Stroudsburg, PA*

- -

Takes: 30 min. • **Makes:** 2 servings

- ¾ cup uncooked penne pasta
- 2 Italian sausage links, casings removed
- ½ cup chopped sweet onion
- 1 garlic clove, minced
- 1 tsp. olive oil
- ⅓ cup white wine or chicken broth
- 1 bay leaf
- ¾ cup chicken broth
- ⅓ cup canned pumpkin
- 3 tsp. minced fresh sage, divided
- ⅛ tsp. each salt, pepper and ground cinnamon
  Dash ground nutmeg
- 3 Tbsp. half-and-half cream
- 2 Tbsp. shredded Romano cheese

1. Cook the pasta according to the package directions. Meanwhile, in a large skillet, cook sausage over medium heat until no longer pink, breaking into crumbles. Remove with a slotted spoon; drain on paper towels. Discard drippings, reserving 1 tsp.
2. Cook and stir the onion and garlic in oil and the reserved drippings over medium-high heat until tender. Add wine and bay leaf. Bring to a boil; cook until the liquid is reduced by half. Stir in broth, pumpkin, 1½ tsp. sage and remaining seasonings; cook 1 minute longer. Add the cream and sausage; heat through. Remove bay leaf.
3. Drain the pasta; transfer to a large bowl. Add the sausage mixture; toss to coat. Sprinkle with cheese and the remaining sage.
1⅓ cups: 490 cal., 23g fat (9g sat. fat), 61mg chol., 950mg sod., 42g carb. (7g sugars, 4g fiber), 21g pro.

FILET MIGNON IN PUFF PASTRY

Horseradish lovers will adore the creamy sauce served with these delicious steak bundles, which turn any meal into something truly special.

—*Kelly Williams, Forked River, NJ*

- -

Prep: 20 min. • **Bake:** 20 min.
Makes: 2 servings

- 2 beef tenderloin steaks (6 oz. each)
- ½ tsp. coarsely ground pepper
- 2 Tbsp. butter, softened
- 1 sheet frozen puff pastry, thawed
- 1 garlic clove, minced
- 2 slices Muenster cheese
- 1 large egg, lightly beaten

SAUCE

- 2 Tbsp. prepared horseradish
- ¼ tsp. Dijon mustard

1. Place steaks on an ungreased baking sheet. Sprinkle with pepper; top with butter. Bake at 425° for 10 minutes. Cool slightly; refrigerate until chilled.

2. Meanwhile, on a lightly floured surface, roll out the puff pastry into a 14x9½-in. rectangle. Cut out two 7-in. squares, reserving scraps.

3. Rub the steaks with garlic and top each with a slice of cheese; place steaks, cheese side down, in the center of each pastry square. Lightly brush the pastry edges with egg. Bring opposite corners of pastry over the steaks; pinch seams to seal tightly. Place seam side down on an ungreased baking sheet. Cut small slits in top of pastry; brush with egg.

4. Using lightly floured small cookie cutters, cut out shapes from the reserved pastry. Arrange shapes over the wrapped steaks; brush with egg.

5. Bake at 425° for 20-25 minutes or until the pastry is golden brown and the meat reaches desired doneness (for medium-rare, a thermometer should read 135°; medium, 140°; medium-well, 170°).

6. In a small bowl, combine the sauce ingredients. Serve with steaks.

1 pastry-wrapped steak with 1 Tbsp. sauce: 1135 cal., 70g fat (24g sat. fat), 230mg chol., 673mg sod., 72g carb. (0 sugars, 9g fiber), 54g pro.

TUNA POTATO SUPPER

Tuna lovers will find this a real treat. My husband and I enjoy it as a nice change from the ordinary baked potato. Along with a salad it makes a simple lunch or dinner.
—*Rosella Peters, Gull Lake, SK*

- -

Takes: 25 min. • **Makes:** 2 servings

- 2 large baking potatoes
- 1 can (6 oz.) light water-packed tuna, drained and flaked
- 1 celery rib with leaves, finely chopped
- 1 green onion, chopped
- ⅓ cup creamy cucumber salad dressing
- ⅛ tsp. each salt and pepper
- ¼ cup shredded Colby-Monterey Jack cheese

1. Scrub and pierce potatoes; place on a microwave-safe plate. Microwave, uncovered, on high until tender, turning once, 7-9 minutes. Cool slightly. Cut a thin slice off the top of each potato; discard top. Scoop out the pulp, leaving a thin shell.

2. In a bowl, mash the pulp. Stir in the tuna, celery, onion, salad dressing, salt and pepper. Spoon into potato shells. Sprinkle with cheese. Place on a baking sheet. Broil 4-6 in. from the heat until cheese is melted, 5-6 minutes.

1 filled potato: 598 cal., 25g fat (6g sat. fat), 38mg chol., 866mg sod., 63g carb. (0 sugars, 6g fiber), 30g pro.

MUSHROOM PORK RAGOUT

Savory, slow-cooked pork is luscious served in a delightful tomato gravy over noodles. It's a nice change from regular pork roast. I serve it with broccoli or green beans on the side.
—*Connie McDowell, Greenwood, DE*

- -

Prep: 20 min. • **Cook:** 3 hours
Makes: 2 servings

- 1 pork tenderloin (¾ lb.)
- ⅛ tsp. salt
- ⅛ tsp. pepper
- 1 Tbsp. cornstarch
- ¾ cup canned crushed tomatoes, divided
- 1 Tbsp. chopped sun-dried tomatoes (not packed in oil)
- 1¼ tsp. dried savory
- 1½ cups sliced fresh mushrooms
- ⅓ cup sliced onion
- 1½ cups hot cooked egg noodles

1. Rub pork with salt and pepper; cut in half. In a 1½-qt. slow cooker, combine the cornstarch, ½ cup crushed tomatoes, sun-dried tomatoes and savory. Top with mushrooms, onion and pork. Pour remaining tomatoes over pork. Cover and cook on low for 3-4 hours or until the meat is tender.

2. Remove pork and cut into slices. Stir the cooking juices until smooth; serve with pork and noodles.

1 serving: 360 cal., 7g fat (2g sat. fat), 122mg chol., 309mg sod., 32g carb. (3g sugars, 3g fiber), 40g pro. **Diabetic exchanges:** 5 lean meat, 2 vegetable, 1 starch.

Baked Mushroom Pork Ragout: Assemble as directed, using a greased 1½-qt. baking dish. Cover dish and bake at 425° for 30-35 minutes or until a thermometer inserted in pork reads 160°. Serve as directed.

SHRIMP PASTA PRIMAVERA

They say the way to a man's heart is through his stomach. So when I invite my special guy to dinner, I like to prepare something equally special. This well-seasoned pasta dish has lots of flavor...and it won't hurt your budget!
—*Shari Neff, Takoma Park, MD*

- -

Takes: 15 min. • **Makes:** 2 servings

- 4 oz. uncooked angel hair pasta
- 8 jumbo shrimp, peeled and deveined
- 6 fresh asparagus spears, trimmed and cut into 2-in. pieces
- ¼ cup olive oil
- 2 garlic cloves, minced
- ½ cup sliced fresh mushrooms
- ½ cup chicken broth
- 1 small plum tomato, peeled, seeded and diced
- ¼ tsp. salt
- ⅛ tsp. crushed red pepper flakes
- 1 Tbsp. each minced fresh basil, oregano, thyme and parsley
- ¼ cup grated Parmesan cheese

1. Cook pasta according to the package directions. Meanwhile, in a large skillet, saute shrimp and asparagus in oil for 3-4 minutes or until the shrimp turn pink. Add garlic; cook 1 minute longer. Add the mushrooms, broth, tomato, salt and pepper flakes; simmer, uncovered, for 2 minutes.

2. Drain the pasta. Add the pasta and seasoning to the skillet; toss to coat. Sprinkle with cheese.

1 serving: 581 cal., 32g fat (6g sat. fat), 89mg chol., 783mg sod., 49g carb. (4g sugars, 3g fiber), 24g pro.

TANGY GLAZED CHICKEN

This finger-licking citrus sauce offers a hint of sweet apple jelly, making it perfect over bone-in chicken breasts. Serve them with potatoes or rice and a salad if you wish.
—*Barbara Haney, St Louis, MO*

- -

Prep: 15 min. • **Cook:** 30 min.
Makes: 2 servings

- 2 bone-in chicken breast halves (8 oz. each)
- ¼ tsp. salt, optional
- 4½ tsp. butter
- 1 small onion, thinly sliced
- 1 celery rib, thinly sliced
- ½ cup chicken broth
- ½ cup apple jelly
- 3 Tbsp. orange juice
- 1 Tbsp. minced fresh parsley
- ¼ to ½ tsp. dried thyme

1. Sprinkle chicken with salt if desired. In a large skillet, melt butter over medium heat; brown chicken on all sides. Remove from skillet and keep warm.

2. In the pan drippings, saute onion and celery until tender. Add the remaining ingredients; cook and stir until jelly is melted. Return chicken to pan. Cook, uncovered, for 30-35 minutes or until a thermometer reads 170°. Remove skin if desired. Top chicken with onion mixture.

1 serving: 505 cal., 13g fat (3g sat. fat), 101mg chol., 363mg sod., 59g carb. (53g sugars, 1g fiber), 39g pro.

SALMON SALAD WITH GLAZED WALNUTS

This main-dish salad was inspired by a meal I enjoyed on a trip. The glazed walnuts make it something special. I'll also top this with grilled chicken or portobello mushrooms.
—*Joanna Kobernik, Berkley, MI*

- -

Takes: 15 min. • **Makes:** 2 servings

  2   **salmon fillets (4 oz. each)**
  6   **Tbsp. reduced-fat balsamic vinaigrette, divided**
  ⅛   **tsp. pepper**
  4   **cups spring mix salad greens**
  ¼   **cup glazed walnuts**
  2   **Tbsp. crumbled blue cheese**

1. Brush salmon with 2 Tbsp. vinaigrette; sprinkle with pepper. On a greased grill rack, cook salmon, covered, over medium heat or broil 4 in. from heat just until the fish begins to flake easily with a fork, 3-4 minutes on each side.

2. In a bowl, toss salad greens with the remaining vinaigrette. Divide between two plates; sprinkle with walnuts and cheese. Top with the salmon.

1 serving: 374 cal., 25g fat (5g sat. fat), 64mg chol., 607mg sod., 13g carb. (8g sugars, 4g fiber), 24g pro. **Diabetic exchanges:** 3 lean meat, 3 fat, ½ starch.

PUFFY APPLE OMELET

This is one omelet you'll never forget because of its unique and delicious flavors!
—*Melissa Davenport, Campbell, MN*

- -

Prep: 15 min. • **Bake:** 20 min.
Makes: 2 servings

  3   **Tbsp. all-purpose flour**
  ¼   **tsp. baking powder**
  2   **large eggs, separated**
  3   **Tbsp. fat-free milk**
  1   **Tbsp. lemon juice**
  3   **Tbsp. sugar**
TOPPING
  1   **large tart apple, peeled and thinly sliced**
  1   **tsp. sugar**
  ¼   **tsp. ground cinnamon**

1. Preheat oven to 375°. In a small bowl, combine flour and baking powder. In another bowl, whisk egg yolks, milk and lemon juice; add to dry ingredients and mix well. Set aside.

2. In a small bowl, beat the egg whites on medium speed until soft peaks form. Gradually beat in sugar, 1 Tbsp. at a time, on high until stiff peaks form. Fold into the yolk mixture.

3. Pour into a shallow 1½-qt. baking dish coated with cooking spray. Arrange apple slices on top. Combine the sugar and cinnamon; sprinkle over the apples.

4. Bake, uncovered, 18-20 minutes or until a knife inserted in the center comes out clean. Cut in half.

½ omelet: 249 cal., 5g fat (2g sat. fat), 212mg chol., 130mg sod., 44g carb. (32g sugars, 2g fiber), 9g pro. **Diabetic exchanges:** 2 starch, 1 lean meat, 1 fruit.

RAINBOW HASH

To get everyone to eat outside their comfort zone, I use lots of color. This happy hash for two combines sweet potato, carrot, purple potato and kale.
—*Courtney Stultz, Weir, KS*

- -

Takes: 30 min • **Makes:** 2 servings

2 Tbsp. olive or coconut oil
1 medium sweet potato, peeled and cubed
1 medium purple potato, peeled and cubed
1 large carrot, peeled and cubed
½ tsp. dried oregano
½ tsp. dried basil
½ tsp. sea salt
½ tsp. pepper
2 cups coarsely chopped fresh kale or spinach
1 small garlic clove, minced

In a large skillet, heat oil over medium heat. Cook and stir potatoes, carrot and seasonings until the vegetables are tender, 10-12 minutes. Add kale and garlic; continue cooking until the vegetables are lightly browned and the kale is tender, 2-4 minutes.

1 cup: 304 cal., 14g fat (2g sat. fat), 0 chol., 523mg sod., 43g carb. (12g sugars, 5g fiber), 4g pro.

LEMONY CHICKEN VELVET SOUP

Here's the perfect antidote to a chilly spring day! The lively flavor of lemon perks up a rich chicken soup accented with sugar snap peas.
—*Celeste Buckley, Redding, CA*

- -

Takes: 25 min. • **Makes:** 2 servings

2 Tbsp. butter
2 Tbsp. all-purpose flour
1 can (14½ oz.) chicken broth
3 Tbsp. lemon juice
1½ cups cubed cooked chicken breast
10 fresh or frozen sugar snap peas
2 Tbsp. minced fresh parsley
1 tsp. grated lemon zest
3 Tbsp. heavy whipping cream

1. In a small saucepan, melt butter. Stir in flour until smooth; gradually add broth and lemon juice. Bring to a boil; cook and stir for 1-2 minutes or until thickened.
2. Stir in the chicken, peas, parsley and lemon zest; cook 2-3 minutes longer or until the chicken is heated through and the peas are crisp-tender. Stir in cream; heat through (do not boil).

1¼ cups: 352 cal., 18g fat (10g sat. fat), 131mg chol., 730mg sod., 13g carb. (4g sugars, 2g fiber), 37g pro.

Slow Cooker

Whether it's a hearty stew waiting for you when you get home, a tasty holiday side cooking away while your oven is full of other dishes, or a perfect party food kept hot and ready to eat on a buffet, slow-cooker recipes are magic. Here are 29 recipes that prove slow cooking is the ultimate in comfort and convenience!

ORANGE SPICE CARROTS

To get my son to eat veggies, I mix and match flavors and spices. My slow-cooker carrots with orange and cinnamon won him over. For a little extra zing, try topping them with some added orange zest.

—*Christina Addison, Blanchester, OH*

- -

Prep: 10 min. • **Cook:** 4 hours
Makes: 6 servings

- 2 lbs. medium carrots or baby carrots, cut into 1-in. pieces
- ½ cup packed brown sugar
- ½ cup orange juice
- 2 Tbsp. butter
- ¾ tsp. ground cinnamon
- ½ tsp. salt
- ¼ tsp. ground nutmeg
- 4 tsp. cornstarch
- ¼ cup cold water

1. In a 3-qt. slow cooker, combine the first seven ingredients. Cook, covered, on low 4-5 hours or until carrots are tender.
2. In a small bowl, mix cornstarch and water until smooth; gradually stir into the carrot mixture until the sauce is thickened, 1-2 minutes.

⅔ cup: 187 cal., 4g fat (3g sat. fat), 10mg chol., 339mg sod., 38g carb. (27g sugars, 4g fiber), 2g pro.

MEAT LOAF FROM THE SLOW COOKER

This easy-to-make meat loaf is one of my personal favorites. The spicy-sweet sauce is a delicious alternative to plain ketchup.

—*Laura Burgess, Mount Vernon, SD*

- -

Prep: 25 min. • **Cook:** 3 hours
Makes: 8 servings

- ½ cup tomato sauce
- 2 large eggs, lightly beaten
- ¼ cup ketchup
- 1 tsp. Worcestershire sauce
- 1 small onion, chopped
- ⅓ cup crushed saltines (about 10 crackers)
- ¾ tsp. minced garlic
- ¼ tsp. seasoned salt
- ⅛ tsp. seasoned pepper
- 1½ lbs. lean ground beef (90% lean)
- ½ lb. reduced-fat bulk pork sausage

SAUCE
- ½ cup ketchup
- 3 Tbsp. brown sugar
- ¾ tsp. ground mustard
- ¼ tsp. ground nutmeg

1. Cut three 25x3-in. strips of heavy-duty foil; crisscross strips so they resemble spokes of a wheel. Place strips on the bottom and up the sides of a 4- or 5-qt. slow cooker. Coat with cooking spray.
2. Combine the first nine ingredients. Crumble the beef and sausage over top and mix well (the mixture will be moist). Shape into a loaf. Place loaf in the center of the strips.
3. Combine all the sauce ingredients; spoon over the meat loaf. Cover and cook on low for 3-4 hours or until no pink remains and a thermometer reads 160°. Using the foil strips as handles, remove loaf to a platter.

1 slice: 284 cal., 14g fat (5g sat. fat), 119mg chol., 681mg sod., 16g carb. (12g sugars, 1g fiber), 24g pro. **Diabetic exchanges:** 3 lean meat, 1 starch.

EASY SLOW-COOKER CHICKEN ROPA VIEJA

When discussing various ways to cook ropa vieja, a friend of mine told me her sister adds apple juice. I thought a Granny Smith apple might give it an extra kick— and it does. This savory stew may be served over hominy or tortillas—but plantains add a special touch.
—Arlene Erlbach, Morton Grove, IL

- -

Prep: 20 min. • **Cook:** 5 hours
Makes: 6 Servings

- 2 medium sweet red peppers, sliced
- 1 medium Granny Smith apple, peeled chopped
- 1 cup fresh cilantro leaves
- 1 cup chunky salsa
- 2 Tbsp. tomato paste
- 1 garlic clove, minced
- 1 tsp. ground cumin
- 5 tsp. adobo seasoning, divided
- 1½ lbs. boneless skinless chicken thighs
- 3 to 6 tsp. lime juice
- ¼ cup butter

- 3 ripe plantains, peeled and thinly sliced into thin rounds
  Hot cooked rice, lime wedges and additional fresh cilantro leaves, optional

1. Place the first seven ingredients and 1 tsp. of the adobo seasoning in a 5- or 6-qt. slow cooker. Rub the remaining adobo seasoning over the chicken; add to the slow cooker. Cook, covered, on low until the chicken is tender, 5-6 hours. Using two forks, shred chicken. Stir in lime juice to taste; heat through.
2. Meanwhile, heat butter in a large skillet over medium heat. Cook plantains in batches until tender and golden brown, about 3 minutes each side. Drain plantains on paper towels.
3. Serve chicken with plantains using a slotted spoon. If desired, serve with rice, lime wedges and cilantro.
1 serving: 387 cal., 16g fat (7g sat. fat), 96mg chol., 1428mg sod., 39g carb. (20g sugars, 4g fiber), 23g pro.

Contest Winner

POTATO CHOWDER

One of the ladies in our church quilting group brought this savory potato soup to a meeting, and everyone loved how the cream cheese and bacon made it so rich. It's easy to assemble in the morning so it can simmer on its own all day.
—Anna Mayer, Fort Branch, IN

- -

Prep: 15 min. • **Cook:** 8 hours
Makes: 12 servings (3 qt.)

- 8 cups diced potatoes
- 3 cans (14½ oz. each) chicken broth
- 1 can (10¾ oz.) condensed cream of chicken soup, undiluted
- ⅓ cup chopped onion
- ¼ tsp. pepper
- 1 pkg. (8 oz.) cream cheese, cubed
- ½ lb. sliced bacon, cooked and crumbled, optional
  Minced chives, optional

1. In a 5-qt. slow cooker, combine the first five ingredients. Cover and cook on low for 8-10 hours or until the potatoes are tender.
2. Add cream cheese; stir until blended. Garnish with bacon and chives if desired.
1 cup: 179 cal., 9g fat (5g sat. fat), 25mg chol., 690mg sod., 21g carb. (2g sugars, 2g fiber), 4g pro.

SLOW-COOKER BACON MAC & CHEESE

I'm all about easy slow-cooker meals. Using more cheese than ever, I've developed an addictive spin on this casserole favorite.
—*Kristen Heigl, Staten Island, NY*

Prep: 20 min. • **Cook:** 3 hours + standing
Makes: 18 servings

2   large eggs, lightly beaten
4   cups whole milk
1   can (12 oz.) evaporated milk
¼   cup butter, melted
1   Tbsp. all-purpose flour
1   tsp. salt
1   pkg. (16 oz.) small pasta shells
1   cup shredded provolone cheese
1   cup shredded Manchego or Monterey Jack cheese
1   cup shredded white cheddar cheese
8   bacon strips, cooked and crumbled

1. Whisk the first six ingredients until blended. Stir in pasta and cheeses; transfer to a 4- or 5-qt. slow cooker.
2. Cook, covered, on low 3-3½ hours or until pasta is tender. Turn off slow cooker; remove insert. Let stand, uncovered, for 15 minutes before serving. Top with bacon.
½ cup: 272 cal., 14g fat (8g sat. fat), 59mg chol., 400mg sod., 24g carb. (5g sugars, 1g fiber), 13g pro.

SLOW-COOKER BANANAS FOSTER

The flavors of caramel, rum and walnut naturally complement fresh bananas in this classic dessert made easy! It's my go-to choice for any family get-together.
—*Crystal Jo Bruns, Iliff, CO*

Prep: 10 min. • **Cook:** 2 hours
Makes: 5 servings

5   medium firm bananas
1   cup packed brown sugar
¼   cup butter, melted
¼   cup rum
1   tsp. vanilla extract
½   tsp. ground cinnamon
⅓   cup chopped walnuts
⅓   cup sweetened shredded coconut
    Vanilla ice cream or sliced pound cake

1. Cut bananas in half lengthwise, then widthwise; layer in the bottom of a 1½-qt. slow cooker. Combine the brown sugar, butter, rum, vanilla and cinnamon; pour over bananas. Cover and cook on low for 1½ hours or until heated through.
2. Sprinkle with walnuts and coconut; cook 30 minutes longer. Serve with ice cream or pound cake.
1 serving: 462 cal., 17g fat (8g sat. fat), 24mg chol., 99mg sod., 74g carb. (59g sugars, 4g fiber), 3g pro.

SECRET'S IN THE SAUCE BBQ RIBS

Slow-cooking makes these ribs so tender the meat literally falls off the bones. And the sweet, rich sauce is simply wonderful. Yum!
—*Tanya Reid, Winston-Salem, NC*

Prep: 10 min. • **Cook:** 6 hours
Makes: 5 servings

- 4½ lbs. pork baby back ribs
- 1½ tsp. pepper
- 2½ cups barbecue sauce
- ¾ cup cherry preserves
- 1 Tbsp. Dijon mustard
- 1 garlic clove, minced

Cut ribs into serving-size pieces; sprinkle with pepper. Place in a 5- or 6-qt. slow cooker. Combine remaining ingredients; pour over the ribs. Cook, covered, on low until the meat is tender, 6-8 hours. Serve with sauce.

1 serving: 921 cal., 58g fat (21g sat. fat), 220mg chol., 1402mg sod., 50g carb. (45g sugars, 2g fiber), 48g pro.

Contest Winner

SLOW-COOKED HAM WITH PINEAPPLE SAUCE

We serve this dish during the holidays—everyone is crazy about it. But we also enjoy it all year long because it's super simple to prepare.
—*Terry Roberts, Yorktown, VA*

Prep: 10 min. • **Cook:** 6 hours
Makes: 12 servings

- 1 fully cooked boneless ham (4 to 5 lbs.)
- 1 Tbsp. cornstarch
- 2 Tbsp. lemon juice
- 1 cup packed brown sugar
- 1 Tbsp. yellow mustard
- ¼ tsp. salt
- 1 can (20 oz.) unsweetened crushed pineapple, undrained

Place ham in a 5-qt. slow cooker. In a small saucepan, mix cornstarch and lemon juice until smooth. Stir in the remaining ingredients; bring to a boil, stirring occasionally. Pour over ham, covering completely. Cook, covered, on low 6-8 hours (a thermometer inserted in ham should read at least 140°).
Note: This recipe is not recommended for a spiral-sliced ham.

4 oz. ham with ¼ cup sauce: 262 cal., 6g fat (2g sat. fat), 77mg chol., 1638mg sod., 27g carb. (25g sugars, 0 fiber), 28g pro.

SLOW-COOKER SAUSAGE LASAGNA

This delicious lasagna is oh, so welcome on especially cold winter days. My family loves mild Italian sausage but I prefer the spicy version, which gives it a bit of a zing.
—Cindi DeClue, Anchorage, AK

- -

Prep: 40 min. • **Cook:** 3½ hours + standing
Makes: 8 servings

- 1   lb. ground beef
- 1   lb. ground mild Italian sausage
- 1   medium onion, finely chopped
- 1   garlic clove, minced
- 1   jar (24 oz.) spaghetti sauce
- 1   can (14½ oz.) diced tomatoes in sauce, undrained
- ½   cup water
- 1   tsp. dried basil
- 1   tsp. dried oregano
- 1   carton (15 oz.) whole-milk ricotta cheese
- 2   large eggs, lightly beaten
- ½   cup grated Parmesan cheese
- 9   uncooked lasagna noodles
- 4   cups shredded part-skim mozzarella cheese
     Minced fresh basil, optional

1. Line the sides of an oval 6-qt. slow cooker with heavy-duty foil; coat foil with cooking spray.

2. In a Dutch oven, cook the beef, sausage, onion and garlic over medium heat for 8-10 minutes or until the meat is no longer pink, breaking up the beef and sausage into crumbles; drain. Stir in spaghetti sauce, tomatoes, water and herbs; heat through.

3. In a small bowl, mix ricotta cheese, eggs and Parmesan cheese. Spread 1½ cups meat sauce onto the bottom of the prepared slow cooker. Layer with three noodles (breaking to fit as necessary), ¾ cup ricotta mixture, 1 cup mozzarella cheese and 2 cups meat sauce. Repeat layers twice. Sprinkle with the remaining mozzarella cheese.

4. Cook, covered, on low 3½-4 hours or until the noodles are tender. Turn off the slow cooker; remove insert. Let stand for 15 minutes. If desired, sprinkle lasagna with fresh basil.

1 serving: 667 cal., 37g fat (17g sat. fat), 164mg chol., 1310mg sod., 41g carb. (14g sugars, 4g fiber), 42g pro.

SLOW-COOKER CINNAMON ROLL PUDDING

A slow cooker turns day-old cinnamon rolls into a comforting, old-fashioned dessert. This dish tastes wonderful topped with lemon or vanilla sauce or whipped cream.

—Edna Hoffman, Hebron, IN

- -

Prep: 15 min. • **Cook:** 3 hours
Makes: 6 servings

- 8 cups cubed day-old unfrosted cinnamon rolls
- 4 large eggs
- 2 cups whole milk
- ¼ cup sugar
- ¼ cup butter, melted
- ½ tsp. vanilla extract
- ¼ tsp. ground nutmeg
- 1 cup raisins

Place cubed cinnamon rolls in a 3-qt. slow cooker. In a small bowl, whisk the eggs, milk, sugar, butter, vanilla and nutmeg. Stir in raisins. Pour over the cinnamon rolls; stir gently. Cover and cook on low for 3 hours or until a knife inserted in the center comes out clean.

Note: 8 slices of cinnamon or white bread, cut into 1-in. cubes, may be substituted for the cinnamon rolls.

1 serving: 570 cal., 27g fat (10g sat. fat), 226mg chol., 468mg sod., 72g carb. (53g sugars, 3g fiber), 13g pro.

SLOW-COOKED MINESTRONE SOUP

When this hearty minestrone has about 30 minutes left to cook, I add the macaroni. Then there's time to toss together a salad and slice some French bread. It all comes together for a deliciously simple meal.

—Kara de la Vega, Santa Rosa, CA

- -

Prep: 15 min. • **Cook:** 7 hours
Makes: 10 servings

- 6 cups chicken broth
- 1 can (15 oz.) garbanzo beans or chickpeas, rinsed and drained
- 1 medium potato, peeled and cubed
- 1 cup cubed deli ham
- ⅓ cup chopped onion
- 1 small carrot, chopped
- 1 celery rib, chopped
- 2 Tbsp. minced fresh parsley
- ½ tsp. minced garlic
- ½ cup uncooked elbow macaroni
- 1 can (14½ oz.) diced tomatoes, undrained
- 1 pkg. (10 oz.) frozen chopped spinach, thawed and squeezed dry

1. In a 5-qt. slow cooker, combine the first nine ingredients. Cover and cook on high for 1 hour. Reduce heat to low; cook for 6-8 hours or until the vegetables are almost tender.

2. During the last 30 minutes of cooking, stir in macaroni. Cover and cook until the macaroni is tender. Stir in tomatoes and spinach; heat through.

1 cup: 112 cal., 2g fat (0 sat. fat), 6mg chol., 885mg sod., 17g carb. (4g sugars, 4g fiber), 8g pro.

Instant Pot™ Perfection

The flip side of cooking it slow is cooking it fast—ultra fast, with an electric pressure cooker. These delicious meals will make gadget-happy home cooks even happier, and get food on the table in an Instant.

PRESSURE-COOKER CHEESY BACON SPAGHETTI SQUASH

This quick casserole is called cheesy for a reason. The recipe calls for Swiss, but feel free to stir in any kind of cheese you have in the fridge—or use a blend of your favorites to make this dish your own.

—Jean Williams, Stillwater, OK

Takes: 30 min. • **Makes:** 4 servings

1   large spaghetti squash (3½ lbs.)
4   bacon strips, chopped
3   Tbsp. butter
1   Tbsp. brown sugar
½   tsp. salt
¼   tsp. pepper
½   cup shredded Swiss cheese

1. Cut the squash in half lengthwise; remove and discard seeds. Place trivet insert and 1 cup water in a 6-qt. electric pressure cooker. Place squash, cut side down, on trivet. Lock lid; close pressure-release valve. Adjust to pressure-cook on high for 7 minutes. Quick-release pressure. Press cancel. Remove the squash, trivet and water from cooker.
2. Select saute setting and adjust for medium heat; add the bacon, stirring occasionally, and cook until crisp. With a slotted spoon, remove the bacon to paper towels; reserve drippings. Stir in the butter, brown sugar, salt and pepper. Separate the squash strands with a fork and add to cooker; toss and heat through. Remove from heat. Press cancel.
3. Transfer to a serving bowl; stir in Swiss cheese. Top with bacon.
1 cup: 383 cal., 26g fat (12g sat. fat), 54mg chol., 643mg sod., 31g carb. (4g sugars, 6g fiber), 10g pro.

PRESSURE-COOKER FABULOUS FAJITAS

When friends ask for new recipes to try, I suggest these flavorful fajitas. It's wonderful to put the beef in the pressure cooker and have a hot, delicious main dish.

—Taste of Home Test Kitchen

Prep: 20 min. • **Cook:** 25 min. + releasing
Makes: 8 servings

1½ lbs. beef top sirloin steak, cut into thin strips
1½ tsp. ground cumin
½   tsp. seasoned salt
½   tsp. chili powder
¼   to ½ tsp. crushed red pepper flakes
2   Tbsp. canola oil
2   Tbsp. lemon juice
1   garlic clove, minced
1   large sweet red pepper, thinly sliced
1   large onion, thinly sliced
8   flour tortillas (8 in.), warmed
    Optional toppings: sliced avocado and jalapeno peppers, shredded cheddar cheese and chopped tomatoes

1. In a bowl, toss the steak with cumin, salt, chili powder and red pepper flakes. On a 6-qt. electric pressure cooker, select the saute setting and adjust for high heat. Add oil. When oil is hot, brown the meat in batches and remove. Add lemon juice and garlic to cooker; stir to loosen any browned bits. Return the beef to cooker. Lock lid; close pressure-release valve. Select manual setting; adjust pressure to high and set time for 20 minutes.
2. When finished cooking, allow pressure to naturally release for 10 minutes, then quick-release pressure. Press cancel. Remove steak; keep warm.
3. Add red pepper and onion to cooker; lock lid. Adjust to pressure-cook on high for 5 minutes. When finished cooking, quick-release pressure. Press cancel. Serve vegetables and steak with tortillas and desired toppings.
1 fajita: 314 cal., 11g fat (2g sat. fat), 34mg chol., 374mg sod., 31g carb. (1g sugars, 2g fiber), 23g pro. **Diabetic exchanges:** 3 lean meat, 2 starch, 1 fat.

PRESSURE-COOKER CHICKEN THIGHS IN WINE SAUCE

I adore this recipe because it has amazing flavor. Everyone who has tried it loves it just as much as I do. For an easy meal, pair it with mashed potatoes and peas to soak up all the delicious sauce.
—*Heike Annucci, Hudson, NC*

Prep: 15 min. • **Cook:** 20 min. + releasing
Makes: 4 servings

- 2 Tbsp. butter, divided
- 1 cup sliced fresh mushrooms
- 6 bone-in chicken thighs, skin removed (about 2¼ lbs.)
- ¼ tsp. salt
- ¼ tsp. pepper
- ¼ tsp. Italian seasoning
- ¼ tsp. paprika
- ⅓ cup all-purpose flour
- ½ cup chicken broth
- ½ cup white wine or additional chicken broth
- 3 green onions, thinly sliced

1. Select saute setting on a 6-qt. electric pressure cooker and adjust for medium heat. Add 1 Tbsp. of the butter. When hot, add mushrooms; cook until tender, 3-4 minutes. Remove. Sprinkle chicken with salt, pepper, Italian seasoning and paprika. Place flour in a shallow bowl. Add the chicken, a few pieces at a time, and toss to coat; shake off excess.
2. Heat the remaining butter in pressure cooker; brown the chicken on both sides. Remove. Add broth and wine to cooker; increase heat to medium-high. Cook for 2-3 minutes, stirring to loosen any browned bits.
3. Return the chicken and mushrooms to the pressure cooker; add green onions. Lock lid; close pressure-release valve. Select manual setting; adjust pressure to high, and set time for 10 minutes. When finished cooking, allow the pressure to naturally release for 10 minutes; then quick-release pressure.
1 serving: 243 cal., 13g fat (5g sat. fat), 97mg chol., 284mg sod., 3g carb. (1g sugars, 0 fiber), 25g pro. **Diabetic exchanges:** 3 lean meat, 1½ fat.

SLOW IT DOWN

To slow-cook this recipe, place browned chicken and mushrooms in slow cooker; add remaining ingredients and cook on low until chicken is tender, 3-4 hours.

EASY RIGATONI WITH SAUSAGE & PEAS

With a tomato-y meat sauce and tangy goat cheese, this weeknight wonder is my personal version of comfort food. You just want to have bowl after bowl.
—*Lizzie Munro, Brooklyn, NY*

Takes: 30 min. • **Makes:** 6 servings

- 1 lb. bulk Italian sausage
- 4 garlic cloves, minced
- ¼ cup tomato paste
- 12 oz. uncooked rigatoni or large tube pasta
- 1½ cups frozen peas
- 1 can (28 oz.) crushed tomatoes
- ½ tsp. dried basil
- ¼ to ½ tsp. crushed red pepper flakes
- 4 cups water
- ½ cup heavy whipping cream
- ½ cup crumbled goat or feta cheese
  Thinly sliced fresh basil, optional

1. Select saute setting on a 6-qt. electric pressure cooker and adjust for high heat. Cook and crumble the sausage until no longer pink, 4-6 minutes. Add the minced garlic; cook 1 minute longer. Add tomato paste; cook and stir until meat is coated, 1-2 minutes. Stir in next five ingredients; pour in water. Lock lid; close pressure-release valve. Select manual setting; adjust pressure to low and set time for 6 minutes. When finished cooking, quick-release pressure. Press cancel.
2. Stir in cream; heat through. Top with cheese and, if desired, fresh basil.
1⅔ cups: 563 cal., 28g fat (12g sat. fat), 75mg chol., 802mg sod., 60g carb. (11g sugars, 7g fiber), 23g pro.

SLOW-COOKED BEANS

This flavorful bean dish adds nice variety to any buffet, because it's a bit different from traditional baked beans. It's a snap to prepare, too, since it uses convenient canned beans, barbecue sauce and salsa.
—*Joy Beck, Cincinnati, OH*

Prep: 10 min. • **Cook:** 2 hours
Makes: 16 servings

  4 cans (15½ oz. each) great northern
     beans, rinsed and drained
  4 cans (15 oz. each) black
     beans, rinsed and drained
  2 cans (15 oz. each) butter
     beans, rinsed and drained
2¼ cups barbecue sauce
2¼ cups salsa
  ¾ cup packed brown sugar
  ½ to 1 tsp. hot pepper sauce

In a 6-qt. slow cooker, gently combine all the ingredients. Cook, covered, on low until heated through, about 2 hours.
1 serving: 134 cal., 1g fat (0 sat. fat), 0 chol., 657mg sod., 27g carb. (16g sugars, 5g fiber), 4g pro.

PARSLEY SMASHED POTATOES

I love mashed potatoes but hate the work involved. So I came up with a simple side dish that my slow cooker made even easier. Save the leftover broth for soup the next day!
—*Katie Hagy, Blacksburg, SC*

Prep: 20 min. • **Cook:** 6 hours
Makes: 8 servings

 16 small red potatoes (about 2 lbs.)
  1 celery rib, sliced
  1 medium carrot, sliced
  ¼ cup finely chopped onion
  2 cups chicken broth
  1 Tbsp. minced fresh parsley
1½ tsp. salt, divided
  1 tsp. pepper, divided
  1 garlic clove, minced
  2 Tbsp. butter, melted
     Additional minced fresh parsley

1. Place the potatoes, celery, carrot and onion in a 4-qt. slow cooker. In a small bowl, mix the broth, parsley, 1 tsp. salt, ½ tsp. pepper and the garlic; pour over the vegetables. Cook, covered, on low for 6-8 hours or until the potatoes are tender.
2. Transfer potatoes from slow cooker to a 15x10x1-in. pan; discard cooking liquid and vegetables. Using the bottom of a measuring cup, flatten the potatoes slightly. Transfer to a large bowl; drizzle with butter. Sprinkle with the remaining salt and pepper; toss to coat. Sprinkle with additional parsley.
2 smashed potatoes: 114 cal., 3g fat (2g sat. fat), 8mg chol., 190mg sod., 20g carb. (2g sugars, 2g fiber), 2g pro. **Diabetic exchanges:** 1 starch, ½ fat.

HEARTY HOMEMADE CHICKEN NOODLE SOUP

This satisfying homemade soup with a hint of cayenne is brimming with vegetables, chicken and noodles. The original recipe was from my father-in-law, but I made some adjustments to give it my own spin.

—Norma Reynolds, Overland Park, KS

Prep: 20 min. • **Cook:** 5½ hours
Makes: 12 servings (3 qt.)

- 12 fresh baby carrots, cut into ½-in. pieces
- 4 celery ribs, cut into ½-in. pieces
- ¾ cup finely chopped onion
- 1 Tbsp. minced fresh parsley
- ½ tsp. pepper
- ¼ tsp. cayenne pepper
- 1½ tsp. mustard seed
- 2 garlic cloves, peeled and halved
- 1¼ lbs. boneless skinless chicken breast halves
- 1¼ lbs. boneless skinless chicken thighs
- 4 cans (14½ oz. each) chicken broth
- 1 pkg. (9 oz.) refrigerated linguine Coarsely ground pepper and additional minced fresh parsley, optional

1. In a 5-qt. slow cooker, combine the first six ingredients. Place the mustard seed and garlic on a double thickness of cheesecloth; bring up the corners of the cloth and tie with kitchen string to form a bag. Place bag in slow cooker. Add the chicken and broth. Cover and cook on low for 5-6 hours or until the meat is tender.

2. Discard the spice bag. Remove chicken; let cool slightly. Stir linguine into the soup; cover and cook on high for 30 minutes or until tender. Cut chicken into pieces and return to soup; heat through. Sprinkle, if desired, with coarsely ground pepper and additional parsley.

1 cup: 199 cal., 6g fat (2g sat. fat), 73mg chol., 663mg sod., 14g carb. (2g sugars, 1g fiber), 22g pro. **Diabetic exchanges:** 3 lean meat, 1 starch.

HERBED TURKEY BREASTS

Tender, moist turkey breast is enhanced with an array of flavorful herbs in this comforting recipe. It's so juicy and delicious!
—*Laurie Mace, Los Osos, CA*

Prep: 25 min. + marinating • **Cook:** 3½ hours
Makes: 12 servings

- 1 can (14½ oz.) chicken broth
- ½ cup lemon juice
- ¼ cup packed brown sugar
- ¼ cup fresh sage
- ¼ cup fresh thyme leaves
- ¼ cup lime juice
- ¼ cup cider vinegar
- ¼ cup olive oil
- 1 envelope onion soup mix
- 2 Tbsp. Dijon mustard
- 1 Tbsp. minced fresh marjoram
- 1½ tsp. paprika
- 1 tsp. garlic powder
- 1 tsp. pepper
- ½ tsp. salt
- 2 boneless skinless turkey breast halves (2 lbs. each)

1. In a blender, process the first 15 ingredients until blended. Pour the marinade into a large bowl; add turkey and turn to coat. Cover; refrigerate for 8 hours or overnight.
2. Transfer turkey and marinade to a 5-qt. slow cooker. Cover and cook on high for 3½-4½ hours or until a thermometer reads 165°.

5 oz. cooked turkey: 219 cal., 5g fat (1g sat. fat), 87mg chol., 484mg sod., 5g carb. (3g sugars, 0 fiber), 36g pro. **Diabetic exchanges:** 5 lean meat, ½ fat.

CONTEST-WINNING CHICKEN CACCIATORE

My husband and I own and operate a busy farm. There are days when there's just no time left for cooking! It's really nice to be able to come into the house at night and smell this wonderful dinner simmering.
—*Aggie Arnold-Norman, Liberty, PA*

Prep: 15 min. • **Cook:** 6 hours
Makes: 6 servings

- 2 medium onions, thinly sliced
- 1 broiler/fryer chicken (3 to 4 lbs.), cut up and skin removed
- 2 garlic cloves, minced
- 1 to 2 tsp. dried oregano
- 1 tsp. salt
- ½ tsp. dried basil
- ¼ tsp. pepper
- 1 bay leaf
- 1 can (14½ oz.) diced tomatoes, undrained
- 1 can (8 oz.) tomato sauce
- 1 can (4 oz.) mushroom stems and pieces, drained, or 1 cup sliced fresh mushrooms
- ¼ cup white wine or water
  Hot cooked pasta

1. Place onions in a 5-qt. slow cooker. Add the chicken, seasonings, tomatoes, tomato sauce, mushrooms and wine.
2. Cover and cook on low for 6-8 hours or until chicken is tender. Discard bay leaf. Serve chicken with sauce over pasta.

1 serving: 207 cal., 6g fat (2g sat. fat), 73mg chol., 787mg sod., 11g carb. (6g sugars, 3g fiber), 27g pro. **Diabetic exchanges:** 4 lean meat, 2 vegetable.

BACON-BEEF BARLEY SOUP

Here's a robust dish that's perfect for hungry teenage boys! Served over creamy mashed potatoes, this quick, comforting soup will really hit the spot.

—Cathy Peterson, Menominee, MI

- -

Prep: 40 min. • **Cook:** 7 hours
Makes: 7 servings

- 4 bacon strips, chopped
- 1½ lbs. beef stew meat, cut into ½-in. pieces
- 1 medium onion, chopped
- 4 medium red potatoes, cut into ½-in. cubes
- 1½ cups fresh baby carrots, cut in half lengthwise
- 1 cup frozen corn
- ¼ cup medium pearl barley
- 2 cans (14½ oz. each) beef broth
- 1 can (14½ oz.) diced tomatoes with basil, oregano and garlic, undrained
- 1 jar (12 oz.) home-style beef gravy
- ½ tsp. pepper
  Mashed potatoes, optional

1. In a large skillet, cook bacon over medium heat until crisp. Using a slotted spoon, remove to paper towels to drain. In the drippings, cook beef and onion until the meat is browned; drain.

2. In a 5-qt. slow cooker, layer the potatoes, carrots, corn and barley. Top with the beef mixture and the bacon. Combine broth, tomatoes, gravy and pepper; pour over top (do not stir).

3. Cover and cook on low for 7-9 hours or until meat and vegetables are tender. Stir before serving. Serve over mashed potatoes if desired.

1¼ cups: 319 cal., 10g fat (3g sat. fat), 68mg chol., 1218mg sod., 32g carb. (7g sugars, 4g fiber), 26g pro.

CHEESY SPINACH

My daughter often serves this cheese and spinach blend at church suppers. Even people who don't usually eat spinach like this flavorful dish—there is never any left!

—Frances Moore, Decatur, IL

- -

Prep: 10 min. • **Cook:** 5 hours
Makes: 8 servings

- 2 pkg. (10 oz. each) frozen chopped spinach, thawed and well drained
- 2 cups (16 oz.) 4% cottage cheese
- 1½ cups cubed process cheese (Velveeta)
- 3 large eggs, lightly beaten
- ¼ cup butter, cubed
- ¼ cup all-purpose flour
- 1 tsp. salt

In a large bowl, combine all ingredients. Pour into a greased 3-qt. slow cooker. Cover and cook on high for 1 hour. Reduce heat to low; cook 4-5 hours longer or until a knife inserted in the center comes out clean.

¾ cup: 230 cal., 15g fat (9g sat. fat), 121mg chol., 855mg sod., 9g carb. (4g sugars, 1g fiber), 14g pro.

CAROLINA SHRIMP & CHEDDAR GRITS

My family loves shrimp and grits, but for the longest time, we couldn't agree on a recipe. This one, with cheddar and Cajun seasoning, seems to make everyone happy.
—*Charlotte Price, Raleigh, NC*

Prep: 15 min. • **Cook:** 2¾ hours
Makes: 6 servings

- 1 cup uncooked stone-ground grits
- 1 large garlic clove, minced
- ½ tsp. salt
- ¼ tsp. pepper
- 4 cups water
- 2 cups shredded cheddar cheese
- ¼ cup butter, cubed
- 1 lb. peeled and deveined cooked shrimp (31-40 per lb.)
- 2 medium tomatoes, seeded and finely chopped
- 4 green onions, finely chopped
- 2 Tbsp. chopped fresh parsley
- 4 tsp. lemon juice
- 2 to 3 tsp. Cajun seasoning

1. Place the first five ingredients in a 3-qt. slow cooker; stir to combine. Cook, covered, on high for 2½-3 hours or until the water is absorbed and the grits are tender, stirring every 45 minutes.
2. Stir in cheese and butter until melted. Stir in the remaining ingredients; cook, covered, on high 15-30 minutes or until heated through.

1⅓ cups: 417 cal., 22g fat (13g sat. fat), 175mg chol., 788mg sod., 27g carb. (2g sugars, 2g fiber), 27g pro.

MOIST CRANBERRY PORK ROAST

I love to serve guests this tender, flavorful pork. You don't have to toil away in the kitchen to prepare it, yet it tastes like a gourmet meal.
—*Kimberley Scasny, Douglasville, GA*

Prep: 5 min. • **Cook:** 4 hours + standing
Makes: 8 servings

- 1 boneless rolled pork loin roast (2½ to 3 lbs.)
- ½ tsp. salt
- ¼ tsp. pepper
- 1 can (14 oz.) whole-berry cranberry sauce
- ¼ cup honey
- 1 tsp. grated orange zest
- ⅛ tsp. ground cloves
- ⅛ tsp. ground nutmeg

Cut roast in half and place in a 3-qt. slow cooker; sprinkle with salt and pepper. Combine the remaining ingredients; pour over roast. Cover and cook on low for 4-5 hours or until a thermometer reads 160°. Let stand 10 minutes before slicing.

6 oz. cooked pork: 289 cal., 7g fat (2g sat. fat), 70mg chol., 201mg sod., 30g carb. (22g sugars, 1g fiber), 27g pro.

CHEESY SLOW-COOKED CORN

Even those who usually don't reach for corn at the table often ask for seconds once they try this side dish. Folks love the flavor, and I love how easy it is to make with ingredients that I usually have on hand.
—*Mary Ann Truitt, Wichita, KS*

Prep: 5 min. • **Cook:** 3 hours
Makes: 12 servings

- 9½ cups (48 oz.) frozen corn
- 11 oz. cream cheese, softened
- ¼ cup butter, cubed
- 3 Tbsp. water
- 3 Tbsp. whole milk
- 2 Tbsp. sugar
- 6 slices process American cheese, cut into small pieces

In a 4- or 5-qt. slow cooker, combine all ingredients. Cook, covered, on low, until heated through and the cheese is melted, 3-4 hours, stirring once.
1 cup: 265 cal., 16g fat (9g sat. fat), 39mg chol., 227mg sod., 27g carb. (6g sugars, 2g fiber), 7g pro.

SLOW-COOKED CHILI

I like to use my own homemade stewed tomatoes and pizza sauce in this recipe. It's the perfect chili—not too spicy, and a cinch to whip up.
—*Sandy McKenzie, Braham, MN*

Prep: 25 min. • **Cook:** 6 hours
Makes: 14 servings

- 2 lbs. ground beef
- ½ cup chopped onion
- 2 garlic cloves, minced
- 2 cans (16 oz. each) dark red kidney beans, rinsed and drained
- 2 cans (16 oz. each) light red kidney beans, rinsed and drained
- 2 cans (14½ oz. each) stewed tomatoes, cut up
- 1 can (15 oz.) pizza sauce
- 1 can (4 oz.) chopped green chiles
- 4 tsp. chili powder
- 1 tsp. dried basil
- ½ tsp. salt
- ⅛ tsp. pepper

In a Dutch oven, cook the beef, onion and garlic over medium heat until the meat is no longer pink; drain. Transfer to a 5-qt. slow cooker; stir in remaining ingredients. Cover and cook on low for 6 hours.
1 cup: 183 cal., 6g fat (3g sat. fat), 32mg chol., 409mg sod., 16g carb. (4g sugars, 4g fiber), 16g pro.

PINEAPPLE UPSIDE-DOWN DUMP CAKE

No matter what the season, this dump cake recipe is wonderful! It works well with gluten-free and sugar-free cake mixes too.
—*Karin Gatewood, Dallas, TX*

- -

Prep: 10 min. • **Cook:** 2 hours + standing
Makes: 10 servings

¾	cup butter, divided
⅔	cup packed brown sugar
1	jar (6 oz.) maraschino cherries, drained
½	cup chopped pecans, toasted
1	can (20 oz.) unsweetened pineapple tidbits or crushed pineapple, undrained
1	pkg. yellow cake mix (regular size) Vanilla ice cream, optional

1. In a microwave, melt ½ cup butter; stir in brown sugar. Spread evenly onto bottom of a greased 5-qt. slow cooker. Sprinkle with cherries and pecans; top with pineapple. Sprinkle evenly with dry cake mix. Melt the remaining butter; drizzle over top.
2. Cook, covered, on high until the fruit mixture is bubbly, about 2 hours. (To avoid scorching, rotate the slow cooker insert one-half turn midway through the cooking time, lifting it carefully with oven mitts.)
3. Turn off the slow cooker; let stand, uncovered, 30 minutes before serving. If desired, serve with ice cream.
Note: To toast nuts, bake in a shallow pan in a 350° oven for 5-10 minutes or cook in a skillet over low heat until lightly browned, stirring occasionally.
½ cup: 455 cal., 22g fat (10g sat. fat), 37mg chol., 418mg sod., 66g carb. (47g sugars, 1g fiber), 3g pro.

KEEP YOUR LAYERS LEVEL
Sprinkle the cake mix in an even layer over the pineapple. If it's piled high in the center, the middle of the cake may be undercooked. A large slow cooker keeps the ingredient layers thin and promotes even cooking. Let the cake stand, uncovered, after cooking to allow the steam to escape. As it cools, the cake and pineapple mixture will set up a bit.

COCONUT-PECAN SWEET POTATOES

These sweet potatoes cook effortlessly in the slow cooker so you can tend to other things. Coconut gives the classic dish new flavor.
—*Raquel Haggard, Edmond, OK*

Prep: 15 min. • **Cook:** 4 hours
Makes: 12 servings

- ½ cup chopped pecans
- ½ cup sweetened shredded coconut
- ⅓ cup sugar
- ⅓ cup packed brown sugar
- ½ tsp. ground cinnamon
- ¼ tsp. salt
- ¼ cup reduced-fat butter, melted
- 4 lbs. sweet potatoes (about 6 medium), peeled and cut into 1-in. pieces
- ½ tsp. coconut extract
- ½ tsp. vanilla extract

1. In a small bowl, combine the first six ingredients; stir in the melted butter. Place the sweet potatoes in a 5-qt. slow cooker coated with cooking spray. Sprinkle with the pecan mixture.
2. Cook, covered, on low 4-4½ hours or until the potatoes are tender. Stir in the extracts.

Note: This recipe was tested with Land O'Lakes light stick butter.
⅔ cup: 211 cal., 7g fat (3g sat. fat), 5mg chol., 103mg sod., 37g carb. (22g sugars, 3g fiber), 2g pro.

SLOW-COOKER BARBACOA

My husband adores this roast simmered in lime juice, chipotle and cumin. I serve it over rice flavored with cilantro and even more zippy lime.
—*Aundrea McCormick, Denver, CO*

Prep: 45 min. • **Cook:** 7 hours
Makes: 8 servings

- ¼ cup lime juice
- ¼ cup cider vinegar
- 3 chipotle peppers in adobo sauce
- 4 garlic cloves, thinly sliced
- 4 tsp. ground cumin
- 3 tsp. dried oregano
- 1½ tsp. pepper
- ¾ tsp. salt
- ½ tsp. ground cloves
- 1 cup reduced-sodium chicken broth
- 1 boneless beef chuck roast (3 to 4 lbs.)
- 3 bay leaves

RICE
- 3 cups water
- 2 cups uncooked jasmine rice, rinsed and drained
- 3 Tbsp. butter
- 1½ tsp. salt
- ½ cup minced fresh cilantro
- 2 Tbsp. lime juice

1. Place the first nine ingredients in a blender; cover and process until smooth. Add broth; pulse to combine.
2. Place roast and bay leaves in a 4- or 5-qt. slow cooker; pour the sauce over top. Cook, covered, on low for 7-9 hours or until the meat is tender.
3. Prepare rice about 30 minutes before serving. In a large saucepan, combine water, rice, butter and salt; bring to a boil. Reduce heat; simmer, covered, for 12-15 minutes or until liquid is absorbed and rice is tender. Remove from heat; gently stir in cilantro and lime juice.
4. Remove roast from slow cooker; cool slightly. Discard bay leaves and skim fat from the cooking juices. Shred the beef with two forks; return to slow cooker. Serve with rice.
½ cup beef mixture with ⅔ cup cooked rice: 513 cal., 21g fat (9g sat. fat), 122mg chol., 882mg sod., 40g carb. (1g sugars, 1g fiber), 37g pro.

Cookies, Bars & Candies

For holiday trays and afternoon snacks, midnight nibbles and bake-sale goodies, look no further than this chapter. With 29 different sweet treats to choose from, you're sure to find just the right recipe to satisfy your craving for an indulgent bite.

BLACK-BOTTOM BANANA BARS

These bars stay very moist, and their rich banana and chocolate taste is even better the second day. My mother-in-law gave me this recipe, and it's a big favorite with both my husband and two sons.
—*Renee Wright, Ferryville, WI*

Prep: 20 min. • **Bake:** 25 min. • **Makes:** 3 dozen

- ½ cup butter, softened
- 1 cup sugar
- 1 large egg
- 1 tsp. vanilla extract
- 1½ cups mashed ripe bananas (about 3 medium)
- 1½ cups all-purpose flour
- 1 tsp. baking powder
- 1 tsp. baking soda
- ½ tsp. salt
- ¼ cup baking cocoa

1. Preheat oven to 350°. Cream butter and sugar until light and fluffy. Beat in egg and vanilla. Stir in bananas. Combine flour, baking powder, baking soda and salt; add to the creamed mixture and mix well.

2. Divide the batter in half. Add cocoa to half; spread into a greased 13x9-in. baking pan. Spoon the remaining batter on top. If desired, swirl with a knife to marble the batter.

3. Bake until a toothpick inserted in the center comes out clean, 25 minutes. Cool on a wire rack.

1 bar: 76 cal., 3g fat (2g sat. fat), 12mg chol., 104mg sod., 12g carb. (7g sugars, 1g fiber), 1g pro.

PISTACHIO THUMBPRINTS

These mild pistachio-flavored cookies disappear in a wink. They're a natural for a holiday cookie plate!
—*Elizabeth Probelski, Port Washington, WI*

Prep: 45 min. • **Bake:** 10 min./batch
Makes: about 4 dozen

- 1 cup butter, softened
- ⅓ cup confectioners' sugar
- 1 large egg
- 1 tsp. vanilla extract
- ¾ tsp. almond extract
- 2 cups all-purpose flour
- 1 pkg. (3.4 oz.) instant pistachio pudding mix
- ½ cup miniature chocolate chips
- 2 cups finely chopped pecans

FILLING
- 2 Tbsp. butter, softened
- 2 cups confectioners' sugar
- 1 tsp. vanilla extract
- 2 to 3 Tbsp. 2% milk

GLAZE
- ½ cup semisweet chocolate chips
- 2 tsp. shortening

1. Preheat oven to 350°. Cream butter and sugar until smooth and fluffy. Beat in egg and extracts. Combine the flour and pudding mix; gradually add to the creamed mixture and mix well. Stir in chocolate chips.

2. Shape into 1-in. balls; roll in nuts. Place 2 in. apart on greased baking sheets; make a thumbprint in center of cookie. Bake 10-12 minutes. Remove to a wire rack to cool.

3. Beat butter, confectioners' sugar, vanilla and enough milk to achieve desired consistency. Spoon filling into center of cooled cookies.

4. Melt chocolate chips and shortening; drizzle over cookies. Let stand until set.

2 cookies: 163 cal., 11g fat (4g sat. fat), 18mg chol., 84mg sod., 17g carb. (11g sugars, 1g fiber), 2g pro.

CINNAMON ALMOND BRITTLE

It simply wouldn't be Christmas at our house without this old-time favorite, a spiced-up twist on peanut brittle. No one believes how easy it is to make!

—Lynette Kleinschmidt, Litchfield, MN

Prep: 15 min. • **Cook:** 20 min. + cooling
Makes: about 2 lbs.

- 1 tsp. plus 3 Tbsp. butter, cubed
- 2 cups sugar
- ¾ cup light corn syrup
- ¼ cup water
- 3 cups slivered almonds, toasted
- 2 tsp. ground cinnamon
- ½ tsp. salt
- 1½ tsp. baking soda
- 1 tsp. vanilla extract

1. Preheat oven to 200°. Grease two baking sheets with 1 tsp. butter; place in oven to warm.
2. In a large heavy saucepan, combine sugar, corn syrup and water. Bring to a boil, stirring constantly to dissolve sugar.

Using a pastry brush dipped in water, wash down the sides of the pan to eliminate sugar crystals. Cook, without stirring, over medium heat until a candy thermometer reads 240° (soft-ball stage). Stir in almonds, cinnamon, salt and the remaining butter; cook until the thermometer reads 300° (hard-crack stage), stirring frequently and brushing sides of pan as needed.
3. Remove from heat; stir in the baking soda and vanilla. Immediately pour onto the prepared pans, spreading to ¼-in. thickness. Cool completely.
4. Break brittle into pieces. Store between layers of waxed paper in an airtight container.

Note: We recommend you test your candy thermometer before each use by bringing water to a boil; the thermometer should read 212°. Adjust your recipe temperature up or down based on your test.

1 ounce: 142 cal., 6g fat (1g sat. fat), 3mg chol., 111mg sod., 21g carb. (19g sugars, 1g fiber), 2g pro.

TRIPLE FUDGE BROWNIES

When you're in a hurry to make dessert, here's a mix of mixes that's convenient and quick. The result is a big pan of rich, fudgy brownies. Friends who ask me for the recipe are amazed it's so simple to make.

—Denise Nebel, Wayland, IA

Prep: 10 min. • **Bake:** 30 min. • **Makes:** 4 dozen

- 1 pkg. (3.9 oz.) instant chocolate pudding mix
- 1 pkg. chocolate cake mix (regular size)
- 2 cups (12 oz.) semisweet chocolate chips
  Confectioners' sugar
  Vanilla ice cream, optional

1. Preheat oven to 350°. Prepare pudding according to package directions. Whisk in dry cake mix. Stir in chocolate chips.
2. Pour into a greased 15x10x1-in. baking pan. Bake for 30-35 minutes or until the top springs back when lightly touched.
3. Dust with confectioners' sugar. Serve with ice cream if desired.

1 brownie: 91 cal., 3g fat (2g sat. fat), 1mg chol., 86mg sod., 15g carb. (10g sugars, 1g fiber), 1g pro.

BUTTERY ORANGE SUGAR COOKIES

My husband's grandmother made a variety of cookies every year at Christmastime. She would box them up and give each grandchild his or her very own box. This crisp, orange-flavored cookie is one of my favorites.
—*Heather McKillip, Aurora, IL*

Prep: 25 min. • Bake: 10 min./batch
Makes: 4 dozen

- 1 cup butter, softened
- 1 cup sugar
- 4 tsp. grated orange zest
- 2 tsp. vanilla extract
- 1¼ cups all-purpose flour
- ¾ cup rye flour
- 1 tsp. baking soda
- ¾ tsp. salt

1. Preheat oven to 350°. In a large bowl, cream butter and sugar until light and fluffy. Beat in orange zest and vanilla. In another bowl, whisk the remaining ingredients; gradually beat into creamed mixture.
2. Shape level tablespoons of dough into balls; place 2 in. apart on ungreased baking sheets. Bake until edges are light brown, 10-12 minutes. Cool on pans for 2 minutes. Remove to wire racks to cool. Store in airtight containers.
1 cookie: 68 cal., 4g fat (2g sat. fat), 10mg chol., 94mg sod., 8g carb. (4g sugars, 0 fiber), 1g pro.

FUDGY LAYERED IRISH MOCHA BROWNIES

My husband and I are big fans of Irish cream, so I incorporated it into this decadent brownie. I started with my mom's brownie recipe, then added frosting and ganache.
—*Sue Gronholz, Beaver Dam, WI*

Prep: 35 min. • Bake: 25 min. + chilling
Makes: 16 servings

- ⅔ cup all-purpose flour
- ½ tsp. baking powder
- ¼ tsp. salt
- ⅓ cup butter
- 6 Tbsp. baking cocoa
- 2 Tbsp. canola oil
- ½ tsp. instant coffee granules
- 1 cup sugar
- 2 large eggs, beaten
- 1 tsp. vanilla extract

FROSTING
- 2 cups confectioners' sugar
- ¼ cup butter, softened
- 3 Tbsp. Irish cream liqueur

GANACHE TOPPING
- 1 cup semisweet chocolate chips
- 3 Tbsp. Irish cream liqueur
- 2 Tbsp. heavy whipping cream
- ½ tsp. instant coffee granules

1. Preheat oven to 350°. Sift together flour, baking powder and salt; set aside. In a small saucepan over low heat, melt butter. Remove from heat; stir in cocoa, oil and instant coffee granules. Cool slightly; stir in sugar and beaten eggs. Gradually add the flour mixture and vanilla; mix well. Spread the batter into a greased 8-in. square pan; bake until the center is set (do not overbake), about 25 minutes. Cool in pan on wire rack.
2. For frosting, whisk together the confectioners' sugar and butter (the mixture will be lumpy). Gradually whisk in Irish cream liqueur; beat until smooth. Spread over slightly warm brownies. Refrigerate until frosting is set, about 1 hour.
3. Meanwhile, prepare ganache: Microwave all ingredients on high for 1 minute; stir. Microwave 30 seconds longer; stir until smooth. Cool slightly until the ganache reaches a spreading consistency. Spread over the frosting. Refrigerate until set, 45-60 minutes.
1 brownie: 295 cal., 14g fat (7g sat. fat), 43mg chol., 116mg sod., 41g carb. (34g sugars, 1g fiber), 2g pro.

WARREN'S OATMEAL JAM SQUARES

At age 102, I still love to bake! I make these bars in my toaster oven for my fellow residents at our assisted living home.
—*Warren Patrick, Townshend, VT*

- -

Prep: 20 min. • **Bake:** 25 min. + cooling
Makes: 16 squares

1¼ cups quick-cooking oats
1¼ cups all-purpose flour
½ cup sugar
½ tsp. baking soda
¼ tsp. salt
¾ cup butter, melted
2 tsp. vanilla extract
1 jar (10 oz.) seedless raspberry jam or jam of your choice
4 whole graham crackers, crushed

1. Preheat oven to 350°. In a large bowl, mix the first five ingredients. In a small bowl, mix melted butter and vanilla; add to the oat mixture, stirring until crumbly. Reserve 1 cup mixture for topping.
2. Press the remaining mixture onto bottom of a greased 9-in. square baking pan. Spread jam over top to within ½ in. of edges. Add crushed graham crackers to reserved topping; sprinkle over jam.
3. Bake for 25-30 minutes or until the edges are golden brown. Cool in pan on a wire rack. Cut into squares.
1 square: 220 cal., 9g fat (6g sat. fat), 23mg chol., 161mg sod., 33g carb. (18g sugars, 1g fiber), 2g pro.

MINI S'MORES

Want to sink your teeth into s'mores all year long? Here's the answer! Just combine marshmallow creme, chocolate, graham crackers and more for an awesome bite.
—*Stephanie Tewell, Elizabeth, IL*

- -

Prep: 50 min. + standing • **Cook:** 5 min.
Makes: about 4 dozen

2 cups milk chocolate chips
½ cup heavy whipping cream
1 pkg. (14.4 oz.) graham crackers, quartered
1 cup marshmallow creme
2 cartons (7 oz. each) milk chocolate, for dipping
4 oz. white candy coating, melted, optional

1. Place chocolate chips in a small bowl. In a small saucepan, bring cream just to a boil. Pour over the chocolate; stir with a whisk until smooth. Cool to room temperature or until mixture reaches a spreading consistency, about 10 minutes.
2. Spread the chocolate mixture over half of the graham crackers. Spread marshmallow creme over the remaining graham crackers; place over chocolate-covered crackers, pressing to adhere.
3. Melt dipping chocolate according to the package directions. Dip each s'more halfway into the dipping chocolate; allow excess to drip off. Place s'mores on waxed paper-lined baking sheets; let stand until the dipping chocolate is set.
4. If desired, drizzle with melted white candy coating; let stand until set. Store in an airtight container in the refrigerator.
1 s'more: 145 cal., 7g fat (4g sat. fat), 5mg chol., 66mg sod., 19g carb. (13g sugars, 1g fiber), 2g pro.

KEEP ON WHISKING!

At first, the chocolate and cream mixture may look separated. But don't panic: It will smooth out with plenty of whisking. For a richer treat, mix peanut butter into the marshmallow creme. A tablespoon or two should do it.

FREEZE IT

GRANDMA KRAUSE'S COCONUT COOKIES

When my two daughters were young, their great-grandma made them cookies with oats and coconut. Thankfully, she shared the recipe!

—Debra Dorn, Homosassa, FL

- -

Prep: 40 min. + freezing • **Bake:** 10 min./batch
Makes: about 4 dozen

- 1 **cup shortening**
- 1 **cup sugar**
- 1 **cup packed brown sugar**
- 2 **large eggs**
- 1 **tsp. vanilla extract**
- 2 **cups all-purpose flour**
- 1 **tsp. baking powder**
- 1 **tsp. baking soda**
- ¼ **tsp. salt**
- 1 **cup old-fashioned oats**
- 1 **cup sweetened shredded coconut**

1. In a large bowl, beat shortening and sugars until blended. Beat in eggs and vanilla. In another bowl, whisk flour, baking powder, baking soda and salt; gradually beat into the sugar mixture. Stir in oats and coconut.

2. Divide dough into four portions. On a lightly floured surface, shape each into a 6-in.-long roll. Wrap each roll in plastic; freeze 2 hours or until firm.

3. Preheat oven to 350°. Unwrap rolls and cut dough crosswise into ½-in. slices, reshaping as needed. Place 2 in. apart on ungreased baking sheets. Bake for 10-12 minutes or until golden brown. Cool on pans 5 minutes. Remove to wire racks to cool completely.

Freeze option: Place wrapped logs in freezer container; return to freezer. To use, unwrap frozen logs and cut into slices. If necessary, let the dough stand a few minutes at room temperature before cutting. Prepare and bake as directed.

1 cookie: 109 cal., 5g fat (2g sat. fat), 8mg chol., 56mg sod., 15g carb. (10g sugars, 0 fiber), 1g pro.

MAINE POTATO CANDY

Years ago, folks in Maine ate potatoes daily, which meant leftovers—to be used in bread, doughnuts and even candy. This is a great traditional recipe from the Pine Tree State.
—*Barbara Allen, Chelmsford, MA*

Prep: 30 min. + chilling
Makes: 2 lbs. (40 servings)

- 4 cups confectioners' sugar
- 4 cups sweetened shredded coconut
- ¾ cup cold mashed potatoes (without added milk and butter)
- 1½ tsp. vanilla extract
- ½ tsp. salt
- 1 lb. dark chocolate candy coating, coarsely chopped

1. In a large bowl, combine the first five ingredients. Line a 9-in. square pan with foil; butter the foil. Spread the coconut mixture into pan. Cover mixture and chill overnight. Cut into 2x1-in. rectangles. Cover and freeze.

2. In a microwave, melt candy coating; stir until smooth. Dip bars in coating; allow excess to drip off. Place on waxed paper to set. Store in an airtight container.

1 piece: 155 cal., 7g fat (6g sat. fat), 0 chol., 55mg sod., 25g carb. (23g sugars, 1g fiber), 1g pro.

BLACKBERRY CHEESECAKE BARS

Sugar cookie dough is a speedy way to turn ricotta and mascarpone cheeses topped with blackberries into beautiful bars.
—*Terri Crandall, Gardnerville, NV*

Prep: 30 min. • **Bake:** 20 min. + cooling
Makes: 12 servings

- 1 tube (16½ oz.) refrigerated sugar cookie dough
- 1½ cups ricotta cheese
- 1 carton (8 oz.) mascarpone cheese
- ½ cup sugar
- 2 large eggs, lightly beaten
- 3 tsp. vanilla extract
- 2 tsp. grated lemon zest
- 1 tsp. lemon juice
- 1 tsp. orange juice
- 1 Tbsp. amaretto, optional
- 1 cup seedless blackberry spreadable fruit
- 2⅔ cups fresh blackberries

1. Preheat oven to 375°. Let cookie dough stand at room temperature for 5 minutes to soften. Press onto bottom and 1 in. up the sides of a greased 13x9-in. baking dish. Bake 12-15 minutes or until golden brown. Cool on a wire rack.

2. Meanwhile, in a large bowl, beat ricotta cheese, mascarpone cheese and sugar until blended. Add eggs; beat on low speed just until combined. Stir in vanilla, lemon zest, citrus juices and, if desired, amaretto. Pour into the crust.

3. Bake for 20-25 minutes or until the center is almost set. Cool for 1 hour on a wire rack.

4. Place the spreadable fruit in a small microwave-safe bowl; microwave on high for 30-45 seconds or until melted. Spread over the cheesecake layer; top with the blackberries. Refrigerate until serving.

1 bar: 414 cal., 21g fat (9g sat. fat), 83mg chol., 224mg sod., 50g carb. (31g sugars, 2g fiber), 8g pro.

Dreaming of Caramel

These four recipes give you a choice of how to get caramel into your desserts: caramel candies, bottled toppings or your own made from scratch. Try one, try them all—it's all sweet, gooey caramel goodness.

PECAN CARAMEL CANDIES

The perfect combination of salty and sweet, these candies make an ideal treat at the holidays! Get kids involved by having them help you to unwrap the candies and place the pretzels on baking sheets. You'll have them ready to give as gifts in no time!

—Julie Wemhoff, Angola, IN

- -

Prep: 30 min. • **Bake:** 5 min. + standing
Makes: 4½ dozen

- 54 pretzels
- 54 Rolo candies (about 11 oz.)
- 54 pecan halves

1. Preheat oven to 250°. Place pretzels 1 in. apart on foil-lined baking sheets. Top each with a Rolo candy.

2. Bake for 3-4 minutes or until candies are softened. (Rolos will still retain their shape.) Immediately top each with a pecan half, pressing to spread the candy into the pretzel. Let stand until set.

1 piece: 44 cal., 2g fat (1g sat. fat), 1mg chol., 24mg sod., 6g carb. (4g sugars, 0 fiber), 1g pro.

CHOCOLATE SALTED CARAMEL BARS

I enjoy experimenting with recipes and combining classic and new flavors. I have been making my favorite shortbread for more than 20 years and finally found the perfect pairing—layered with salted caramel and dark chocolate. For even more gooey goodness, drizzle bottled caramel sauce over the top.

—Lisa Glenn, Sarasota, FL

- -

Prep: 20 min. • **Bake:** 50 min. + cooling
Makes: 2½ dozen

- 2 cups butter, softened
- 1½ cups confectioners' sugar
- 1 cup sugar
- 6 tsp. vanilla extract
- 4 cups all-purpose flour
- 1 pkg. (14 oz.) caramels
- ⅓ cup heavy whipping cream
- 1 tsp. kosher salt
- 1 pkg. (12 oz.) dark chocolate chips
  Bottled caramel sauce, optional

1. Preheat oven to 325°. Beat butter, sugars and vanilla until light and fluffy. Gradually beat in flour, mixing well. Press 3 cups of dough onto the bottom of a greased 13x9-in. pan. Bake until set, 20-22 minutes.

2. Cool for 10 minutes on a wire rack. Meanwhile, in a small saucepan, melt caramels with cream over low heat until smooth. Pour caramel mixture over the crust. Sprinkle with salt, then chocolate chips. Drop the remaining dough over top by teaspoonfuls. Bake until light golden brown, 30-35 minutes longer. Cool on a wire rack.

1 bar: 334 cal., 18g fat (11g sat. fat), 37mg chol., 199mg sod., 43g carb. (28g sugars, 1g fiber), 3g pro.

CHOCOLATE CARAMEL KISS COOKIES

I make this cookie every Christmas with my family. It's a fun twist on a classic peanut butter blossom because of the cinnamon in the batter and the caramel kiss on top.
—*Kristen Heigl, Staten Island, NY*

Prep: 15 min. • **Bake:** 10 min./batch + cooling
Makes: about 2 dozen

- ½ cup butter, softened
- ½ cup packed brown sugar
- 1 cup sugar, divided
- 1 large egg plus 1 large egg yolk
- 1½ tsp. vanilla extract
- 1¼ cups all-purpose flour
- ¾ cup baking cocoa
- 1 tsp. baking soda
- 1 tsp. ground cinnamon
- ¾ tsp. salt
- 24 caramel-filled milk chocolate kisses

1. Preheat oven to 350°. Cream butter, brown sugar and ½ cup granulated sugar until light and fluffy. Beat in egg, egg yolk and vanilla. In another bowl, whisk the next five ingredients; gradually beat into the creamed mixture.

2. Shape rounded tablespoonfuls of dough into balls. Roll balls in the remaining sugar, then place 2 in. apart on ungreased baking sheets. Bake until the edges begin to brown, 8-10 minutes. Immediately press a chocolate kiss into the center of each cookie (cookie will crack around the edges). Cool on pans 2 minutes. Remove to wire racks to cool.

1 cookie: 143 cal., 6g fat (3g sat. fat), 27mg chol., 170mg sod., 23g carb. (15g sugars, 1g fiber), 2g pro.

SOFT CHEWY CARAMELS

One of my first experiences with cooking was helping my mother make these caramels—we'd make as many as 12 batches each year. Today I do at least 95 percent of the cooking at home, but my wife handles most of the baking duties.
—*Robert Sprenkle, Hurst, TX*

Prep: 5 min. • **Cook:** 20 min. + cooling
Makes: about 2½ lbs.

- 1 Tbsp. plus 1 cup butter, divided
- 2¼ cups packed brown sugar
- 1 can (14 oz.) sweetened condensed milk
- 1 cup dark corn syrup

1. Line a 15x10x1-in. pan with foil; grease the foil with 1 Tbsp. butter. Set aside. In a heavy saucepan over medium heat, melt the remaining butter. Add brown sugar, milk and corn syrup. Cook and stir until candy thermometer reads 250° (hard-ball stage).

2. Pour into the prepared pan (do not scrape the saucepan). Cool completely before cutting.

Note: We recommend you test your candy thermometer before each use by bringing water to a boil; the thermometer should read 212°. Adjust your recipe temperature up or down based on your test.

1 caramel: 58 cal., 2g fat (1g sat. fat), 7mg chol., 32mg sod., 9g carb. (8g sugars, 0 fiber), 0 pro.

GIANT MOLASSES COOKIES

My family always requests these soft and deliciously chewy cookies. While we enjoy them at home, they're also great for shipping as gifts or to troops overseas.

—*Kristine Chayes, Smithtown, NY*

Prep: 30 min. • **Bake:** 15 min./batch
Makes: 2 dozen

1½ cups butter, softened
 2 cups sugar
 2 large eggs, room temperature
½ cup molasses
4½ cups all-purpose flour
 4 tsp. ground ginger
 2 tsp. baking soda
1½ tsp. ground cinnamon
 1 tsp. ground cloves
¼ tsp. salt
¼ cup chopped pecans
¾ cup coarse sugar

1. Preheat oven to 350°. In a large bowl, cream butter and sugar until light and fluffy. Beat in the eggs and molasses. Combine the flour, ginger, baking soda, cinnamon, cloves and salt; gradually add to the creamed mixture and mix well. Fold in pecans.
2. Shape dough into 2-in. balls and roll in coarse sugar. Place balls 2½ in. apart on ungreased baking sheets. Bake for 13-15 minutes or until tops are cracked. Remove to wire racks to cool.
1 cookie: 310 cal., 13g fat (7g sat. fat), 48mg chol., 219mg sod., 46g carb. (27g sugars, 1g fiber), 3g pro.

COOKIES & CREAM BROWNIES

You won't want to frost these brownies, since the marbled top is too pretty to cover up. Besides, the tasty cream cheese layer makes them taste as if they're already frosted. Crushed cookies add extra chocolate flavor and a fun crunch.

—*Darlene Brenden, Salem, OR*

Prep: 15 min. • **Bake:** 25 min. + cooling
Makes: 2 dozen

 1 pkg. (8 oz.) cream cheese, softened
¼ cup sugar
 1 large egg
½ tsp. vanilla extract
BROWNIE LAYER
½ cup butter, melted
½ cup sugar
½ cup packed brown sugar
½ cup baking cocoa
 2 large eggs
 1 tsp. vanilla extract
½ cup all-purpose flour
 1 tsp. baking powder
12 Oreo cookies, crushed
 8 Oreo cookies, coarsely chopped

1. Preheat oven to 350°. Beat cream cheese, sugar, egg and vanilla until smooth; set aside. For the brownie layer, combine butter, sugars and cocoa. Beat in eggs. Combine the flour and baking powder; gradually add to the cocoa mixture. Stir in crushed cookie crumbs.
2. Pour batter into a greased 11x7-in. baking pan. Spoon the cream cheese mixture over batter. Sprinkle with the coarsely chopped cookies. Bake 25-30 minutes or until a toothpick inserted in the center comes out with moist crumbs. Cool completely on a wire rack. Cut into bars. Store in the refrigerator.
1 bar: 159 cal., 9g fat (5g sat. fat), 47mg chol., 130mg sod., 18g carb. (13g sugars, 1g fiber), 2g pro.

RHUBARB CUSTARD BARS

Once I tried these rich, gooey bars, I just had to have the recipe so I could make them for my family and friends. The shortbread-like crust and rhubarb and custard layers inspire people to find rhubarb they can use to fix a batch for themselves.

—Shari Roach, South Milwaukee, WI

- -

Prep: 25 min. • **Bake:** 50 min. + chilling
Makes: 3 dozen

- 2 cups all-purpose flour
- ¼ cup sugar
- 1 cup cold butter

FILLING

- 2 cups sugar
- 7 Tbsp. all-purpose flour
- 1 cup heavy whipping cream
- 3 large eggs, beaten
- 5 cups finely chopped fresh or frozen rhubarb, thawed and drained

TOPPING

- 6 oz. cream cheese, softened
- ½ cup sugar
- ½ tsp. vanilla extract
- 1 cup heavy whipping cream, whipped

1. Preheat oven to 350°. Combine the flour and sugar; cut in butter until the mixture resembles coarse crumbs. Press into a greased 13x9-in. baking pan. Bake for 10 minutes.

2. For the filling, combine sugar and flour. Whisk in cream and eggs. Stir in the rhubarb. Pour over the crust. Bake until the custard is set, 40-45 minutes. Cool.

3. For topping, beat cream cheese, sugar and vanilla until smooth; fold in whipped cream. Spread over top. Cover and chill. Cut into bars. Store in the refrigerator.

1 bar: 198 cal., 11g fat (7g sat. fat), 52mg chol., 70mg sod., 23g carb. (16g sugars, 1g fiber), 2g pro.

CHANGE IT UP

Heavy whipping cream gives custard fillings a luscious, decadent texture, but half-and-half cream or whole milk can be substituted with nice results. If you prefer your bars on the tart side, bump up the rhubarb to 6-6½ cups or reduce the sugar in the filling to 1½ cups. Try adding the seeds of one vanilla bean or 1 tsp. of rosewater to the filling. Both pair beautifully with rhubarb and take these already fab bars to another level.

This is a potluck hero: It makes a mountain of bars. If you're cooking for a smaller crew, however, just halve the recipe and use a 9- or 8-in. square baking dish.

CHOCOLATE GINGERSNAPS

When my daughter Jennifer was 15 years old she created this recipe as a way to combine two of her favorite flavors. They're great with a glass of milk.
—*Paula Zsiray, Logan, UT*

Prep: 45 min. + chilling • **Bake:** 10 min./batch
Makes: about 3½ dozen

- ½ cup butter, softened
- ½ cup packed light brown sugar
- ¼ cup molasses
- 1 Tbsp. water
- 2 tsp. minced fresh gingerroot
- 1½ cups all-purpose flour
- 1 Tbsp. baking cocoa
- 1¼ tsp. ground ginger
- 1 tsp. baking soda
- 1 tsp. ground cinnamon
- ¼ tsp. ground nutmeg
- ¼ tsp. ground cloves
- 7 oz. semisweet chocolate, finely chopped
- ¼ cup course sugar

1. In a large bowl, cream butter and brown sugar until light and fluffy. Beat in the molasses, water and gingerroot. Combine the flour, cocoa, ginger, baking soda, cinnamon, nutmeg and cloves; gradually add to creamed mixture and mix well. Stir in chocolate. Cover and refrigerate until easy to handle, about 2 hours.
2. Shape dough into 1-in. balls; roll in sugar. Place balls 2 in. apart on greased baking sheets.
3. Bake at 350° until the tops begin to crack, 10-12 minutes. Cool for 2 minutes before removing to wire racks to cool completely.
1 cookie: 80 cal., 4g fat (2g sat. fat), 6mg chol., 47mg sod., 9g carb. (6g sugars, 0 fiber), 1g pro.

SOUR CREAM & CRANBERRY BARS

I turned sour cream raisin pie into a cookie bar with a crunchy oatmeal crust, custard-style filling and crisp topping.
—*Shelly L. Bevington, Hermiston, OR*

Prep: 35 min. • **Bake:** 35 min. + cooling
Makes: 2 dozen

- 3 large egg yolks
- 1½ cups (12 oz.) sour cream
- 1 cup sugar
- 3 Tbsp. cornstarch
- ⅛ tsp. salt
- 1 cup dried cranberries
- 1 tsp. vanilla extract

CRUST

- 1 cup butter, softened
- 1 cup sugar
- 2 tsp. vanilla extract
- 1¾ cups all-purpose flour
- 1⅓ cups quick-cooking oats
- 1 tsp. salt
- 1 tsp. baking soda
- 1 cup sweetened shredded coconut

1. Preheat oven to 350°. In the top of a double boiler or in a metal bowl over simmering water, whisk the first five ingredients until blended; then stir in cranberries. Cook and stir 15-20 minutes until the mixture is thickened. Remove from heat; stir in vanilla.
2. Meanwhile, in a large bowl, cream the butter and sugar until light and fluffy. Beat in vanilla. In another bowl, whisk flour, oats, salt and baking soda; gradually beat into creamed mixture. Stir in coconut. Reserve half of the dough for topping. Press remainder onto bottom of a greased 13x9-in. baking dish. Bake 8-10 minutes or until set.
3. Spread the sour cream mixture over the crust; crumble the reserved dough over top. Bake for 25-30 minutes or until the filling is set and the top is golden brown. Cool in pan on a wire rack. Cut into bars.
1 bar: 260 cal., 13g fat (8g sat. fat), 53mg chol., 241mg sod., 34g carb. (22g sugars, 1g fiber), 3g pro.

Contest Winner

BUTTERSCOTCH HARD CANDY

I love making this classic butterscotch recipe. We think these irresistible bites are better than the store-bought variety...and they sure don't last long!

—*Darlene Smithers, Elkhart, IN*

Prep: 10 min. • **Cook:** 30 min. + cooling
Makes: about 1½ lbs.

- 1 tsp. plus 1 cup butter, divided
- 2½ cups sugar
- ¾ cup water
- ½ cup light corn syrup
- ¼ cup honey
- ½ tsp. salt
- ½ tsp. rum extract

1. Butter a 15x10x1-in. pan with 1 tsp. butter; set aside. Cube the remaining butter and set aside.
2. In a heavy saucepan, combine the sugar, water and corn syrup. Cover and bring to a boil over medium heat without stirring. Cook, uncovered, until a candy thermometer reads 270° (soft-crack stage). Add the honey, salt and remaining butter; stir constantly until the mixture reaches 300° (hard-crack stage).
3. Remove from the heat. Stir in the rum extract. Pour into the prepared pan without scraping; do not spread. Cool until the candy is almost set, 1-2 minutes. Score into 1-in. squares; cool completely. Break squares apart. Store candy in an airtight container.
Note: We recommend you test your candy thermometer before each use by bringing water to a boil; the thermometer should read 212°. Adjust your recipe temperature up or down based on your test.
1 candy: 144 cal., 6g fat (4g sat. fat), 17mg chol., 109mg sod., 23g carb. (21g sugars, 0 fiber), 0 pro.

CHOCOLATE CHIP PEANUT BUTTER COOKIES

Add peanut butter to the traditional chocolate chip cookie, and you get the best of both worlds.

—*Clarice Schweitzer, Sun City, AZ*

Takes: 30 min. • **Makes:** 2 dozen

- ½ cup butter, softened
- ½ cup sugar
- ⅓ cup packed brown sugar
- ½ cup chunky peanut butter
- 1 large egg
- 1 tsp. vanilla extract
- 1 cup all-purpose flour
- ½ cup old-fashioned oats
- 1 tsp. baking soda
- ¼ tsp. salt
- 1 cup semisweet chocolate chips

1. Preheat oven to 350°. In a bowl, cream butter and sugars; beat in peanut butter, egg and vanilla. Combine the flour, oats, baking soda and salt; stir into the creamed mixture. Stir in chocolate chips.
2. Drop by rounded tablespoonfuls onto ungreased baking sheets. Bake until golden brown, 10-12 minutes. Cool for 1 minute before removing to a wire rack.
2 cookies: 310 cal., 18g fat (8g sat. fat), 38mg chol., 293mg sod., 36g carb. (23g sugars, 2g fiber), 5g pro.

OLD-TIME BUTTER CRUNCH CANDY

My children and my grandchildren say the holiday season wouldn't be the same without the big tray of sweets I prepare each year. These nutty pieces draped in chocolate are a popular part of my collection.

—Mildred Duffy, Bella Vista, AR

- -

Prep: 15 min. + cooling • **Cook:** 25 min.
Makes: about 2 lbs.

    1   cup butter
    1¼ cup sugar
    2   Tbsp. light corn syrup
    2   Tbsp. water
    2   cups finely chopped toasted almonds
    8   milk chocolate candy
         bars (1.55 oz. each)

1. Line a 13x9-in. pan with foil; set aside. Using part of the butter, grease the sides of a large heavy saucepan. Add the remaining butter to the saucepan; melt over low heat. Add sugar, corn syrup and water. Cook and stir over medium heat until a candy thermometer reads 300° (hard-crack stage).
2. Remove from the heat and stir in the almonds. Quickly pour into the prepared pan, spreading to cover bottom of pan. Cool completely. Carefully invert pan to remove candy in one piece; remove foil.
3. Melt half the chocolate in a double boiler or microwave-safe bowl; spread over top of candy. Let cool. Turn candy over and repeat with the remaining chocolate; cool. Break into 2-in. pieces. Store in an airtight container.
2 ounces: 375 cal., 26g fat (12g sat. fat), 35mg chol., 137mg sod., 34g carb. (29g sugars, 3g fiber), 5g pro.

PEANUT BUTTER SANDWICH COOKIES

With two children, a job in our school office and helping my husband on our farm, I don't have much time to bake. So when I do, I like to make it special. Creamy filling gives traditional peanut butter cookies a new twist.

—Debbie Kokes, Tabor, SD

- -

Prep: 20 min. • **Bake:** 10 min./batch + cooling
Makes: 44 sandwich cookies

    1   cup butter-flavored shortening
    1   cup creamy peanut butter
    1   cup sugar
    1   cup packed brown sugar
    3   large eggs
    1   tsp. vanilla extract
    3   cups all-purpose flour
    2   tsp. baking soda
    ¼   tsp. salt
  FILLING
    ½   cup creamy peanut butter
    3   cups confectioners' sugar
    1   tsp. vanilla extract
    5   to 6 Tbsp. milk

1. In a large bowl, cream the shortening, peanut butter and sugars until light and fluffy, about 4 minutes. Beat in eggs and vanilla. Combine the flour, baking soda and salt; add to the creamed mixture and mix well.
2. Shape into 1-in. balls and place 2 in. apart on ungreased baking sheets. Flatten to ⅜-in. thickness with fork. Bake at 375° for 7-8 minutes or until golden. Remove to wire racks to cool.
3. For filling, in a large bowl, beat the peanut butter, confectioners' sugar, vanilla and enough milk to achieve spreading consistency. Spread filling on half of the cookies and top each with another cookie.
1 sandwich cookie: 197 cal., 9g fat (2g sat. fat), 15mg chol., 119mg sod., 26g carb. (18g sugars, 1g fiber), 4g pro.

CHERRY PECAN DREAMS

Packed with fruit, nuts and vanilla chips, these are always a treat. To vary the flavor, swap dried cranberries or apricots for the cherries, and pistachios for the pecans.

—*Mary Ann Mariotti, Plainfield, IL*

Prep: 25 min. • **Bake:** 10 min./batch + cooling
Makes: about 3 dozen

- 1 cup butter, softened
- ½ cup sugar
- ½ cup packed brown sugar
- 1 large egg
- 1 Tbsp. grated orange zest
- 2¼ cups all-purpose flour
- 1 tsp. baking soda
- ½ tsp. salt
- 2 cups white baking chips
- 1 cup dried cherries, coarsely chopped
- 1 cup chopped pecans

1. Preheat oven to 350°. In a large bowl, cream butter and sugars until light and fluffy. Beat in egg and orange zest. Combine the flour, baking soda and salt; gradually add to creamed mixture and mix well. Fold in chips, cherries and pecans.
2. Drop by rounded tablespoonfuls 2 in. apart onto greased baking sheets. Bake for 10-12 minutes or until the edges are golden brown. Cool for 2 minutes before removing to wire racks.
1 cookie: 166 cal., 10g fat (5g sat. fat), 19mg chol., 108mg sod., 19g carb. (13g sugars, 1g fiber), 2g pro.

GRANDMA BRUBAKER'S ORANGE COOKIES

At least two generations of my family have enjoyed the recipe for these light, delicate, orange-flavored cookies.

—*Sheri DeBolt, Huntington, IN*

Prep: 20 min. • **Bake:** 10 min./batch + cooling
Makes: about 6 dozen

- 1 cup shortening
- 2 cups sugar
- 2 large eggs, room temperature, separated
- 1 cup buttermilk
- 5 cups all-purpose flour
- 2 tsp. baking powder
- 2 tsp. baking soda
- Pinch salt
- Juice and grated zest of 2 medium navel oranges

ICING
- 2 cups confectioners' sugar
- ¼ cup orange juice
- 1 Tbsp. butter
- 1 Tbsp. grated orange zest

1. Preheat oven to 325°. In a bowl, cream the shortening and sugar. Beat in egg yolks and buttermilk. Sift together flour, baking powder, soda and salt; add to the creamed mixture alternately with orange juice and zest. Add egg whites and beat until smooth.
2. Drop by rounded teaspoonfuls onto greased cookie sheets. Bake until set, about 10 minutes. Remove to wire racks to cool completely.
3. For icing, combine all ingredients and beat until smooth. Frost cooled cookies.
1 cookie: 97 cal., 3g fat (1g sat. fat), 6mg chol., 58mg sod., 16g carb. (9g sugars, 0 fiber), 1g pro.

FROSTED RASPBERRY TRUFFLE BROWNIES

On the outside, these look like traditional brownies. Inside is a pleasantly surprise—it's almost like eating a filled chocolate candy.

—Leslie Knicl, Mahomet, IL

- -

Prep: 30 min. • **Bake:** 30 min. + chilling
Makes: about 2½ dozen

- ½ cup butter, cubed
- 1¼ cups semisweet chocolate chips
- 2 large eggs
- ¾ cup packed brown sugar
- 1 tsp. instant coffee granules
- 2 Tbsp. hot water
- ¾ cup all-purpose flour
- ½ tsp. baking powder

FILLING
- 1 cup semisweet chocolate chips
- 1 pkg. (8 oz.) cream cheese, softened
- ¼ cup confectioners' sugar
- ⅓ cup seedless red raspberry jam

GLAZE
- ¼ cup semisweet chocolate chips
- 1 tsp. shortening

1. Preheat oven to 350°. In a microwave, melt the butter and chocolate chips; stir until smooth. Cool slightly. In a large bowl, beat the eggs and brown sugar until blended. Dissolve coffee granules in water; add to the egg mixture. Beat in the chocolate until well blended. Combine flour and baking powder; stir into chocolate mixture just until blended.

2. Spread in a greased 9-in. square baking pan. Bake for 30-35 minutes or until brownies test done. Cool on a wire rack.

3. For the filling, in a microwave, melt chocolate chips; stir until smooth. Cool. In a small bowl, beat the cream cheese and confectioners' sugar until smooth. Beat in jam; stir in the melted chocolate. Spread over cooled brownies.

4. For glaze, in a microwave, melt the chocolate chips and shortening; stir until smooth. Drizzle over filling. Chill before cutting. Store in the refrigerator.

1 brownie: 171 cal., 10g fat (6g sat. fat), 31mg chol., 68mg sod., 20g carb. (17g sugars, 1g fiber), 2g pro.

ALMOND TOFFEE SANDIES

I knew after sampling these cookies from a friend that I had to add the recipe to my bulging files!
—*Vicki Crowley, Monticello, IA*

Prep: 15 min. • **Bake:** 10 min./batch
Makes: 9 dozen

- 1 cup butter, softened
- 1 cup sugar
- 1 cup confectioners' sugar
- 2 large eggs
- 1 cup canola oil
- 1 tsp. almond extract
- 4½ cups all-purpose flour
- 1 tsp. baking soda
- 1 tsp. cream of tartar
- 1 tsp. salt
- 2 cups sliced almonds
- 1 pkg. (8 oz.) toffee bits

1. Preheat oven to 350°. In a large bowl, cream butter and sugars until blended. Add eggs, one at a time, beating well after each addition. Gradually beat in oil and extract. Combine the flour, baking soda, cream of tartar and salt; gradually add to the creamed mixture and mix well. Stir in almonds and toffee bits.

2. Drop by teaspoonfuls 2 in. apart onto ungreased baking sheets. Bake until golden brown, 10-12 minutes. Remove to wire racks to cool.

2 cookies: 178 cal., 11g fat (4g sat. fat), 19mg chol., 134mg sod., 18g carb. (9g sugars, 1g fiber), 2g pro.

Pecan Toffee Sandies: Substitute 2 cups coarsely chopped pecans for the almonds.

BUTTERY COCONUT BARS

My coconut bars are an American version of a Filipino coconut cake called *bibingka*. These are a crispier, sweeter take on the Christmas tradition I grew up with.
—*Denise Nyland, Panama City, FL*

Prep: 20 min. + cooling
Bake: 40 min. + cooling • **Makes:** 3 dozen

- 2 cups all-purpose flour
- 1 cup packed brown sugar
- ½ tsp. salt
- 1 cup butter, melted

FILLING
- 3 large eggs
- 1 can (14 oz.) sweetened condensed milk
- ½ cup all-purpose flour
- ¼ cup packed brown sugar
- ¼ cup butter, melted
- 3 tsp. vanilla extract
- ½ tsp. salt
- 4 cups sweetened shredded coconut, divided

1. Preheat oven to 350°. Line a 13x9-in. baking pan with parchment, letting the ends extend up the sides of the pan.

2. In a large bowl, mix flour, brown sugar and salt; stir in 1 cup melted butter. Press onto bottom of prepared pan. Bake until light brown, 12-15 minutes. Cool for 10 minutes on a wire rack. Reduce oven setting to 325°.

3. In a large bowl, whisk the first seven filling ingredients until blended; stir in 3 cups coconut. Pour over the crust; sprinkle with the remaining coconut. Bake until light golden brown, 25-30 minutes. Cool in the pan on a wire rack. Lifting with parchment, remove from pan. Cut into bars.

1 bar: 211 cal., 12g fat (8g sat. fat), 36mg chol., 166mg sod., 25g carb. (18g sugars, 1g fiber), 3g pro.

Dazzling Desserts

Wrap up dinner with a luscious pie, a decadent cake or a comforting homemade cobbler. The 29 recipes in this chapter include favorites like strudel and bundt cake—plus a special selection of frosty desserts perfect for cooling you down. Go ahead—treat yourself and your loved ones!

QUICK ICEBOX SANDWICHES

My mother liked making these cool, creamy treats when I was growing up in the States because she could make them so quickly. Now my three kids enjoy them!

—*Sandy Armijo, Naples, Italy*

- -

Prep: 20 min. + freezing • **Makes:** 2 dozen

- 1 pkg. (3.4 oz.) instant vanilla pudding mix
- 2 cups cold whole milk
- 2 cups whipped topping
- 1 cup miniature semisweet chocolate chips
- 24 whole graham crackers, halved

1. Mix pudding and milk according to the package directions; refrigerate until set. Fold in the whipped topping and chocolate chips.

2. Place 24 graham cracker halves on a baking sheet; top each with about 3 Tbsp. filling. Place another graham cracker half on top. Wrap individual sandwiches in plastic; freeze for 1 hour or until firm. Serve frozen.

1 sandwich: 144 cal., 5g fat (3g sat. fat), 3mg chol., 162mg sod., 23g carb. (13g sugars, 1g fiber), 2g pro.

DOUBLE NUT BAKLAVA

It may take some time to make this rich, buttery treat, but it's well worth the effort! The tropical-tinged blend of coconut, macadamia nuts and pecans is an irresistible spin on traditional baklava.

—*Kari Kelley, Plains, MT*

- -

Prep: 25 min. • **Bake:** 30 min. + standing
Makes: about 3 dozen

- 1¼ cups sweetened shredded coconut, toasted
- ½ cup finely chopped macadamia nuts
- ½ cup finely chopped pecans
- ½ cup packed brown sugar
- 1 tsp. ground allspice
- 1¼ cups butter, melted
- 1 pkg. phyllo dough (16 oz., 14x9-in.- sheet size), thawed
- 1 cup sugar
- ½ cup water
- ¼ cup honey

1. Preheat oven to 350°. In a large bowl, combine the first five ingredients; set aside. Brush a 13x9-in. baking pan with some of the butter. Unroll the sheets of phyllo dough; trim to fit into pan.

2. Layer 10 sheets of phyllo in prepared pan, brushing each with butter. (Keep the remaining dough covered with plastic wrap and a damp towel to prevent it from drying out until it's ready to use.) Sprinkle with a third of the nut mixture. Repeat layers twice. Top with five phyllo sheets, brushing each with butter.

3. Using a sharp knife, cut into diamond shapes. Bake for 30-35 minutes or until golden brown. Set pan on a wire rack to cool completely.

4. In a small saucepan, bring the sugar, water and honey to a boil. Reduce heat; simmer for 5 minutes. Pour hot syrup over the baklava. Cover and let stand overnight.

1 piece: 174 cal., 10g fat (5g sat. fat), 17mg chol., 134mg sod., 20g carb. (12g sugars, 1g fiber), 2g pro.

HOT CHOCOLATE TIRAMISU

Instead of using coffee and rum, I let the cinnamon shine in my version of tiramisu. This dish tastes best if eaten within two days—if it even lasts that long!
—*Cathy Geniti, Saratoga Springs, NY*

- -

Prep: 25 min. • **Cook:** 10 min. + chilling
Makes: 12 servings

- 3 Tbsp. baking cocoa
- 3 Tbsp. sugar
- 2 Tbsp. water
- 2 cups whole milk

TIRAMISU

- 3 large egg yolks
- 1 cup sugar, divided
- 2 cups mascarpone cheese
- 1 cup heavy whipping cream
- 45 crisp ladyfinger cookies (about 13 oz.)
- ¼ cup miniature semisweet chocolate chips
- 2 tsp. ground cinnamon

1. For hot cocoa, in a small saucepan, mix the cocoa, sugar and water until smooth. Bring to a boil; cook, stirring constantly, 2 minutes. Stir in the milk until blended; transfer to a shallow bowl to cool completely.

2. For tiramisu, in a heatproof bowl of a stand mixer, whisk egg yolks and ½ cup sugar until blended. Place over simmering water in a large saucepan over medium heat. Whisking constantly, heat mixture until a thermometer reads 160°, about 2-3 minutes.

3. Remove from heat. With the whisk attachment of the mixer, beat on high speed until thick and pale yellow, about 5 minutes. Add mascarpone; beat on medium speed until smooth, scraping down sides of bowl as needed.

4. In another bowl, beat cream until it begins to thicken. Add remaining sugar; beat until soft peaks form. Fold whipped cream into mascarpone mixture.

5. To assemble, spread one-third of the cream mixture into a 13x9-in. baking dish. Quickly dip half of the ladyfingers halfway into the cooled cocoa; arrange over the cream. Repeat layers. Spread with the remaining cream mixture. Sprinkle with semisweet chocolate chips and cinnamon. Refrigerate, covered, for at least 8 hours or overnight.

Note: This recipe was prepared with Alessi brand ladyfinger cookies.

1 piece: 638 cal., 46g fat (25g sat. fat), 199mg chol., 112mg sod., 49g carb. (38g sugars, 1g fiber), 11g pro.

BLUEBERRY SLUMP

My mother-in-law used to make slump with wild blueberries and serve it warm with a pitcher of cream on the table. My husband and I have been eating it for over 65 years, but the recipe is even older!
—*Eleanore Ebeling, Brewster, MN*

- -

Takes: 30 min. • **Makes:** 6 servings

- 3 cups fresh or frozen blueberries
- ½ cup sugar
- 1¼ cups water
- 1 tsp. finely grated lemon zest
- 1 Tbsp. lemon juice
- 1 cup all-purpose flour
- 2 Tbsp. sugar
- 2 tsp. baking powder
- ½ tsp. salt
- 1 Tbsp. butter
- ½ cup milk
  Cream or whipped cream, optional

1. In a large heavy saucepan, combine the blueberries, sugar, water, lemon zest and juice; bring to a boil. Reduce heat and simmer, uncovered, for 5 minutes.

2. Meanwhile, in a large bowl, combine the flour, sugar, baking powder and salt; cut in butter until the mixture resembles coarse crumbs. Add milk quickly; stir until moistened.

3. Drop dough by spoonfuls onto berries (makes six dumplings). Cover and cook over low heat for 10 minutes. Do not lift lid while simmering. Spoon dumplings into individual serving bowls; top with sauce. Serve warm with cream or whipped cream if desired.

1 serving: 228 cal., 3g fat (2g sat. fat), 8mg chol., 361mg sod., 48g carb. (29g sugars, 2g fiber), 3g pro.

CRANBERRY-ALMOND APPLE PIE

My grandmother made this treat every year for Christmas. It's much better than everyday apple pie. The recipe is a family treasure.
—*Maxine Theriault, Nashua, NH*

- -

Prep: 15 min. • **Bake:** 1 hour
Makes: 8 servings

- 1 cup sugar
- ¼ cup all-purpose flour
- 3 Tbsp. butter, melted
- ½ tsp. ground nutmeg
- ⅛ tsp. salt
- 6 medium tart apples, peeled and thinly sliced
- 1 cup fresh or frozen cranberries
- 1 pastry shell (9 in.)

TOPPING
- ½ cup packed brown sugar
- ⅓ cup all-purpose flour
- ½ tsp. ground cinnamon
- 3 Tbsp. cold butter
- ⅓ cup sliced almonds, toasted

1. Preheat oven to 350°. In a bowl, combine the sugar, flour, butter, nutmeg and salt. Add apples and cranberries; stir gently. Pour into the pastry shell.
2. In a small bowl, combine the brown sugar, flour and cinnamon; cut in butter until crumbly. Stir in almonds; sprinkle over filling. Bake for 1 hour or until apples are tender.

1 slice: 453 cal., 18g fat (9g sat. fat), 28mg chol., 230mg sod., 73g carb. (50g sugars, 3g fiber), 3g pro.

AUNT MURNA'S JAM CAKE

I remember Aunt Murna telling me that she created her jam cake recipe as a young girl. She made some improvements to it over the years, such as soaking the raisins in crushed pineapple. This cake is a favorite at our annual family reunions.
—*Eddie Robinson, Lawrenceburg, KY*

- -

Prep: 20 min. + soaking
Bake: 50 min. + cooling • **Makes:** 16 servings

- 1 cup raisins
- 1 can (8 oz.) crushed pineapple, undrained
- 1 cup butter, softened
- 1 cup sugar
- 4 large eggs
- 1 jar (12 oz.) blackberry jam or 1 cup homemade blackberry jam
- ⅔ cup buttermilk
- 2½ cups all-purpose flour
- ⅓ cup baking cocoa
- 1 tsp. baking soda
- 1 tsp. ground cinnamon
- 1 tsp. ground nutmeg
- ½ tsp. ground cloves
- 1 cup chopped pecans

CARAMEL ICING
- 1 cup butter, cubed
- 2 cups packed brown sugar
- ½ cup whole milk
- 3½ to 4 cups sifted confectioners' sugar

1. Soak raisins in pineapple and juice several hours or overnight.
2. Preheat oven to 350°. Grease and flour two 9-in. round baking pans; set aside. In a large bowl, cream butter and sugar until light and fluffy. Add eggs, one at a time, beating well after each addition. Add jam and buttermilk; beat until well blended. Sift together dry ingredients; add to batter. Beat on low just until combined. Stir in the raisins, pineapple and pecans.
3. Pour into prepared pans. Bake until a toothpick inserted in the center comes out clean, about 50 minutes. Cool in pans for 10 minutes before removing to wire racks to cool completely.
4. For icing, melt butter in a saucepan over medium heat. Stir in brown sugar and milk; bring to a boil. Remove from the heat. Cool just until warm; beat in enough of the confectioners' sugar for icing to reach spreading consistency. Add more sugar for thicker icing, more milk to thin it. Frost cooled cake.

1 slice: 694 cal., 30g fat (15g sat. fat), 116mg chol., 353mg sod., 105g carb. (83g sugars, 2g fiber), 6g pro.

IVA'S PEACH COBBLER

My mother received this recipe from a friend of hers many years ago and shared it with me. Boise is situated right between two large fruit-producing areas in our state, so sweet, juicy peaches are plentiful in the summer.
—*Ruby Ewart, Boise, ID*

Prep: 15 min. • **Bake:** 45 min.
Makes: 12 servings

- 6 to 8 large ripe peaches, peeled and sliced
- 2½ Tbsp. cornstarch
- ¾ to 1 cup sugar

CRUST
- 1 cup all-purpose flour
- 2 large egg yolks. room temperature
- ¼ cup butter, melted
- 1 tsp. baking powder
- 1 cup sugar
- 2 large egg whites, room temperature, stiffly beaten

Preheat oven to 375°. Combine peaches, cornstarch and sugar; place in a greased 13x9-in. baking dish. For crust, combine flour, egg yolks, butter, baking powder and sugar in a bowl. Gently fold in egg whites. Spread over peaches. Bake until the fruit is bubbling around edges and the top is golden, about 45 minutes.
½ cup: 224 cal., 5g fat (3g sat. fat), 46mg chol., 83mg sod., 44g carb. (33g sugars, 1g fiber), 3g pro.

HAZELNUT PEAR CAKE

From the hazelnuts to the yummy browned butter glaze, this dessert is a little different from an everyday pound cake.
—*Elisabeth Larsen, Pleasant Grove, UT*

Prep: 30 min. • **Bake:** 55 min. + cooling
Makes: 16 servings

- 1½ cups whole hazelnuts, toasted and skins removed
- 1 cup unsalted butter, softened
- 2 cups sugar
- 4 large eggs
- 2 tsp. vanilla extract
- 1 tsp. almond extract
- 2½ cups all-purpose flour
- ½ tsp. salt
- ½ tsp. baking soda
- 1 cup ricotta cheese
- 3 ripe medium pears, peeled and chopped (about 2 cups)

BROWNED BUTTER GLAZE
- ½ cup butter, cubed
- 3 Tbsp. 2% milk
- 1 tsp. vanilla extract
- 1¾ to 2 cups confectioners' sugar

1. Preheat oven to 350°. Grease and flour a 10-in. fluted tube pan. Chop 1 cup hazelnuts. Place remaining hazelnuts in a food processor; pulse until finely ground.

2. In a large bowl, cream butter and sugar until light and fluffy. Add eggs, one at a time, beating well after each addition. Beat in extracts.

3. In another bowl, whisk the flour, salt, baking soda and ground hazelnuts; add to the creamed mixture alternately with the ricotta cheese, beating after each addition just until combined. Fold in pears and chopped hazelnuts.

4. Transfer batter to prepared pan. Bake for 55-65 minutes or until a toothpick inserted in center comes out clean. Cool in pan 10 minutes before removing to a wire rack to cool completely.

5. For glaze, in a small heavy saucepan, melt butter over medium heat. Heat for 5-7 minutes or until golden brown, stirring constantly. Transfer to a bowl. Stir in milk, vanilla and enough confectioners' sugar to reach desired consistency. Drizzle over cooled cake.

Note: To remove cakes easily, use solid shortening to grease plain and fluted tube pans. • To toast whole hazelnuts, spread hazelnuts in a 15x10x1-in. baking pan. Bake in a 350° oven 7-10 minutes or until fragrant and lightly browned, stirring occasionally. To remove skins, wrap hazelnuts in a tea towel; rub with towel to loosen skins.
1 slice: 533 cal., 30g fat (13g sat. fat), 104mg chol., 193mg sod., 62g carb. (42g sugars, 3g fiber), 8g pro.

FAVORITE COCONUT CAKE

When I need an impressive dessert for a special occasion, this is the recipe I always depend on. My guests are glad I do!
—*Edna Hoffman, Hebron, IN*

- -

Prep: 45 min. • **Bake:** 15 min. + cooling
Makes: 16 servings

  4 **large egg whites**
  ¾ **cup butter, softened**
1½ **cups sugar, divided**
  1 **tsp. almond extract**
  1 **tsp. vanilla extract**
2¾ **cups cake flour**
  4 **tsp. baking powder**
  ¾ **tsp. salt**
  1 **cup whole milk**
FROSTING
  5 **large egg whites**
1⅔ **cups sugar**
  1 **Tbsp. water**
  ½ **tsp. cream of tartar**
  1 **tsp. vanilla extract**
2½ **cups unsweetened coconut flakes**
     Colored sprinkles, optional

1. Place egg whites in a large bowl; let stand at room temperature 30 minutes. Line bottoms of three greased 9-in. round baking pans with parchment; grease the paper. Preheat oven to 350°.

2. Cream butter and 1 cup sugar until light and fluffy; beat in the extracts. In another bowl, whisk together the flour, baking powder and salt; add to creamed mixture alternately with milk.

3. With clean beaters, beat egg whites on medium speed until soft peaks form. Gradually add remaining sugar, 1 Tbsp. at a time, beating on high after each addition until sugar is dissolved. Continue beating until stiff glossy peaks form. Fold egg white mixture into the batter.

4. Transfer to prepared pans. Bake until a toothpick inserted in center comes out clean, 13-17 minutes. Cool in pans 10 minutes before removing to wire racks; remove paper. Cool completely.

5. For frosting, in a large heatproof bowl, whisk the egg whites, sugar, water and cream of tartar until blended. Place over simmering water in a large saucepan over medium heat; whisking constantly, heat mixture until a thermometer reads 160°, 2-3 minutes. Remove from heat; add vanilla. Beat on high speed until stiff glossy peaks form, about 7 minutes.

6. Spread frosting between layers and over top and sides of cake. Cover with coconut flakes. If desired, decorate with sprinkles. Store cake, uncovered, in refrigerator.

1 slice: 400 cal., 16g fat (11g sat. fat), 24mg chol., 341mg sod., 62g carb. (41g sugars, 2g fiber), 5g pro.

LAYERED LEMON DESSERT SQUARES

I found this recipe in an old cookbook and changed it to be extra citrusy. If you love Key lime pie, change the lemon flavors to lime.
—*Dawn Lowenstein, Huntingdon Valley, PA*

- -

Prep: 30 min. + chilling • **Makes:** 12 servings

- 3½ cups graham cracker crumbs
- 1¾ cups sugar, divided
- 1 Tbsp. ground cinnamon
- 1¼ cups butter, melted
- 2 pkg. (8 oz. each) cream cheese, softened
- 2 cups heavy whipping cream
- 1 tsp. lemon extract
- 2 jars (10 oz. each) lemon curd or 1 can (15¾ oz.) lemon pie filling

1. In a large bowl, mix cracker crumbs, ¾ cup sugar and cinnamon; stir in butter. Reserve half of mixture for topping. Press remaining crumb mixture onto bottom of a greased 13x9-in. baking dish.

2. In a large bowl, beat cream cheese and remaining sugar until smooth. Gradually beat in cream and extract until soft peaks form. Spread half of the cream cheese mixture over crust. Gently spread lemon curd over the cream cheese layer. Spread with the remaining cream cheese mixture. Sprinkle with reserved cracker crumbs. Refrigerate, covered, overnight.

1 serving: 676 cal., 42g fat (25g sat. fat), 136mg chol., 361mg sod., 71g carb. (56g sugars, 1g fiber), 5g pro.

RHUBARB STRAWBERRY COBBLER

Mom's yummy cobbler is a truly wonderful finale to any meal. This sweet-tart family favorite is brimming with berries and rhubarb and has a thick, easy-to-make crust.
—*Susan Emery, Everett, WA*

- -

Prep: 20 min. • **Bake:** 40 min.
Makes: 8 servings

- 1⅓ cups sugar
- ⅓ cup all-purpose flour
- 4 cups sliced fresh or frozen rhubarb, thawed (½-in. pieces)
- 2 cups halved fresh strawberries
- 2 Tbsp. butter, cubed

CRUST
- 2 cups all-purpose flour
- ½ tsp. salt
- ⅔ cup canola oil
- ⅓ cup warm water
- 1 Tbsp. 2% milk
- 1 Tbsp. sugar
  Vanilla ice cream, optional

1. Preheat oven to 425°. In a large bowl, mix sugar and flour. Add fruit; toss to coat. Transfer to a greased 11x7-in. baking dish. Dot with butter.

2. For crust, in a bowl, mix flour and salt. In another bowl, whisk oil and water; add to flour mixture, stirring with a fork until a dough is formed (dough will be sticky).

3. Roll dough between two pieces of waxed paper into an 11x7-in. rectangle. Remove top piece of waxed paper; invert rectangle over filling. Gently peel off waxed paper. Brush pastry with milk; sprinkle with sugar.

4. Bake 40-50 minutes or until golden brown. If desired, serve with ice cream.

Note: If using frozen rhubarb, measure while still frozen, then thaw completely. Drain in a colander, but do not press liquid out.

1 serving: 479 cal., 22g fat (4g sat. fat), 8mg chol., 181mg sod., 68g carb. (38g sugars, 3g fiber), 5g pro.

Frosty Homemade Desserts

If we all scream for ice cream, what will we do for sorbet, frozen yogurt and gelato? These flavorful, ultra cool treats are good any time of year, and all can be created in the kitchen with easy-to-get ingredients.

PUMPKIN ICE CREAM

With or without the added gingersnaps, this recipe really captures the flavor of fall.
—*Linda Young, Longmont, CO*

- -

Takes: 30 min. • **Makes:** 6 servings

1   cup canned pumpkin
¼   tsp. pumpkin pie spice
1   qt. vanilla ice cream, softened
    Gingersnaps, optional

In a large bowl, combine the pumpkin and pie spice until well blended. Stir in ice cream. Freeze until serving. Garnish with gingersnaps if desired.

1 cup: 190 cal., 10g fat (6g sat. fat), 39mg chol., 72mg sod., 24g carb. (17g sugars, 2g fiber), 4g pro.

BLACKBERRY FROZEN YOGURT

Pairing blackberries with tangy vanilla yogurt churns out this luscious purple delight. You could also use boysenberries, raspberries or strawberries—or even huckleberries, if you can get them!
—*Rebecca Baird, Salt Lake City, UT*

- -

Prep: 30 min. + freezing • **Makes:** 8 servings

5   cups fresh or frozen blackberries
⅓   cup water
2   Tbsp. lemon juice
1   cup sugar
2   tsp. vanilla extract
4   cups (32 oz.) fat-free frozen vanilla yogurt

1. In a food processor, puree the blackberries, water and lemon juice. Strain blackberries, reserving juice and pulp. Discard seeds. Return pureed berries to food processor; add sugar and vanilla. Cover and process until smooth.

2. In a large bowl, combine yogurt and blackberry mixture. Fill cylinder of an ice cream freezer two-thirds full; freeze according to manufacturer's directions. (Refrigerate the remaining mixture until ready to freeze.) When yogurt is frozen, transfer to a freezer container; freeze 2-4 hours before serving.

¾ cup: 248 cal., 1g fat (0 sat. fat), 2mg chol., 78mg sod., 57g carb. (0 sugars, 5g fiber), 6g pro.

WATERMELON CHOCOLATE CHIP SORBET

Summertime and watermelon go hand in hand. My melon sorbet is fresh, fruity and without the gluten and eggs you get in many other frozen desserts.
—*Rachel Lewis, Danville, VA*

- -

Prep: 15 min. + chilling
Process: 30 min. + freezing • **Makes:** 1 qt.

- 1 cup sugar
- ½ cup water
- 3 cups chopped seedless watermelon
- 1 cup orange juice
- 2 Tbsp. lime juice
- ½ cup miniature semisweet chocolate chips, optional

1. In a small saucepan, bring the sugar and water to a boil. Reduce the heat; simmer, uncovered, for 5 minutes, stirring occasionally to dissolve the sugar. Cool mixture slightly.
2. Place watermelon in a food processor; process until pureed. Add orange juice, lime juice and the cooled syrup; process until blended. Transfer to a large bowl; refrigerate, covered, 3 hours or until cold.
3. Pour into cylinder of ice cream freezer. Freeze according to the manufacturer's directions; if desired, add chocolate chips during the last 10 minutes of processing. Transfer sorbet to freezer containers, allowing headspace for expansion. Freeze 2-4 hours or until firm.

½ cup: 129 cal., 0 fat (0 sat. fat), 0 chol., 1mg sod., 33g carb. (32g sugars, 0 fiber), 1g pro.

LEMON GELATO

On a recent trip to Italy, I became addicted to gelato. My favorite choice was lemon because Italian lemons have an intense flavor. This recipe brings back memories of our vacation.
—*Gail Wang, Troy, MI*

- -

Prep: 30 min. • **Process:** 20 min. + freezing
Makes: 1½ qt.

- 1 cup whole milk
- 1 cup sugar
- 5 large egg yolks, lightly beaten
- 3 Tbsp. grated lemon zest
- ¾ cup fresh lemon juice (about 5 lemons)
- 2 cups heavy whipping cream

1. In a small heavy saucepan, heat milk to 175°; stir in sugar until dissolved. Whisk a small amount of the hot mixture into egg yolks. Return all to the pan, whisking constantly. Add lemon zest. Cook over low heat until the mixture is just thick enough to coat a metal spoon and a thermometer reads at least 160°, stirring constantly. Do not allow to boil.
2. Remove immediately from heat; stir in lemon juice and cream. Place in a bowl. Press plastic wrap on surface of custard; refrigerate several hours or overnight.
3. Fill the cylinder of an ice cream freezer two-thirds full; freeze according to the manufacturer's directions. (Refrigerate remaining mixture until ready to freeze.) Transfer ice cream to freezer containers, allowing headspace for expansion. Freeze 2-4 hours or until firm. Repeat with the remaining mixture.

⅔ cup: 361 cal., 26g fat (15g sat. fat), 213mg chol., 40mg sod., 31g carb. (27g sugars, 0 fiber), 4g pro.

LEMON PEELS DO DOUBLE DUTY

For an elegant (and fun!) presentation, spoon the gelato into the hollowed-out halves of the lemons. You can keep the "bowls" filled with gelato in the freezer until you're ready to serve.

CHOCOLATE CAKE WITH CHOCOLATE FROSTING

I once sent this rich chocolate cake to my kids' teachers, and it vanished, so I had to make another one. Who swipes a whole cake? When it's this one, it's a risk!
—*Megan Moelbert, Springville, NY*

- -

Prep: 40 min. • **Bake:** 30 min. + cooling
Makes: 16 servings

- 2 **cups sugar**
- 2 **cups water**
- ⅔ **cup canola oil**
- 2 **Tbsp. white vinegar**
- 2 **tsp. vanilla extract**
- 3 **cups all-purpose flour**
- ⅓ **cup plus 1 Tbsp. baking cocoa, sifted**
- 2 **tsp. baking soda**
- 1 **tsp. salt**

FROSTING

- 3¾ **cups confectioners' sugar**
- ⅓ **cup baking cocoa**
- 1 **cup butter, softened**
- 1 **tsp. vanilla extract**
- 3 **to 5 Tbsp. 2% milk**

1. Preheat oven to 350°. Line bottoms of two greased 9-in. round baking pans with parchment; grease paper. Set aside.
2. In a large bowl, beat sugar, water, oil, vinegar and vanilla until well blended. In a large bowl, whisk flour, sifted cocoa, baking soda and salt; gradually add to the sugar mixture, beating until smooth.
3. Transfer batter to prepared pans. Bake for 30-35 minutes or until a toothpick inserted in center comes out clean. Cool in pans for 10 minutes before removing to wire racks; remove paper. Cool the cakes completely.
4. For frosting, sift confectioners' sugar and cocoa together. In a large bowl, beat butter and vanilla until blended. Beat in confectioners' sugar mixture alternately with enough of the milk to reach desired consistency. Spread frosting between layers and over the top and sides of cake.
For sheet cake: Make batter as directed and transfer to a greased 13x9-in. baking pan. Bake in a preheated 350° oven for 30-35 minutes or until a toothpick inserted in center comes out clean. Frosting recipe may be halved.
1 slice: 491 cal., 22g fat (8g sat. fat), 31mg chol., 399mg sod., 74g carb. (53g sugars, 1g fiber), 3g pro.

PEACH AND BERRY COBBLER

This is one of my favorite summer recipes, as it features seasonal peaches and berries. However, it's just as delicious with frozen fruit, so you can indulge year-round. A quick biscuit topping brings it all together.
—*Lauren Knoelke, Des Moines, IA*

- -

Prep: 20 min. • **Bake:** 40 min.
Makes: 8 servings

- ½ **cup sugar**
- 3 **Tbsp. cornstarch**
- ½ **tsp. ground cinnamon**
- ¼ **tsp. ground cardamom**
- 10 **medium peaches, pealed and sliced**
- 2 **cups mixed blackberries, raspberries and blueberries**
- 1 **Tbsp. lemon juice**

TOPPING

- 1 **cup all-purpose flour**
- ¼ **cup sugar**
- 2 **tsp. grated orange zest**
- ¾ **tsp. baking powder**
- ¼ **tsp. salt**
- ¼ **tsp. baking soda**
- 3 **Tbsp. cold butter**
- ¾ **cup buttermilk**
  Vanilla ice cream, optional

1. Preheat oven to 375°. In a large bowl, mix sugar, cornstarch, cinnamon and cardamom. Add the peaches, berries and lemon juice; toss to combine. Transfer to a 10-in. cast-iron skillet.
2. In a small bowl, whisk the first six topping ingredients; cut in butter until the mixture resembles coarse crumbs. Add buttermilk; stir just until moistened. Drop mixture by tablespoonfuls over peach mixture.
3. Bake, uncovered, for 40-45 minutes or until the topping is golden brown. Serve warm. If desired, top with vanilla ice cream.
1 serving: 279 cal., 5g fat (3g sat. fat), 12mg chol., 238mg sod., 57g carb. (38g sugars, 5g fiber), 4g pro.

OMA'S APFELKUCHEN

Translated from German, the name of this recipe means "Grandma's apple cake," and my husband's family has been making it for more than 150 years. It's that scrumptious! Try it with any apples you have on hand. I used Granny Smith.

—Amy Kirchen, Loveland, OH

- -

Prep: 20 min. • **Bake:** 45 min. + cooling
Makes: 10 servings

- 5 **large egg yolks**
- 2 **medium tart apples, peeled, cored and halved**
- 1 **cup plus 2 Tbsp. unsalted butter, softened**
- 1¼ **cups sugar**

- 2 **cups all-purpose flour**
- 2 **Tbsp. cornstarch**
- 2 **tsp. cream of tartar**
- 1 **tsp. baking powder**
- ½ **tsp. salt**
- ¼ **cup 2% milk**
  Confectioners' sugar

1. Preheat oven to 350°. Let the egg yolks stand at room temperature for 30 minutes. Grease a 9-in. springform pan and wrap it in foil; set aside. Starting ½ in. from one end, cut the apple halves lengthwise into ¼-in. slices, leaving them attached at the top so they fan out slightly. Set aside.
2. Cream butter and sugar until light and fluffy. Add the egg yolks, one at a time;

beat well after each addition. In another bowl, sift flour, cornstarch, cream of tartar, baking powder and salt twice. Gradually beat into the creamed mixture. Add milk; mix well (batter will be thick).
3. Spread the batter into the prepared pan. Gently press apples, round side up, into the batter. Bake until a toothpick inserted in the center comes out with moist crumbs, 45-55 minutes. Cool on a wire rack for 10 minutes. Loosen sides from pan with a knife; remove foil. Cool 1 hour longer. Remove rim from pan. Dust with confectioners' sugar.
1 slice: 422 cal., 23g fat (14g sat. fat), 148mg chol., 177mg sod., 50g carb. (28g sugars, 1g fiber), 4g pro.

JUICY PEACH & STRAWBERRY CRUMB PIE

You've had peach pie and strawberry pie, and maybe even peach-strawberry pie. But throw in some garden-fresh basil and you're in for a real treat!

—*Lindsay Sprunk, Brooklyn, NY*

Prep: 25 min. • **Bake:** 45 min. + cooling
Makes: 8 servings

- 1   sheet refrigerated pie crust
- 3½ cups sliced peeled peaches (about 4 medium)
- 2½ cups sliced fresh strawberries
- 2   Tbsp. lemon juice
- ¾   cup sugar
- ¼   cup cornstarch
- 2   Tbsp. minced fresh basil
- ¾   cup all-purpose flour
- ½   cup packed brown sugar
- 6   Tbsp. cold butter

1. Preheat oven to 375°. Unroll crust into a 9-in. pie plate; flute edge. In a large bowl, combine the peaches, strawberries and lemon juice. In a small bowl, mix the sugar, cornstarch and basil. Add to fruit and toss gently to coat. Transfer to crust.
2. In a small bowl, mix flour and brown sugar; cut in butter until crumbly. Sprinkle over filling. Place the pie on a foil-lined baking pan.
3. Bake on a lower oven rack until the topping is golden brown and filling is bubbly, 45-55 minutes. Cool pie on a wire rack.
1 piece: 424 cal., 16g fat (9g sat. fat), 28mg chol., 174mg sod., 69g carb. (41g sugars, 2g fiber), 3g pro.

TART CHERRY MERINGUE DESSERT

I've made this cherry dessert for years to serve at baby showers, birthday parties and other special occasions. People really enjoy the tender crust, cherry filling and melt-in-your-mouth meringue.

—*Kathryn Dawley, Gray, ME*

Prep: 25 min. • **Bake:** 25 min. + chilling
Makes: 12 servings

- 2   cups all-purpose flour
- 1   tsp. salt
- 1   cup shortening
- 1   large egg, lightly beaten

TOPPING AND FILLING
- 3   large eggs, separated
- 1   tsp. vanilla extract
- ¼   tsp. cream of tartar
- 1½ cups sugar, divided
- ¾   cup finely chopped almonds
- 1   can (14½ oz.) pitted tart cherries
- 3   Tbsp. quick-cooking tapioca
- 2   tsp. lemon juice
- 6   to 8 drops red food coloring, optional

1. Preheat oven to 375°. In a small bowl, mix flour and salt; cut in shortening until crumbly. Add egg, stirring with a fork.

Press mixture onto bottom and up sides of a greased 11x7-in. baking dish. Bake for 20-22 minutes or until lightly browned. Cool on a wire rack. Reduce oven setting to 350°.
2. In a small bowl, beat egg whites with vanilla and cream of tartar on medium speed until soft peaks form. Gradually add ¾ cup sugar, 1 Tbsp. at a time, beating on high after each addition until sugar is dissolved. Continue beating until stiff glossy peaks form. Fold in almonds.
3. Drain cherries, reserving juice. Add enough water to the juice to measure 1 cup; pour into a saucepan. Stir in tapioca, egg yolks and the remaining sugar; let stand 5 minutes. Bring to a boil over medium heat, stirring constantly; cook and stir 2 minutes or until thickened. Stir in cherries, lemon juice and, if desired, food coloring.
4. Pour into crust. Immediately spread meringue over top, sealing edges to crust. Bake 22-25 minutes or until meringue is golden brown.
5. Cool 1 hour on a wire rack. Refrigerate at least 3 hours before serving.
1 piece: 554 cal., 28g fat (6g sat. fat), 94mg chol., 294mg sod., 69g carb. (42g sugars, 2g fiber), 8g pro.

BUTTERMILK CAKE WITH CARAMEL ICING

This fabulous cake is so tender, it melts in your mouth. It's been a family favorite since the '70s and always goes over really well at our church potluck meals.
—*Anna Jean Allen, West Liberty, KY*

- -

Prep: 35 min. • **Bake:** 45 min. + cooling
Makes: 16 servings

- 1 cup butter, softened
- 2⅓ cups sugar
- 1½ tsp. vanilla extract
- 3 large eggs
- 3 cups all-purpose flour
- 1 tsp. baking powder
- ½ tsp. baking soda
- 1 cup buttermilk

ICING
- ¼ cup butter, cubed
- ½ cup packed brown sugar
- ⅓ cup heavy whipping cream
- 1 cup confectioners' sugar

1. Preheat oven to 350°. Grease and flour a 10-in. fluted tube pan. Cream butter and sugar until light and fluffy. Beat in vanilla and eggs, one at a time, beating well after each addition. In another bowl, whisk together the flour, baking powder and baking soda; add to the creamed mixture alternately with buttermilk (batter will be thick). Transfer to the prepared pan.
2. Bake until a toothpick inserted in the center comes out clean, 45-50 minutes. Cool in pan 10 minutes before removing to a wire rack to cool completely.
3. For icing, in a small saucepan, combine butter, brown sugar and cream; bring to a boil over medium heat, stirring constantly. Remove from heat; cool 5-10 minutes. Gradually beat in confectioners' sugar; spoon over cake.
Note: To remove the cakes easily, use solid shortening to grease either a plain and fluted tube pan.
1 slice: 419 cal., 17g fat (11g sat. fat), 79mg chol., 230mg sod., 63g carb. (44g sugars, 1g fiber), 4g pro.

NUTELLA HAND PIES

These pint-size Nutella hand pies made with puff pastry are too good to keep to yourself!
—*Taste of Home Test Kitchen*

- -

Prep: 10 min. • **Bake:** 20 min.
Makes: 9 servings

- 1 large egg
- 1 Tbsp. water
- 1 sheet frozen puff pastry, thawed
- 3 Tbsp. Nutella
- 1 to 2 tsp. grated orange zest

ICING
- ⅓ cup confectioners' sugar
- ½ tsp. orange juice
- ⅛ tsp. grated orange zest
  Additional Nutella, optional

1. Preheat oven to 400°. In a small bowl, whisk egg with water.
2. Unfold the puff pastry; cut into nine squares. Place 1 tsp. Nutella in the center of each square; sprinkle with orange zest. Brush the edges of each pastry with egg mixture. Fold one corner over filling to form a triangle; press edges to seal. Transfer to an ungreased baking sheet.
3. Bake until pies are golden brown and puff pastry has cooked through, 17-20 minutes. Cool slightly.
4. In a small bowl, mix confectioners' sugar, orange juice and orange zest; drizzle over pies. If desired, warm additional Nutella in a microwave and drizzle over top.
1 hand pie: 190 cal., 10g fat (2g sat. fat), 21mg chol., 100mg sod., 24g carb. (8g sugars, 2g fiber), 3g pro.

STRAWBERRY CREAM CHEESE PIE

Cheesecake lovers will savor every bite of this light and pretty pie, even if they don't have to watch their diets. Our whole family enjoys it.
—*Kenny Van Rheenen, Mendota, IL*

Prep: 20 min. + chilling
Bake: 30 min. + cooling • **Makes:** 8 servings

```
     Pastry for a single-crust pie (9 in.)
 1   pkg. (8 oz.) reduced-fat
     cream cheese
 ½   cup egg substitute
 3   Tbsp. honey
 1   tsp. vanilla extract
3½   cups sliced fresh strawberries
 1   Tbsp. cornstarch
 ½   cup cold water
 ½   cup reduced-sugar strawberry
     preserves
     Fat-free whipped topping, optional
```

1. Preheat oven to 350°. Roll out crust to fit a 9-in. pie plate; transfer to plate. Trim to ½ in. beyond the edge of plate; flute edges. Bake for 13-15 minutes or until lightly browned.

2. Meanwhile, in a large bowl, beat the cream cheese, egg substitute, honey and vanilla until smooth. Pour into the crust. Bake 15-18 minutes longer or until the center is almost set. Cool completely on a wire rack.

3. Arrange strawberries over the filling. In a saucepan over low heat, combine cornstarch and water until smooth. Stir in preserves. Bring to a boil; cook and stir for 2 minutes or until thickened. Spoon or brush over the strawberries. Refrigerate for 2 hours before cutting. Garnish with whipped topping if desired.

1 piece: 268 cal., 12g fat (6g sat. fat), 21mg chol., 119mg sod., 34g carb. (0 sugars, 2g fiber), 5g pro.

TOFFEE TRUFFLE CHEESECAKE

I combined two of my favorite cheesecake recipes and added delicious homemade caramel sauce for a cheesecake that's now my favorite!
—*Hannah Halstead, Blair, NE*

Prep: 40 min. • **Bake:** 45 min. + chilling
Makes: 12 servings (¾ cup sauce)

```
1½   cups graham cracker crumbs
 3   Tbsp. sugar
 1   Tbsp. baking cocoa
 ⅓   cup butter, melted
```
FILLING
```
 2   pkg. (8 oz. each) cream cheese,
     softened
 ⅔   cup sugar
 8   oz. bittersweet chocolate, melted
     and cooled
 1   Tbsp. all-purpose flour
 1   tsp. vanilla extract
 3   large eggs, lightly beaten
 1   cup milk chocolate English toffee bits
```
SAUCE
```
 ¼   cup butter, cubed
 ⅔   cup packed brown sugar
 1   Tbsp. corn syrup
 ¼   cup heavy whipping cream
 2   Tbsp. plus ½ cup milk chocolate
     English toffee bits, divided
```

1. Preheat oven to 325°. In a small bowl, mix cracker crumbs, sugar and cocoa; stir in butter. Press onto bottom of a greased 9-in. springform pan.

2. In a large bowl, beat cream cheese and sugar until smooth. Beat in the cooled chocolate, flour and vanilla. Add eggs; beat on low speed just until blended. Fold in toffee bits. Pour over crust. Place pan on a baking sheet.

3. Bake 45-50 minutes or until center is almost set. Cool on a wire rack for 10 minutes. Loosen the sides from the pan with a knife. Cool 1 hour longer. Refrigerate overnight, covering when completely cooled.

4. For the sauce, melt butter in a small saucepan. Stir in brown sugar and corn syrup; bring to a boil. Reduce heat to medium; cook and stir until sugar is completely dissolved, about 2 minutes. Stir in cream; return to a boil. Remove from heat; stir in 2 Tbsp. toffee bits.

5. Remove the rim from springform pan. Sprinkle the remaining toffee bits over top of cheesecake. Warm sauce if necessary; serve with cheesecake.

1 slice with 1 Tbsp. sauce: 672 cal., 44g fat (25g sat. fat), 146mg chol., 396mg sod., 69g carb. (44g sugars, 2g fiber), 7g pro.

BREAD PUDDING WITH NUTMEG

I always make this recipe for my dad on his birthday and holidays. He says it tastes exactly like the bread pudding he enjoyed as a child.

—Donna Powell, Montgomery City, MO

Prep: 15 min. • **Bake:** 40 min.
Makes: 6 servings

    2   large eggs, room temperature
    2   cups whole milk
    ¼   cup butter, cubed
    ¾   cup sugar
    ¼   tsp. salt
    1   tsp. ground cinnamon
    ½   tsp. ground nutmeg
    1   tsp. vanilla extract
 4½ to 5 cups soft bread cubes
        (about 9 slices)
    ½   cup raisins, optional
VANILLA SAUCE
    ⅓   cup sugar
    2   Tbsp. cornstarch
    ¼   tsp. salt
 1⅔   cups cold water
    3   Tbsp. butter
    2   tsp. vanilla extract
    ¼   tsp. ground nutmeg

1. Preheat oven to 350°. In a large bowl, lightly beat eggs. Combine milk and butter; add to eggs along with sugar, salt, spices and vanilla. Add the bread cubes and the raisins if desired; stir gently.
2. Pour into a well-greased 11x7-in. baking dish. Bake for 40-45 minutes or until a knife inserted 1 in. from edge comes out clean.
3. Meanwhile, for sauce, combine the sugar, cornstarch and salt in a saucepan. Stir in water until smooth. Bring to a boil over medium heat; cook and stir for 2 minutes or until thickened. Remove from the heat. Stir in the butter, vanilla and nutmeg. Serve with warm pudding.
1 piece: 419 cal., 19g fat (11g sat. fat), 118mg chol., 534mg sod., 56g carb. (40g sugars, 1g fiber), 7g pro.

APPLE STRUDEL

My family always loves it when I make this wonderful dessert. Old-fashioned strudel was too fattening and time-consuming, but this revised classic is just as good. It's best served warm from the oven.

—Joanie Fuson, Indianapolis, IN

Prep: 30 min. • **Bake:** 35 min.
Makes: 6 servings

    ⅓   cup raisins
    2   Tbsp. water
    ¼   tsp. almond extract
    3   cups coarsely chopped peeled apples
    ⅓   cup plus 2 tsp. sugar, divided
    3   Tbsp. all-purpose flour
    ¼   tsp. ground cinnamon
    2   Tbsp. butter, melted
    2   Tbsp. canola oil
    8   sheets phyllo dough (14x9-in.)
        Confectioners' sugar, optional

1. Preheat oven to 350°. Place raisins, water and extract in a large microwave-save bowl; microwave, uncovered, on high for 1½ minutes. Let stand 5 minutes. Drain. Add apples, ⅓ cup sugar, flour and cinnamon; toss to combine.

2. In a small bowl, mix the melted butter and oil; remove 2 tsp. for brushing top. Place one sheet of phyllo dough on a work surface; brush lightly with some of the butter mixture. (Keep the remaining remaining phyllo covered with plastic wrap and a damp towel to prevent it from drying out.) Layer with seven additional phyllo sheets, brushing each layer with some of the butter mixture. Spread the apple mixture over the phyllo to within 2 in. of one long side.
3. Fold the short edges of the phyllo over the filling. Roll up jelly-roll style, starting from the side with a 2-in. border. Transfer to a baking sheet coated with cooking spray. Brush with the reserved butter mixture; sprinkle with the remaining sugar. With a sharp knife, cut diagonal slits in the top of the strudel.
4. Bake until strudel is golden brown, 35-40 minutes. Cool on a wire rack. If desired, dust with confectioners' sugar before serving.
1 slice: 229 cal., 9g fat (3g sat. fat), 10mg chol., 92mg sod., 37g carb. (24g sugars, 2g fiber), 2g pro.

CHOCOLATE CHIP COOKIE DOUGH CHEESECAKE

I created this recipe to combine two of my all-time favorites: cheesecake for the grown-up in me and chocolate chip cookie dough for the little girl in me. Sour cream offsets the sweetness and adds a nice tang. It's got all the age and flavor bases covered!
—*Julie Craig, Kewaskum, WI*

- -

Prep: 25 min. • **Bake:** 45 min. + chilling
Makes: 14 servings

1¾ cups crushed chocolate chip cookies or chocolate wafer crumbs
¼ cup sugar
⅓ cup butter, melted
FILLING
3 pkg. (8 oz. each) cream cheese, softened
1 cup sugar
1 cup sour cream
½ tsp. vanilla extract
3 large eggs, lightly beaten
COOKIE DOUGH
¼ cup butter, softened
¼ cup sugar
¼ cup packed brown sugar
1 Tbsp. water
1 tsp. vanilla extract
½ cup all-purpose flour
1½ cups miniature semisweet chocolate chips, divided

1. In a small bowl, combine the cookie crumbs and sugar; stir in butter. Press onto the bottom and 1 in. up the sides of a greased 9-in. springform pan. Place pan on a baking sheet; set aside.
2. In a large bowl, beat cream cheese and sugar until smooth. Beat in sour cream and vanilla. Add eggs; beat on low speed just until combined. Pour over the crust; set aside.
3. In another bowl, cream butter and sugars until light and fluffy. Add water and vanilla. Gradually add flour and mix well. Stir in 1 cup of the chocolate chips.
4. Drop the dough by teaspoonfuls over the filling, gently pushing dough below surface (the dough should be completely covered by the filling). Place pan on a baking sheet.
5. Bake at 350° for 45-55 minutes or until the center is almost set. Cool on a wire rack for 10 minutes. Carefully run a knife around the edge of the pan to loosen; cool 1 hour longer. Refrigerate overnight.
6. Remove sides of pan. Sprinkle with remaining chips. Refrigerate leftovers.

1 slice: 551 cal., 36g fat (22g sat. fat), 131mg chol., 328mg sod., 52g carb. (37g sugars, 2g fiber), 8g pro.

FRESH PLUM CRUMB DESSERT

Talk about comfort food! This old-fashioned dessert has the perfect sweet-tart balance with its fresh-plum tang and sweet, crispy topping. Imagine it warm from the oven, served with a scoop of ice cream...yum!
—*Janet Fahrenbruck-Lynch, Cincinnati, OH*

- -

Prep: 25 min. • **Bake:** 40 min. + cooling
Makes: 8 servings

- 7 large plums, pitted and quartered
- ½ cup packed brown sugar
- 3 Tbsp. plus 1 cup all-purpose flour, divided
- 1 tsp. ground cinnamon
- 1 cup sugar
- 1 tsp. baking powder
- ¼ tsp. salt
- ¼ tsp. ground mace
- 1 large egg, lightly beaten
- ½ cup butter, melted

1. Preheat oven to 375°. In a large bowl, combine plums, brown sugar, 3 Tbsp. of flour and the cinnamon. Spoon into a greased 2-qt. baking dish.

2. In a small bowl, combine sugar, baking powder, salt, mace and the remaining flour. Add egg; stir with a fork until crumbly. Sprinkle over plum mixture. Drizzle with butter.

3. Bake 40-45 minutes or until plums are tender and top is golden brown. Cool for 10 minutes before serving. Serve warm or at room temperature.

1 piece: 358 cal., 13g fat (7g sat. fat), 57mg chol., 253mg sod., 60g carb. (44g sugars, 2g fiber), 3g pro.

BANANA CREAM PIE

Made from our farm-fresh dairy products, this pie was a sensational creamy treat anytime that Mom served it. Her recipe is a treasure; I've never found one better!
—*Bernice Morris, Marshfield, MO*

- -

Prep: 20 min. + cooling • **Makes:** 8 servings

- ¾ cup sugar
- ⅓ cup all-purpose flour
- ¼ tsp. salt
- 2 cups whole milk
- 3 large egg yolks, room temperature, lightly beaten
- 2 Tbsp. butter
- 1 tsp. vanilla extract
- 3 medium, firm bananas
- 1 pastry shell (9 in.), baked
  Whipped cream and additional
  sliced bananas, optional

1. In a saucepan, combine the sugar, flour and salt; stir in the milk and mix well. Cook over medium-high heat until mixture is thickened and bubbly. Cook and stir for 2 minutes longer. Remove from the heat. Stir a small amount of the mixture into egg yolks; return all to saucepan. Bring to a gentle boil. Cook and stir 2 minutes; remove from the heat. Add butter and vanilla; cool slightly.

2. Slice the bananas into the pastry shell; pour filling over top. Cool on wire rack for 1 hour. Store in the refrigerator. If desired, before serving, garnish with whipped cream and sliced bananas.

1 slice: 338 cal., 14g fat (7g sat. fat), 101mg chol., 236mg sod., 49g carb. (30g sugars, 1g fiber), 5g pro.

HOW TO LOSE THE LUMPS

To ensure a smooth, lump-free filling, stir the sugar mixture constantly during cooking, and scrape the sides and bottom of the saucepan with a heatproof rubber spatula. For an Elvis-approved variation of this pie, spread a layer of peanut butter on the bottom of the pastry shell before adding the bananas.

Substitutions & Equivalents

EQUIVALENT MEASURES

3 teaspoons	= 1 tablespoon		16 tablespoons	= 1 cup	
4 tablespoons	= ¼ cup		2 cups	= 1 pint	
5⅓ tablespoons	= ⅓ cup		4 cups	= 1 quart	
8 tablespoons	= ½ cup		4 quarts	= 1 gallon	

FOOD EQUIVALENTS

GRAINS

Macaroni	1 cup (3½ ounces) uncooked	=	2½ cups cooked
Noodles, medium	3 cups (4 ounces) uncooked	=	4 cups cooked
Popcorn	⅓ -½ cup unpopped	=	8 cups popped
Rice, long grain	1 cup uncooked	=	3 cups cooked
Rice, quick-cooking	1 cup uncooked	=	2 cups cooked
Spaghetti	8 ounces uncooked	=	4 cups cooked

CRUMBS

Bread	1 slice	=	¾ cup soft crumbs, ¼ cup fine dry crumbs
Graham crackers	7 squares	=	½ cup finely crushed
Buttery round crackers	12 crackers	=	½ cup finely crushed
Saltine crackers	14 crackers	=	½ cup finely crushed

FRUITS

Bananas	1 medium	=	⅓ cup mashed
Lemons	1 medium	=	3 tablespoons juice, 2 teaspoons grated zest
Limes	1 medium	=	2 tablespoons juice, 1½ teaspoons grated zest
Oranges	1 medium	=	¼ -⅓ cup juice, 4 teaspoons grated zest

VEGETABLES

Cabbage	1 head	= 5 cups shredded	Green pepper	1 large	= 1 cup chopped	
Carrots	1 pound	= 3 cups shredded	Mushrooms	½ pound	= 3 cups sliced	
Celery	1 rib	= ½ cup chopped	Onions	1 medium	= ½ cup chopped	
Corn	1 ear fresh	= ⅔ cup kernels	Potatoes	3 medium	= 2 cups cubed	

NUTS

Almonds	1 pound	= 3 cups chopped	Pecan halves	1 pound	= 4½ cups chopped	
Ground nuts	3¾ ounces	= 1 cup	Walnuts	1 pound	= 3¾ cups chopped	

EASY SUBSTITUTIONS

WHEN YOU NEED...   USE...

Baking powder	1 teaspoon	½ teaspoon cream of tartar + ¼ teaspoon baking soda
Buttermilk	1 cup	1 tablespoon lemon juice or vinegar + enough milk to measure 1 cup (let stand 5 minutes before using)
Cornstarch	1 tablespoon	2 tablespoons all-purpose flour
Honey	1 cup	1¼ cups sugar + ¼ cup water
Half-and-half cream	1 cup	1 tablespoon melted butter + enough whole milk to measure 1 cup
Onion	1 small, chopped (⅓ cup)	1 teaspoon onion powder or 1 tablespoon dried minced onion
Tomato juice	1 cup	½ cup tomato sauce + ½ cup water
Tomato sauce	2 cups	¾ cup tomato paste + 1 cup water
Unsweetened chocolate	1 square (1 ounce)	3 tablespoons baking cocoa + 1 tablespoon shortening or oil
Whole milk	1 cup	½ cup evaporated milk + ½ cup water

Cooking Terms

Here's a quick reference for some of the most common cooking terms used in recipes:

BASTE To moisten food with melted butter, pan drippings, marinades or other liquid to add more flavor and juiciness.

BEAT A rapid movement to combine ingredients using a fork, spoon, wire whisk or electric mixer.

BLEND To combine ingredients until just mixed.

BOIL To heat liquids until bubbles form that cannot be stirred down. In the case of water, the temperature will reach 212°.

BONE To remove all meat from the bone before cooking.

CREAM To beat ingredients together to a smooth consistency, usually in the case of butter and sugar for baking.

DASH A small amount of seasoning, less than ⅛ teaspoon. If using a shaker, a dash would be a quick flick of the container.

DREDGE To coat foods with flour or other dry ingredients. Most often done with pot roasts and stew meat before browning.

FOLD To incorporate several ingredients by careful and gentle turning with a spatula. Often used with beaten egg whites or whipped cream when mixing into the rest of the ingredients to keep the batter light.

JULIENNE To cut foods into long thin strips much like matchsticks. Used most often for salads and stir-fry dishes.

MINCE To cut into very fine pieces. Used often for garlic or fresh herbs.

PARBOIL To cook partially. Usually used in the case of chicken, sausages and vegetables.

PARTIALLY SET Describes the consistency of gelatin after it has been chilled for a short amount of time. Mixture should resemble the consistency of egg whites.

PUREE To process foods to a smooth mixture. Can be prepared in an electric blender, food processor, food mill or sieve.

SAUTE To fry quickly in a small amount of fat, stirring almost constantly. Most often done with onions, mushrooms and other chopped vegetables.

SCORE To cut slits partway through the outer surface of foods. Often used with ham or flank steak.

STIR-FRY To cook meats and/or vegetables with a constant stirring motion in a small amount of oil in a wok or skillet over high heat.

Alphabetical Index